THE LOGIC OF NOTE

NANZAN LIBRARY
OF ASIAN RELIGION
AND CULTURE

James W. Heisig & John Maraldo, eds., *Rude Awakenings: Zen, the Kyoto School, & the Question of Nationalism* (1995)

Jamie Hubbard & Paul L. Swanson, eds., *Pruning the Bodhi Tree: The Storm over Critical Buddhism* (1997)

Mark R. Mullins, *Christianity Made in Japan: A Study of Indigenous Movements* (1998)

Jamie Hubbard, *Absolute Delusion, Perfect Buddhahood: The Rise and Fall of a Chinese Heresy* (2001)

James W. Heisig, *Philosophers of Nothingness: An Essay on the Kyoto School* (2001)

Victor Sōgen Hori, *Zen Sand: The Book of Capping Phrases for Kōan Practice* (2003)

Robert J. J. Wargo, *The Logic of Nothingness: A Study of Nishida Kitarō* (2005)

The Logic
of Nothingness

A STUDY OF NISHIDA KITARŌ

Robert J. J. Wargo

University of Hawai'i Press

HONOLULU

10 09 08 07 06 05   6 5 4 3 2 1

Library of Congress Cataloging-in-Publication Data

Wargo, Robert.
   The logic of nothingness : a study of Nishida Kitarō / Robert J. J.
Wargo.
       p. cm. — (Nanzan library of Asian religion and culture)
   Includes bibliographical references and index.
   ISBN 0-8248-2930-1 (cloth : alk. paper)
   ISBN 0-8248-2969-7 (pbk. : alk. paper)
   1. Nishida Kitarō, 1870–1945. 2. Nothing (Philosophy) I. Title.
II. Series.
   B5244.N554W35 2005
   181'.12—dc22

                                                        2004063785

The typesetting for this book was done by the Nanzan Institute for
Religion and Culture.

Contents

Foreword

Thomas P. Kasulis

NISHIDA KITARŌ, the founder of the so-called Kyoto school of philosophy, was the most influential thinker of modern (post-1868) Japan. His influence has gradually spread beyond the boundaries of his homeland, gaining him recognition as a major world philosopher of the twentieth century. Especially since the early 1980s, the Kyoto school of philosophy has achieved notable visibility in Western philosophical and theological circles, reflected in the steady flow of translations of the philosophical works by the major philosophers of the school, including Nishida Kitarō, Nishitani Keiji, Tanabe Hajime, Takeuchi Yoshinori, and Ueda Shizuteru. In the last decade or so, over a dozen important studies of Kyoto school thinkers have been published in Western languages. Most of the excitement has been generated in the philosophy of religion and philosophical theology. There are two reasons for this. First, because the Kyoto school developed in Japan, a country where the nontheistic tradition of Buddhism has been predominant, its philosophers have developed contemporary, systematic philosophical analyses of religion and religious experience that do not depend on, or grow out of, theistic assumptions. This challenges the modern Western philosophies of religion that have assumed the universality of religious categories like supreme being and faith. Second, the Kyoto school thinkers are well-versed in Western philosophy and have developed their perspective in response to, and often out of criticism against, various prevailing tendencies in modern Western philosophy. They meet Western philosophers on their own turf.

Although the West has engaged the Kyoto school mainly as a philosophy of religion, this is only one aspect of the school's concerns. For many members of the school, the primary interest has been in epistemology, rather than religion. Certainly this is true of the school's founder, Nishida Kitarō, which brings us to the importance of the present volume.

Robert Wargo's study masterfully takes us into the core of Nishida's epistemological theories. Drawing on the insights of Nishida's early commentators, the philosophers who were his direct students, Wargo develops his own characterization of Nishida's thought that is at once engaging and philosophically persuasive. For example, Wargo explains the immediate questions motivating Nishida's philosophical projects more clearly than has any other scholar in the West (and perhaps Japan as well). Whereas most other studies of modern Japanese philosophy look forward in history to emphasize Nishida's impact on subsequent thinkers in the Kyoto school, Wargo takes pains to situate Nishida's thought as a response to philosophical questions arising from the preceding Meiji period (1868–1912): How can the newly introduced positivistic and empirical traditions from the West harmonize with traditional Japanese systems based on the models of mentorship and apprenticeship? What is the role of the self in the knowing act? Is the nature of the self fixed, or does the self have to be cultivated in order to reach deeper levels of understanding? How can the different approaches to knowledge developed by such Western and Asian theories as realism, idealism, and Buddhist immediacy be reconciled? What is the relation between fact and value? For Nishida these were all primarily epistemological questions. Their answers may have implications for our understanding and appreciating the role of spirituality in human experience, but this does not imply that Nishida's philosophy was exclusively or even primarily motivated by religious interests. Therefore, the common Western perception that the Kyoto school is a school of religious philosophy may need some adjustment, at least if we are to take full account of Nishida's original agenda.

To a great extent, Nishida's basic philosophical questions remained consistent throughout his career, but his answers were continuously being revised, often assuming radically new forms. In many ways, Nishida could be his own severest critic, never hesitant to scrap one philosophical articulation for a new one. Although different scholars have categorized Nishida's philosophical development in different ways, to appreciate the significance of Wargo's approach we need to characterize three phases to Nishida's writings. His early work explored the general character of experience in order to explain the bases of thought, will, and value. In so doing, Nishida drew on ideas from such Western thinkers as William James, Henri Bergson, Johann Gottlieb Fichte, the psychologist Wilhelm Wundt, and (somewhat later) the German Neo-Kantians. Eventually, however, Nishida questioned this approach as overly "psychologistic" or even "mystical." This spurred him to rethink his philosophical point of departure and to develop a perspective more distinctively his own. In this middle period he turned to analyzing the structure of judgment and how different kinds of judgment relate to each other. He characterized this as leaving behind the earlier psychologism for the purpose of developing a new "logic." Finally, in his later years he developed yet another approach (or perhaps we could say he added a new dimension to the second phase of his thinking). In those final years, no doubt influenced by the political events swirling around him during the war, he turned increasing to analyzing the relevance of culture and history on the development of knowledge and spirituality. Most Western studies up to now have focused primarily on the first and third phases of Nishida's system-building.

What are we to make of these three stages in the evolution of Nishida's thought? My own evaluation—and, if I understand him correctly, it is close to Wargo's—is that Nishida secured himself a place in Japanese philosophical history already with his maiden work, *An Inquiry into the Good*. Prior to Nishida, creative academic philosophizing in Japan had mainly been articulated within the framework of one or another of the traditional schools of thought—Buddhist, Confucian, Neo-Confucian, or Shintō. With the establishment of the imperial, national universities (including Kyoto University) in the late nineteenth century, philosophy (*tetsugaku*) came on the scene as a modern academic discipline. In the early years, the effort was to make sense of the new ways of thinking being introduced from the West. With Nishida's *Inquiry,* however, there was a shift from the descriptive study of Western philosophy or the development of a particular tradition of Asian thought to something quite new—the constructive enterprise of philosophizing itself. This new philosophizing, Nishida argued, did not take place from the standpoint of any particular Western or Eastern school of thought, but from a standpoint behind, beneath, or in some way prior to these differentiations. This was to set modern Japanese philosophy on a new course. If Nishida had never written anything after *Inquiry*, he would still be honored as one of Japan's great thinkers.

Nishida's status as a world-class philosopher, however, derives more from the second and third periods of his writing. Traditional philosophy, whether Western or Asian, was no longer a direct influence on his thought so much as a resource to use or ignore as needed. In this second phase of his development Nishida's philosophizing became both more rigorous and independent. He was now constituting his own system and these years of creativity were the origin of many motifs and terms associated with the Kyoto school: *basho*, absolute nothingness, the self-consciousness of the universal, *soku*, the logic of the predicate, and action-intuition. These concepts continue to drive the philosophy done in the Kyōto school vein and are essential for appreciating the intellectual engagement of later Kyōto school figures.

Even the third phase of Nishida's own thinking must be understood in terms of the second. We do an injustice to Nishida if we read his insights into the concrete world of history and culture as bolts of lightning falling unexpectedly from a clear sky. The fire that burns in the philosophy of his later years emerged from the patient working and reworking of earlier ideas. It is as if his insights were not ignited by some sudden flash of insight, but rather out of the smoldering heat arising from the friction of steadily rubbing two sticks together. The rigor of abstract analysis and the painstaking attention to philosophical detail from Nishida's middle period made his later insights possible. We see this intensity in the trenchant prose from the essay included as the appendix to this volume: "General Summary." Reading the essay—whether in Japanese or in Wargo's precise English translation—is not easy going. Happily Wargo's explanations and analyses help us see the essay for what it is: nothing less than a crystallization of the moment in Japanese philosophy when the past Meiji period philosophical problems are addressed brilliantly and at the same time the basis is laid for future philosophizing.

Robert Wargo's study of Nishida fills an important lacuna in Western studies of both Nishida and the Kyoto school. But this is more than merely an analysis of a major historical thinker. Wargo succeeds in making intelligible Nishida's most abstruse phase of thinking. In so doing, he challenges us to work through philosophical issues with the attention to subtleties of argument that only a great philosopher like Nishida can supply. The outstanding accomplishment of the book is that it takes us beyond Nishida Kitarō, the major thinker who founded an influential school of philosophy in twentieth-century Japan, into the heart of his philosophical project itself. In time, we find ourselves thinking along with the master. In the final analysis, Wargo's study is not a study *about* Nishida as much as it is a study *in* Nishida. Readers who work through these pages will find themselves sharing in the birth of one of the most important movements in the intellectual history of Japan.

Introduction

NISHIDA KITARŌ (1870–1945) is without question the best-known and most influential philosopher that Japan has produced in the past hundred years. He is the only thinker in Japan around whom a recognizable philosophical school (the Kyoto school) has been formed. This alone would be sufficient reason to study his work in detail, but the greater reason lies in the fact that his work represents a monumental attempt to do no less than provide a solution to problems that have vexed philosophy since its beginnings.

While the present volume will make no attempt to evaluate or even describe in detail the influence that Nishida's work has had on Japanese culture, I do not think it out of place to remark briefly on his status and the historical importance of his work. The success of Nishida's first work, *An Inquiry into the Good*, catapulted him into a position of prominence among Japanese thinkers and his subsequent writings solidified that position. Not only did he create a philosophical system that sought to synthesize insights from the Japanese tradition with those of the European philosophical tradition, but the way he constructed his synthesis seemed to strike a sympathetic chord in the minds and hearts of large numbers of Japanese intellectuals. Nishida had given them, it seemed, a philosophy that expressed the underlying worldview of most Japanese. Far from a mere Japanese adaptation of a philosophy imported from abroad, his was a complex systematization of their own implicit views. The fact that his philosophy was regarded as a creative and accurate expression of the Japanese spirit is, I believe, important both for an understanding of Nishida's thought itself and for an understanding of the intellectual history of Japan since the Taishō period (1912–1926).

There are any number of scholars who could be cited to substantiate this point. Even Marxist writers such as Miyakawa Tōru, Tōsaka Jun, Miyajima Hajime, Yamada Munemitsu, and Funayama Shin'ichi acknowledge this to be the case, however strongly they happen to disagree on specific points of content.

It should also be noted that virtually all the prominent names in philosophy during the Shōwa period (1926–1989) were either direct disciples of Nishida or acknowledged a profound debt to him. They include figures influential in fields other than philosophy, such as educators and political advisors. There were even attempts to apply Nishida's thought to such disciplines as economics. The influence has not always been direct, nor even entirely welcome. One thinks of the ongoing dispute over the extent to which Nishida's thought was used to provide a philosophical grounding to the chauvinism of the 1930s in Japan. (Questions of this sort, although intrinsically interesting and indicative of the breadth of Nishida's influence, are beyond the scope of this essay, and are well covered in a volume edited by James Heisig and John Maraldo, *Rude Awakenings: Zen, the Kyoto School and the Question of Nationalism*.) In any case, Nishida's thought has continued to attract attention up to this day, especially in recent years, to judge from the number of articles and books devoted to him. In attempting to reassess the cultural heritage of Japan more and more intellectuals have turned to Nishida for guidance.

It is not, however, only because of his historical importance that Nishida is of interest. As a philosopher he grappled with some of the most fundamental problems of philosophy. Our primary focus here will be on the intrinsic nature and merits of his philosophic system. As will be seen, his proposals are not mere "variations on a theme" derived from Aristotle or Kant or some other leading Western philosopher. They more in the nature of a radical change in the basic conceptual scheme for viewing experience. What Nishida requires is a reworking of our basic philosophical conceptual scheme, and what he proposes as the instrument for this revolution is a new logic. The core of Nishida's work is best illustrated by a passage from the preface of *From the Acting to the Seeing*:

> It goes without saying that in the spectacular development of Western culture, which took form as existence and becoming as good, there are a great number of things that must be admired and learned, but at the core of Oriental culture that has nourished our ancestors for thousands of years is there not hidden something like "seeing the form of the formless, hearing the sound of the soundless"? Our hearts cannot help but

search for this sort of thing. I would like to attempt to provide a philosophical foundation for this demand. (NKZ IV, 6)

In a sense it seems that Nishida is trying to provide a logic for mysticism, which, at least on the face of it, sounds absurd. After all, mysticism is commonly understood as an orientation away from the limitations imposed by the laws of logic, beginning with the law of non-contradiction. What the mystic wants to express is a truth thought to be of such profundity that it transcends language and the rules of logic. To be bound by these laws would leave one with only half-truths, distortions, and inadequacies. To express what has been experienced, the mystic sets aside the limitations of logic. For this reason, talk of a "logic of mysticism" sound meaningless in the extreme.

Nishida's aims are different. He is not out to translate the content of "enlightenment" into academic terms or anything of the sort. While it seems clear that he regards the religious experience as the deepest and most meaningful of experiences, he is not attempting to lead the reader to such an experience nor to relate accounts of the experiences of others. What he does try to do is give a precise formulation of the structure of the world that takes into account this kind of experience. In presenting his view of the logical structure of reality, Nishida means to include and relate all of experience. The support for his description does not rest on any external authority but on its capacity to provide reasonable and acceptable solutions to some of the most vexing of philosophical problems: self-consciousness, the relationship of fact and value, the objectivity of knowledge, and the relation of universals to particulars.

There is a side to Nishida's work that reminds one of philosophy as conceptual therapy. He claims that the various "unsolvable problems" of Western philosophy are neither problems solvable with more research in one of the traditional systems nor problems that are necessarily unsolvable. Rather, they are problems that cannot be solved within their traditional framework for the simple reason that the structure does not permit a solution. Nishida is not simply rejecting particular solutions, but the very context in which these solutions have been generated. The idea of a "traditional framework" is every bit as broad as it sounds, including everything from materialism to idealism to empiricism to rationalism. What concerns Nishida is the assumption, shared across a wide spectrum of philosophical positions, of a dichotomy between subject and object, between knower and known. However differently these positions are elaborated, it is the common tendency to depict the structure of experience in what we might call "intellectualistic terms" that Nishida draws our attention to. The logic that underlies each of these views is essentially a logic oriented to the grammatical subject; it is a logic of objects, a logic of substance (as witnessed in Aristotle's definition of "substance" as that which could be subject but never predicate).

It is precisely this interconnection of logic and metaphysical views that Nishida considers critical to the solution of the various problems and that accounts for the failure of traditional solutions. The attempt to sever the connection between logic and one's metaphysical views by appealing to the formality of logic is likewise doomed to failure. The formality of logic precludes its dealing with truth or its supplying knowledge, for without content there is no knowledge.

This does not imply that knowledge is somehow an amalgamation of the form provided by logic and the content supplied by some other means. In fact, any metaphysical system based on an Aristotelian logic is seen as incapable of solving problems such as the relation between the universal and particular. In a word, Nishida, considers this (grammatical) subject-oriented logic an insufficient foundation for an adequate description of reality. This is not to say that formal logic is useless, false, or in any sense simple mistaken, but only that it is inadequate to describe reality. Nishida proposes an "alternate logic," a logic of *topos* oriented toward the predicate rather than toward the subject. This logic stands at the heart of Nishida's achievement.

As has often been observed, the fervor that drove the development of Nishida's thought from beginning to end was primarily religious. Yet, religious insight, no matter how deep or how personally rewarding, cannot serve as a philosophical interpretation of the world and experience. While it is neither advisable—nor even possible—to disengage Nishida's religious motivations from the logical structure of his philosophy, it is equally misleading to think of his philosophy as an apologetic for a particular religious doctrine.

The central theme of the present volume will be the development of Nishida's logic of *basho*. It was construed as a constructive response to a specific philosophical critique, namely, that no basic epistemological or metaphysical theory that assumes the subject-object distinction as an ultimate distinction is capable of giving an adequate account of the whole of experience. This means that not only positions like materialism and idealism but *any* form of of dualism is to be rejected.

In dealing with this problem I will approach it as a "problem of stand-points" in Chapters 1 and 2, and as the "problem of completeness" in later chapters. There are thus two questions involved here:

1. Are all metaphysical theories that assume the ultimacy of the subject-object distinction inadequate?

2. Is it possible to think at all without that assumption?

Already from his early works Nishida was convinced that the subject-object dichotomy is a false one, but the construction of an alternative was a long and winding path. His initial conviction rested, in part, on his Zen experience, but he was also aware of others who had tried to point out the consequences of adhering to the subject-object dichotomy. It is a tribute to his integrity as a philosopher that he did not embrace this early intuition uncritically but tried to argue it rigorously and pursue a viable position of his own.

As Nishida realized from the start, an awareness of the limitations of the subject-object distinction, as well as indications of how to overcome, is to be found in the Buddhist tradition, especially in the Madhyamika tradition of the Middle Path. This is not to say that the critique is laid out in clear and distinct language in the Buddhist texts, or that any alternative position is presented with any logical precision—nor, indeed, should it have been. The focus of the Buddhist scriptures is not on solving philosophical puzzles but on pointing the way to enlightenment.

No attempt will be made in these pages to conduct an exhaustive study of all of Nishida's predecessors or even to catalogue the major figures. Rather, in order to place Nishida in the intellectual history of his age we shall begin with a general historical note and follow with a more detailed examination of the first two modern Japanese philosophers: Inoue Enryō and Inoue Tetsujirō. This represents a break from the usual way of studying Nishida, which is to view his work as an attempt to adopt Western philosophical concepts to express Buddhist, specifically Zen, insights in a systematic fashion.

This view is correct as far as it goes; indeed, the passage cited earlier clearly shows Nishida referring to his philosophy as a logical basis for certain insights into the Buddhist tradition. The difficulty with this approach lies not so much in what it says as in what it fails to say. The tendency is to treat the appearance of Nishida's philosophy as a unique and unprecedented phenomenon that can be explained solely in terms of his dual interests in the practice of Zen and the reading of Western philosophers, thus in

effect detaching his thought from the wider story of modern Japanese philosophy. I will argue, on the contrary, that Nishida's philosophy is the
working out of a position enunciated earlier, albeit somewhat naively, by
the two Inoues. By seeing his thought as the flowering of a fundamental
orientation that was to become the mainstream of Japanese philosophy, we
are better able to gain a clear understanding of the nature and importance
of his work.

Chapter 1 examines the arguments advanced by the Inoues to justify their
identification of a basic philosophical problem, and of the solution that
they offer in terms of a dynamic unity of standpoints, a concept borrowed
from Madhyamika Buddhism. Our basic criticism, aside from the overall
charge of simplistic reasoning, will be that they failed to provide rational
grounds for their solution. Nevertheless, an examination of their efforts is
instructive not only because it highlights the problem but also because it
alerts us to the pitfalls awaiting attempts to resolve it.

In Chapter 2 Nishida's first two major works will be treated as responses
to the challenge presented by the failures of the Inoues to find a grounding
principle for their idea of dynamic unity. *An Inquiry into the Good* shows
Nishida attempting a solution in terms of the notion of pure experience.
His aim there is to develop a complete metaphysical theory with this
notion, conceiving it as utter subjectivity. Unfortunately, the notion of
pure experience, although suggestive, is not given sufficient epistemological foundation and thus fails to provide a solution. What makes it important to consider the work in detail, however, is the fact that it sets the
course his thought is to take in the years ahead on three main points: (1) an
intuition that a solution can be achieved only through a radical subjectivity,
one that encompasses the richness and centrality of the religious experience; (2) a fascination with self-consciousness; and (3) a deep concern for
structure.

In a somewhat more cursory examination of his second major work,
Intuition and Reflection in Self-Consciousness, we find Nishida conducting a
detailed inquiry into the relation of fact and value. In this study he relies
heavily on a critique of the Neo-Kantians, Fichte, and Bergson, culminating in a voluntaristic solution of the problem of standpoints, couched in
the language of what he terms "absolute will." In terms of content, this
absolute will is hardly more than a sophisticated expression of the fact that
we can take various standpoints. In terms of form, it represents a retreat
into mysticism, as Nishida himself was to realize.

The defects common to both of his initial attempts at a solution to the problem of standpoints are the result of his seeking a solution in terms of "activity." His next move, and it is a crucial one, is to propose a solution in terms of "place" (basho) and its defining characteristic, "nothingness."

This brings us to the most crucial stage in the development of Nishida's philosophy, and Chapter 3 examines this transition more closely. The concept of nothingness, with its complex intertwining of logical, ontological, and epistemological characteristics, merits particular attention here because it is only with the advent of the notion of basho that nothingness comes to play a structural role in his thought.

Chapter 4 presents an initial exposition of this concept of basho, which is claimed to be the mechanism for solving the problem of standpoints, and Chapter 5 elaborates the logical structure based on basho. A concluding chapter attempts a tentative assessment of the significance and philosophical value of Nishida's logic of basho as a mechanism for the solution of the problem of completeness.

Although it there are other developments of Nishida's thought worthy of note, including his dialectic, I believe that the introduction of the logic of basho marks the decisive turning point of his philosophical thought and is thus a suitable note on which to end this study. With few exceptions, I have spent very little time discussing Nishida's life. I would refer the reader to Michiko Yusa's excellent and amply documented *Zen and Philosophy: An Intellectual Biography of Nishida Kitarō*.

As Appendix I have included my translation of the "General Summary" of Nishida's *The System of Self Consciousness of the Universal* in which Nishida presents a holistic view of the system that he has developed, emphasizing the nature of judgment and self-consciousness.

Portions of Chapter 1 devoted to Inoue Enryō have been published in the *Proceedings of the International Pen Conference on Japanese Studies*, and a somewhat altered version of Chapter 4 is to be published in the pages of the *International Journal for Field Being*.

I should like to thank my wife, Michiko, and the many friends and colleagues, especially Thomas Kasulis, Agustín Jacinto, and June Spohn, who have encouraged me over the years to publish my research. I should particularly like to thank Noda Matao, Takeuchi Yoshinori, and Minamoto Ryōen for the invaluable insights they gave me into Nishida's thought.

A word of gratitude is due to Richard L. Spear for his editorial assistance in smoothing out the awkwardness in my style. I should also like to express my deepeest appreciation to the staff of the Nanzan Institute for Religion and Culture for their professionalism, their thoughtfulness, their diligence, and their excellent suggestions in editing and preparing the manuscript for publication. In more than one place Jim Heisig worked his editorial magic on the text to transform my turgid and convoluted prose into eminently readable form. His acute eye and keen intellect found lacunae, vagaries, and misstatements, giving me the opportunity to restate my arguments in a clearer and more coherent fashion. Needless to say, all the errors that remain are the sole responsibility of the author.

Tokyo, Japan
1 August 2004

I

Nishida's Predecessors

NISHIDA DID NOT philosophize in a vacuum; a philosopher never does. What I have termed the central theme or objective of Nishida's philosophy, namely the creation of a philosophical viewpoint that would transcend both materialism and idealism, is not new with Nishida. Indeed, this vision might be said to form the Zeitgeist of the Meiji (1868–1911) and Taishō (1911–1925) periods, manifesting itself, in one form or other, in every aspect of the culture. Contact with the West after two and a half centuries of isolation, coupled with the internal political and social changes that were taking shape, produced great mental turmoil and confusion.

Miyakawa Tōru argues that there were essentially two reactions to the new concepts and techniques introduced from the West: (1) a holistic and uncritical acceptance of the new systems, and (2) an attempt to reduce the new systems to "mere technique."[1] This second reaction was was embodied dramatically by Sakuma Shōzan (1811–1864) in the slogan "Western technique, Eastern morality." In this approach the attempt is made to dissociate Western technical advancements from the cultural and philosophical foundation that gave rise to them and to claim further that these techniques could then be put to use to strengthen traditional values.

Miyakawa places such people as Nishi Amane (1828–1897) in the first category. Nishi is often referred to as the father of Japanese philosophy, not only because he was one of the first scholars to be sent to study in the West, but also because of the large number of philosophical works he wrote on his return, works setting forth a strongly positivistic view in matters ranging from epistemology to ethics to politics. In the second category, Miyakawa places thinkers like Nishimura Shigeki (1828–1892) whose primary goal was to show that Western philosophy, which he understands to stand in opposition to Christianity, was congruent to and compatible with Confucianism.[2] The point of his argument, of course, was that the authority that had accrued to Western philosophical thought by virtue of its association with the admittedly advanced state of Western technology could be transmitted to the Confucian tradition and at the same time work to the detriment of Buddhism and Christianity. Miyakawa does not restrict this category to Nishimura but extends it to include any and all philosophers who attempted to find some mode of synthesizing traditional views with the philosophic views being introduced from the West, thus creating the strangest of bedfellows, from Nishimura to Nishida.

It is not my intention to discuss the merits of Miyakawa's classification at this point, but I should like to point out that a large number of thinkers whom Miyakawa places in this second category claim to be interested not in any form of apologetics but rather in the development of a position that would go beyond all previous positions, a position capable of offering an adequate description of reality itself. Their desire to "tell it like it is" is nothing new; it is a hallmark of the philosopher, including those who conclude that no such adequate description is possible. In any case, the explicit aim of these thinkers is not an apology for traditional values or ways of thought but a sincere attempt to tackle the basic problems of philosophy and come up with answers that could stand on their own merits rather than having to rely on the authority of tradition, even though partial answers may be intimated from Buddhist or Confucian intellectual traditions.

In what follows I should like to examine the thought of two philosophers who propounded such a synthesis in the form of an overcoming of the subject-object distinction. Such an examination will help to establish the foundation on which Nishida was able to build. The two philosophers in question are Inoue Enryō (1858–1919) and Inoue Tetsujirō (1855–1944), both important not only because of their status among Meiji thinkers but also because of a much more intimate contact with Nishida. Although Nishida never considered himself the disciple of either man, did not make explicit use of their distinctive philosophical vocabulary (with the possible exception of one term[3]), and never made explicit reference to them in his own writings, there is good evidence that he was familiar with their work.[4]

The significance of these two philosophers for the study of Nishida's work is both historical and philosophical. Historically, the two Inoues' works marked the beginning of a trend that has dominated Japanese philosophy ever since, including such thinkers as Miyake Yūjirō (1860–1945), Kiyozawa Manshi (1863–1903), Nishida, Tanabe Hajime (1885–1962), and Takahashi Satomi (1886–1966). Marxist historians refer to this as the idealistic stream of philosophy. Whether the term is really fitting or not, there is no denying the strong interest in German Idealism, Buddhism, and the problems of consciousness that the work of the two Inoues typified. Philosophically, they felt that the traditional philosophical positions of idealism and materialism were incapable of providing an adequate theory of the nature of the world in that each theory was an answer to a question that was framed in such a way that it precluded the possibility of an answer. That is to say, their respective attempts to describe the world rested on the unquestioned assumption of a radical dichotomy between subjects and objects. This criticism led the Inoues to what one might call "the problem of standpoints," the solution to which they sought in the Buddhist concept of a "Middle Path."

I will argue that Nishida makes a sophisticated version of this problem the pivot of his philosophy and that the solution he offers, while a far cry from the rather simplistic solutions offered by the Inoues, is based on the same insight.

THE PERFECT PATH OF INOUE ENRYŌ

I begin with a disucssion of Inoue Enryō for two reasons: first, because his work seems to have been instrumental in Nishida's decision to specialize in philosophy; and second, because his appeal to Buddhist sources for a solution is much more explicit than it is in the work of Inoue Tetsujirō.

Reading Enryō's *An Evening of Philosophical Conversation*[5] left a deep impression on the young Nishida[6] and is regarded by the historian Funayama Shin'ichi[7] as on a par in historical importance with Nishida's *An Inquiry into the Good*. Not only did this book represent the introduction of German thought into a philosophical climate dominated by positivism but it was the first attempt by a Japanese thinker to render in strictly Western philosophical terms intuitions that owed their origin to the Buddhist tradition.

The work is divided into three sections, originally published as separate volumes: Ontology, Theology, and Epistemology. The form of the work, as the title would indicate, is reminiscent of Plato's dialogues and Berkeley's dialogues between Hylas and Philonous. The difference is that the disputants are not in a protagonist-antagonist relation, resolved when one of the two emerges victorious. Rather, the disputants flail at each other hammer and tong, each skillfully pointing out the weaknesses of the other's argument without being able to resolve the dispute successfully. When all the traditional arguments have been run through without success, Inoue does not have them walk away frustrated at each other's stupidity, let alone abandon intellectual discussion for some other way of resolving the disagreement. He has them appeal to a Master for arbitration.[8]

In the arbitration Inoue begins by laying out certain extreme and diametrically opposed positions and then goes on to show how each of these is inadequate as a total view and must of necessity be seen as part of a larger view, which he calls the Middle Path or the Perfect Path. (Playing on Inoue's personal name, Enryō, which means "perfect," we could as well call it the Enryō Path.) In particular, his discussion of the ontological problem presents three partial, one-sided views, each of which is shown to be the result of a fascination with one particular feature of experience and an attempt to build a philosophical world view that imposes that feature on the whole fabric of experience. In so doing he exposes the mental cramps that afflict materialism, idealism, and what might be termed archism.[9] This last view is not immediately thought of in connection with cosmological disputes, but amounts to the view that matter and spirit are not independent ontological categories but are rooted in a principle (*ri* in Japanese, *li* in Chinese) that is neither matter nor spirit.

Archism is a kind of first approximation of a middle path but ends up in the same mistake as the views it is attempting to reconcile insofar as it rejects both matter and spirit as an ontological basis only to turn around and locate the foundation in principles. Here again, a dichotomy is set up in such a way as to suggest that one of the categories is nothing more than appearance while the other is the reality underlying the appearance. One of the categories must always be explained away or reduced to the other. When it is seen that this cannot be done, the next move is to posit some other distinct category that is then contrasted to the two already at hand. This new category in turn becomes the real of which the others are but appearances. The dichotomy of the real versus the merely phenomenal survives the exercise intact.

It is precisely this dichotomy, Enryō argues, that leads to one-sided views and the failure to attain any adequate picture of the nature of reality. According to Enryō, whenever we attempt to localize reality in a particular category, we invariably land ourselves in a biased view. The true middle path consists not in attempting to localize reality in principles (the intelligible world), but rather in seeing that the intelligible is immediately identical with matter and spirit.[10]

While not attempting a detailed analysis of Enryō's work here, I do think it relevant to note the form of his arguments and the specific nature of his solution, in order to make his relationship to Nishida clear. The section on cosmology in *A Conversation* begins with a discussion between Enyū (a materialist) and Ryōchū (an idealist) about the ultimate nature and constitution of the universe. The conversation proceeds pretty much as one would expect, with Enyū remarking on the insignificance of the human individual vis-à-vis the vastness of the universe, and Ryōchū replying that it is only through the mind that we are aware of this vastness. There follows an exchange that reads like a shortened version of Berkeley's *Dialogues*. On reaching the point where Ryōchū argues that even if there is something outside the mind, it is unknowable and the positing of its existence is mere speculation, he is forced by Enyū to admit that the positing of the non-existence of anything outside the mind is equally speculative.[11] Ryōchū quickly goes on to state that since all these distinctions are made in the mind and since it is only through the power of thought that one can speak of certain things being knowable or unknowable, it can also be said that there is nothing outside the mind. To the objection that if this were true then one would know everything there is to know, and since it is obvious that this is not the case, Ryōchū replies that both knowing and not knowing are equally conscious activities, including the whole of their present discussion. The distinction of mind and matter, as well as the statements about the existence or non-existence of mind itself, are equally mental acts. This leads him to claim that all things are in one mind without distinctions—disposing rather tidily, if somewhat summarily, of the solipsist's predicament.

Enyū objects that this monism flies in the face of the obvious fact that the discussants are facing each other in conversation and are most assuredly not undifferentiated. Further, he goes on, the same could be said with respect to other distinctions that are made and must, in fact, be made, but that have no ground in the view offered by Ryōchū. This objection is acknowledged by Ryōchū with the words: "I haven't researched that point yet."[12]

The focus of the discussion then turns to Enyū's views on explaining the origin of the differentiation, which is crucial to his own position. The pattern of the argument takes a rather surprising turn at this point. Enyū, who started the discussion as a materialist (perhaps naturalist would be a better term), is now forced to argue that the distinction of mind and matter is not merely a relative one. He claims that the characteristics of mind and those of matter are quite different and that this distinction is a distinction rooted in the nature of the universe. He is made to imply further that death does not mean a blurring of the distinction, and it begins to sound as if he is arguing for the existence of an eternal soul (a rather odd position for a materialist). When this is dismissed by Ryōchū as an unwarranted assumption, Enyū retreats to the position that whether certain individuals cease to exist or not has no bearing on the fact that some differences will still exist since other people and objects will still be there. Ryōchū counters that, just as we think of the universe as having evolved from some undifferentiated substance, so, too, it is entirely possible that there will come a time when the universe will "devolve" and all objects will be annihilated, leaving nothing but an undifferentiated universe similar to the initial state. Now it is Enyū's turn to parry the objection with the words: "I haven't researched that point yet."[13]

The last round of the discussion, devoid as it is of cogency, sophistication, or philosophical merit, would seem reason enough for Nishida to avoid referring directly to Enryō in his writings. The conversation seems to lump such an odd assortment of philosophical positions together that one begins to suspect that somewhere along the line, someone—the printer or perhaps Enryō himself—attached the wrong name to a line in the dialogue and sent the arguments spinning out of control. Still, Inoue was no fool and we must avoid too hastily jumping to such conclusions without a careful consideration of the possible reasons for Enyū's shift in position.

It is clear that, for Enyū, the distinction of materialism and idealism was a subsidiary distinction derivable from the fundamental distinction of unity and difference. The views of Enyū and Ryōchū are, in fact, contrasted in terms of whether unity or diversity is emphasized. Enryō saw idealism as a view that was wholly monistic, one stressing unity to the point that the obvious facts of diversity could not be explained. Materialism, on the other hand, he saw as essentially pluralistic, to the extent that it could not tolerate or explain the possibility of total entropy. Thus it is plausible to view this argument as merely undergoing a shift of emphasis with the two disputants changing their positions accordingly. The dialogue starts with the confrontation between materialism and idealism, but the arguments presented against both views lead to a new level of discourse where the opposition is between matter-mind on the one hand and some principle that claims to incorporate mind and matter as mere manifestations on the other. It is at this point that the distinction of diversity and unity becomes primary. The materialist's position is dialectically changed on this level to a position that maintains the ultimate reality of the particular objects in the world and the fundamental nature of the categories into which they fall. Enyū now argues a form of naturalism against the all-embracing archism into which Ryōchū's idealism had been transformed.

It is at this point that the Master arrives to point out the errors in which his students have been caught. His solution is that both arguments are correct, up to a point. Reality manifests diversity, but it also manifests unity. The fundamental confusion that misled both students was the assumption that the diversity-unity distinction was a fundamental bifurcation, and that, if reality could be said to have either of these characteristics, then by that very fact the other characteristic would need to be excluded. But these two characteristics are not independent of each other, and trying to "reduce" one side of the distinction to the other destroys the distinction. The Middle Path—the Enryō Path—consists in seeing that both are one-sided viewpoints.

> From the point of view of diversity you are merely a part of *enryō* (reality), but from the point of view of non-differentiation you and *enryō* are one and the same. Your mind is a part of nature but in that mind you include all the things of heaven and earth and it is as if the world and the mind become one thing (body).[14]

As the Master speaks, he sets forth a doctrine of degrees of universal consciousness similar to that of Leibniz. Reality (*enryō*), he says, is not to be characterized exclusively in terms of either pole of the dichotomy, for unity has diversity implied within it and, conversely, diversity implies a unity in which the diversity is seen as diversity.

The force of this move to a position in which the various conflicting characteristics are seen to be nothing more than shifts of points of view is most clearly brought out in the third section, where Enryō expounds on epistemology.[15] The argument in this section becomes more complicated since there are more participants and, consequently, more points of view.

Roughly, the arguments turn on the question: "Where does the ground of truth reside?" Is it in the material world, in the mind, in the relation between the two, or in some other realm of ideas? After another protracted argument that results again in a stalemate, the Master steps in to show his students their mistake in trying to establish a delimited specific ground for truth, whereas one can arrive at an adequate assessment of the matter only if one is aware of the relativity of these distinctions. To say that the distinctions are relative is not to say that they are worthless or spurious. It is only that they depend on a certain point of view, a limited point of view that cannot give the entire picture precisely because these distinctions are specific. He gives an example of the inseparability of difference and non-difference by referring to the snow in the garden. In its constitution the snow is frozen water and can be seen simply as water, that is, purely in terms of its general character. But at the same time each particle of snow is a particular individual object capable of being distinguished from all others. Snow particles do not exist apart from water; thus, both the homogeneity and the differentiation return to the same basis: the snow particle that is immediately water.[16]

The Perfect Path is the unity of both views. This is not merely to say that that it acknowledges truth to lie in both the mental and physical worlds, since this is only their homogeneity aspect. The Perfect Path has a gate of differentiation that sees the distinction of true and false as "waves on that ocean of the principle of homogeneity."[17] The Master then compares the disputations of his disciples to the sea at night when clouds have obscured the light of the moon. At such times the various waves, and so too their thoughts, appear independent and in mutual conflict (reflecting the relative standards for truth), but once the clouds have dispersed, the various patterns are recognized as patterns of the same body of water.[18] But, of course, while it is clear that the waves could not exist except as modifications of some body of water, it is equally clear that the body of water could not exist but with some surface pattern or other. Thus, he states:

> Not recognizing the non-separateness of the absolute standard and the relative standards and thinking that they exist apart is the illusion of the dark night, while knowing that the absolute and the relative are inseparable is the enlightenment brought about by the clear moon.[19]

Basically, the problem is that a standard can be established only in terms of some sort of difference, but various standards, each quite different, seem to have equal claim to being the absolute standard. The very possibility of these standards further implies that there is a standard of standards in which they are grounded. The example given is that of color: one can make a distinction in terms of white-nonwhite, red-nonred, and the like, where each of these distinctions is made in terms of a color system, even though color itself is not a specific color. The same sort of relation must hold for good-evil, true-false, and a host of similiar distinctions we commonly rely on. Differences can only exist in the context of unity, and unity cannot manifest itself except in differences. The difficulty is, of course, that Inoue only presents us with analogies and metaphors. The problem of individuation is as old as philosophy, and it is not going to be disposed of merely by insisting that it is not a question of choosing between the one and the many but that the one is the many and the many are the one. Not that Enryō's solution to the problem is wrong: he has not really offered a solution at all, only the hint of a direction to seek a solution through consideration of the nature of distinctions in general rather than opting for a particular distinction as the basis for an explanation.

From the beginning, this concern with the ground of distinctions characterizes Nishida's work. The notion of a "standard of standards" is echoed in Nishida's talk of an "a priori of a prioris" and a "universal of universals." Inoue had partially uncovered the roots of the problem, a problem endemic to Western philosophy, and had attempted to bring to bear on it a concept fundamental to Māhāyana Buddhism. He did not, however, succeed fully in understanding the problem and his solutions, such as they are, were entirely too facile. Still, he did make it plain that nothing short of a radical approach was needed. To Nishida, a brilliant young man steeped in the tradition of Buddhism, this was more than sufficient.

INOUE TETSUJIRŌ'S IDENTITY PHILOSOPHY

Another attempt at overcoming the subject-object dichotomy along the lines laid out by Inoue Enryō is to be seen in the work of Inoue Tetsujirō. Although it is more difficult to document his direct influence on Nishida than is the case with Inoue Enryō, I would suggest that the influence was considerable.

Inoue was perhaps the most prominent figure in the philosophy department at Tokyo University when Nishida entered as a special student in 1891.[20] It was inevitable that Nishida would come to know of his work during his three years there. Except for a short, polite article he contributed to a volume celebrating Inoue's seventy-seventh birthday,[21] Nishida makes no specific reference to Inoue Tetsujirō in his philosophical works. For at least three reasons, there is nothing surprising about this. First of all, Nishida was in the habit of quoting only from philosophers he was actively reading at the time. An exception is made for those philosophers whose works he had poured over so many times that they seemed a part of him, Aristotle and Kant for example. Secondly, Nishida was rather bitter about the treatment he had received at Tokyo University as a special student. He was openly considered inferior in rank, someone who should consider himself fortunate to be allowed to associate, even at a distance, with such exalted personages as Inoue.[22] Finally, Nishida was continually at odds with the nationalistic and authoritarian views held by Inoue.[23] These reasons seem sufficient to account for the lack of reference to Inoue Tetsujirō in Nishida's writing. In any case, it is of secondary importance whether or to what extent Nishida consciously felt his ideas to be a development of Inoue's. Far more important is the way in which he creatively and systematically synthesized what had been no more than intuitions for Inoue: the nature of the interrelationship of the categories of the one and the many, phenomenon and reality, subject and object. The essential identity of epistemology and ontology, which is only implicit in Inoue, becomes explicit in Nishida.

The two articles by Tetsujirō to which I will refer in what follows are "A Particle of My World View" (1894) and "An Outline of Phenomena Reality Theory" (1897).[24] As is evident from the Japanese title of the second of these articles, Inoue specifically uses the term *soku* in the designation of name of his own view which may be taken as an equivalent of *Identitäts-realismus*. In the first of these articles Inoue proposes a categorization of philosophical views. He begins with a distinction between skepticism, which he contends is self-defeating, and non-skepticism. The latter is further divided into two main branches, idealism and realism, which are characterized summarily by saying that realism argues there is something independent of our subjectivity, whereas idealism argues that "objectivity" is not independent but rather originates in and is dependent on our subjectivity. The realist position is divided into two positions. The first he calls "excessive realism," the view that although the objects of knowledge are phenomena, these phenomena are grounded in some noumena that are forever beyond our grasp. The second he calls "phenomena-realism," the view that something objective exists outside subjective consciousness and that it is precisely these phenomena that constitute reality. This latter position is then further subdivided into positivism, which holds that the phenomenal stands in contradistinction to the real, and "true" phenomena-realism, which states that one can make a conceptual distinction between phenomena and reality for certain purposes, although they are basically identical.

Inoue admits that the notion of an identity theory is not transparent and proceeds to give some examples to clarify what he means. We can view phenomena, he states, in either of two ways: as phenomena that appear through our senses or as something that exists independently of sensation. In this regard we can speak of the radiation of a certain wavelength (independent of sensation) or the color red (sensation). Again, our ascribing the predicate "hard" to a body may depend on the strength of our own body. However, it may be defined objectively in terms of a scale of hardness that makes no reference to our sensations. From this he does not conclude that we should thereby divest ourselves of one of these modes of speech or attempt to show, at least in principle, how one might be reduced to the other, but simply states that "the various qualities given to us as sensations exist objectively." "Phenomena and their reality are not the sorts of things that can be established separately."[25] Adopting the analogy of cells and organic bodies (sense organs, etc.) he remarks that there can be no organic body without cells just as, in the same manner, there can be no cells apart from organic bodies. This also applies to the distinction between phenomena and reality.

Just how much does this discussion help to clarify Inoue's position? It is, of course, obvious that the examples of the relativity of sensation and the distinction of a physical description of light and the sensual quality of color did not originate with Inoue. Furthermore, it is not immediately apparent how the analogy of cells and organic bodies is related to the distinction of objective properties and sensual properties. It is most certainly not the case that the notion of a light wave of a certain length and the notion of a color are logically identical. One has only to think of light waves either just a bit longer or a bit shorter than the relatively narrow limits of our vision. What color is ultraviolet light? The question seems senseless. There is no difficulty whatsoever in speaking of the radiation of a wavelength of two thousand angstroms, for example, without any reference to a color sensation of any sort; but one cannot speak of organic bodies without implying something about cells. What then is the point of the comparison?

It seems that the main point of the analogy is precisely that we do make a distinction between the objective and the subjective spheres, and with good reason, but that attempts to completely reduce one of these spheres to the other are spurious. In certain instances, such a reduction would be useful and even necessary, for example, in explaining why two people see the same object as being of different colors, but a wholesale reduction cannot be carried out. Thus Inoue seems to be saying that any attempt to speak exclusively in terms of radiation or in terms of color sensations would be like speaking of organic bodies without cells or talking of cells without organic bodies. He plainly regards this latter attempt as absurd. Idealism, on the one hand, and materialism, on the other, attempt to carry out such a reduction.[26] The consciousness-only position, as produced in Greece, India (with Buddhism), and Germany (including Kant), represents an excessive form of idealism in its attempt to reduce the world to a product of subjectivity. This view contradicts common sense: facts are not conformable to will. Conversely, materialism, an excess of realism, is rejected because it is simply incapable of adequately accounting for mental phenomena.

Inoue subscribes to the correspondence theory of truth. Indeed he considers it self-evident and can only conclude that the idealist position, since it views all phenomena as produced by subjectivity, cannot provide a standard for truth. The interesting point here is his insistence that all our knowledge is derived through experience of the world. He notes three possible approaches to the application of experiential knowledge. It can refer (1) to previous experience only, (2) to that which has not as yet been experienced but in principle can be experienced, and (3) to a realm beyond experience. The first alternative is rejected as leading essentially to skepticism and the denial of certain knowledge; the third is rejected as nonsensical in an almost positivistic sense. Only the second alternative provides a ground for the truth claims in scientific laws while not going beyond experience. As to whether there are any universally valid truths, Inoue replies that the only universally valid truths are those that have been repeatedly demonstrated through experience and have never met with a counter instance. If scientific laws and the like are not counted as knowledge, then we have no knowledge. By the same token, their universality is questionable when it comes to the world that lies outside the possibility of our experience.[27] Inoue's views on truth are of interest to us because of the strong empiricist streak that runs through them. This empiricism is also a fundamental element of Nishida's philosophy, and it is important to see how this concurs with his attempt to transcend both idealism and materialism.

To further clarify the precise relations between the various views, it will be necessary to examine "An Outline of the Phenomena-Reality Theory." In this article, Inoue Tetsujirō, as would Nishida later, accepts the Kantian criticism of treating a reality that is supposedly beyond experience as an object of knowledge. To use Walsh's delicious phrase, Inoue rejects the "news from nowhere" approach.[28] This is not to deny that we have a concept of reality or to suggest that this concept is useless. Without bringing in the notion of reality, it is impossible to explain the human condition. If the task of philosophy is to uncover the meaning of reality by dealing with phenomena, Tetsurō argues, it does not treat them as as the physical sciences do but rather views phenomena as a means to clarify reality.

This is all highly obscure, but it would seem that what he is trying to say is that doing philosophy means trying to clarify the structure of experience in the most general way. When the distinction between reality and phenomena hardens into a rift between the two, the philosopher will opt for one side of the distinction as a ground for explaining everything. Inoue wishes to show that either of these options leads to unsatisfactory theories, and that the root of the difficulties lies precisely in the assumption that one of the options must be taken. Here, in somewhat cruder form, lies the core of the intuition we have already seen in the work of Inoue Enryō and that will form the cornerstone of Nishida's thought.

If one understands the reality-phenomena distinction as representing a dichotomy of two worlds, then one is faced with the problem of explaining how phenomena are derived from what one considers reality. If we take the two to be identical in the sense that the terms *phenomena* and *reality* do not refer to different things but are merely differenent orientations toward the same thing, then we would have a view that would satisfy our demands. It is not that phenomena are derived from reality, but that phenomena and reality are identical. The distinction between phenomena and reality is a distinction of points of view: viewing the world as phenomena leads one to think in terms of diversity and change, while thinking of it as reality leads one to think in terms of unity and permanence. The realization of this fact is what Tetsurō means by reality-phenomenalism or *enyūjitsuzairon*.

He is at pains to argue that his theory is not bound to an insight into some limited range of experience, but that it can be shown to be inevitable from any number of approaches. To this end he offers a subjective proof, an objective proof, and a logical proof. The proof in the subjective realm consists of the attempt to show that the concept of a self underlying a particular mental phenomenon is essential and inevitable, and further, that the concept of an individual self is no more than a phenomenon. Any attempt to consider it as something other than a phenomenon fails because it cannot account for the unity of experience or the development of personality. To be sure, philosophy cannot be reduced to psychology, which remains stuck in the realm of phenomena. But this, Tetsruō contends, is not to say that we can intuit a distinct self apart from the phenomena of consciousness. Mental reality can be represented as the common unifying feature of conscious phenomena, but this commonality cannot be found apart from the phenomena themselves; in fact, they are identical with it.[29]

The same spirit or psyche can be seen as mental phenomena and as mental reality. From the point of view of mental reality, the distinction between "I" and "he" disappears into a single vast sea, but it is precisely these phenomena that constitute the basis of the individual self. The distinction of phenomena versus reality is drawn only for the sake of convenience. Inoue claims that we gain the concept of the real by means of an internal intuition, not an intuition of a specific object but an intuition of a unity. The reason that philosophical thinking leans in the subjective direction is simply that this concept is attainable only through direct internal reflection. At the same time, precisely because we are not speaking of the intuition of a determinate object or quality, the content of the intuition will be expressed or represented differently by different individuals. For this reason it is necessary to obtain an objective ground for concepts.

For his objective proof, Tetsurō follows the same line of attack as he does in his subjective proof. First, he offers as examples various phenomena—for example, white light that is broken up when passed through a prism into a complex of colors—to indicate that the properties of things seem to change when the conditions of their perception change. The reason is that we perceive objects through the senses, and alterations in prevailing conditions will produce alterations of the perceptions. The point here is that there is an inherent duality of viewpoints with respect to objects of the physical world and it is the aim of science to show that such apparent diversity can have a common ground. The whole of the causal network rests on the notion of movement and this in turn has as its basis the notions of matter and energy. Changes in the mechanical sphere can be reduced to changes in distribution. Energy becomes the common element that unifies all the phenomena of mechanics. To see a unity underlying the diverse phenomena is to approach the concept of reality.[30] The law of the conservation of energy may form the foundation for a coherent and unified view of mechanics, but this question cannot be pursued further: when we ask what energy is, we are left without an answer. Energy is, for mechanics, the origin and as such it is not analyzable. In this respect the notion of energy approaches the notion of reality.

When it comes to organic things we seem to reach an impasse at the obvious and crucial dissimilarities between organic objects and the objects of mechanics. Organic things develop internally, grow, subsume the environment, and reproduce. Inorganic matter has none of these characteristics. It would seem that the two types are irreconcilable. If, however, we consider that all organic bodies are composed of cells and that cells are composed of chemical elements that are inorganic, the reduction can be carried through. Once again the unity is extended and the notion of reality is approached.

Science is the attempt to unify the diversity of phenomena by uncovering the common ground or universal nature of the phenomena. But science, Tetsurō claims, does not go beyond phenomena. It can go as far as it does because there is a concept of reality lurking in the background, but it cannot itself completely uncover this concept. Thus he states:

> Interpreting the world is not accomplished merely through cognition. Even though cognition has the unique ability to clarify phenomena, reality is not the object of cognition."[31]

Now this is a most curious statement. It could mean any number of things—or nothing at all. In the context of this essay, it seems to come down to this: science can display the interrelatedness of phenomena by showing that the various individual phenomena are instances of certain general categories that interact in specifiable ways, but this procedure does not go beyond a formal structuring. Although laws of wider and wider scope are produced, and in the process more and more diverse phenomena are shown to be interrelated, still this does not count as an interpretation. Why should this be the case? What is involved in interpretation that is not present in this procedure? Tetsurō seems to suggest that for there to be an interpretation there must be an analysis of the basic categories used in science and in all cognitive enterprises. In addition, there must be a concept of reality to ground the phenomena being interpreted. This reality, however, cannot be an object of study, because if it were, it would be on a par with the phenomena of which it is the ground. Further, to be recognized is to be limited in some way and the concept of reality is precisely that concept that gives rise to or grounds all limitations and distinctions.[32]

The objective reality he discusses is no different from the intuited reality that was discussed in the section on subjective proof. Tetsurō claims they are, in fact, the same reality and cannot be differentiated into the objective and the subjective. This comes down to the simple claim that there is no objective reality opposed to a subjective reality, although reality can be represented either subjectively or objectively. He uses the example of a man who has no eyes. Obviously the man's experience is different from someone with vision. Extending the example to a man who has no functioning sense organs whatsoever, it would still be the case that his world and our world of sight, sound, tactile sensations are identical. The representation of the world would differ, but the world itself would be the same. We can picture the world as differentiated or as undifferentiated as our experience deepens and accumulates. We can see it as both because it *is* both. Similarly he uses the example of a desk. The desk can be seen both as a particular object and, at the same time, as a grouping of atoms. In the latter case the desk does not look to be any different from anything else in the universe. Both aspects, universality and particularity, are applicable to the desk. To attempt to see the desk exclusively in either way is fruitless; it must be seen in both aspects.

This last example is remarkably like the example of the snow in the courtyard used by Inoue Enryō, and indeed it seems that Tetsujirō was trying to make much the same point. The question is whether it is worth making at all. If the point is merely that things can be considered with reference to the characteristics that they share with other things and that they also can be considered with reference to the manner in which they differ from other things, then it would seem that he could have said as much without the preceding discussion. In fact, when he develops a logical justification of the concept of reality, he does speak of the fact that any two objects will always have some point of difference and some point of similarity but that there are no absolute differences or similarities. This commonsense position seems so self-evident that one wonders why he should take the trouble to make so much of it. Both of the Inoues seem to be using examples of this sort to show the interrelationship of the notions of a particular and a universal. Particulars must display universal characteristics and universal characteristics must be displayed in some particular.

That this is the sort of thing Tetsujirō meant can be seen by a look at his justification for the reality-phenomena theory based on logic (in the broad sense). As was remarked above, he notes that similarity and difference are concepts relative to specific conditions, and that this relativization is not merely accidental but part of the logic of the concepts. Understanding or interpreting is precisely the attempt to reduce diversity to unity, in the sense that one interprets or explains individual phenomena by means of features common to mankind. In other words, human minds postulate laws. These laws are also explained by subsuming them under still more general laws, although no law is absolutely general. Tetsurō makes reference to the theory of evolution in this context, remarking on its extreme generality and immense usefulness, but goes on to observe that it provides no philosophical interpretation of the world. He argues that it is a scientific theory that displays the interrelationship of diverse phenomena, but that is all. It is not, and could not be, the basis of an adequate philosophical worldview because it does not go beyond phenomena.

What would it mean to go beyond phenomena? Clearly it cannot mean, for either of the Inoues, a transition to a world of things independent of the phenomena they give rise to. Both of them explicitly reject such a move. What sense then can be attached to the phrase? It would seem that what is meant is that the notion of a unity, a reality, underlying the diverse phenomena is necessary in order even to have the notion of phenomena. These two notions are complementary and the attempt to exclude one in favor of the other is to misunderstand their logic. The terms *reality* and *phenomena* do not refer to different things (the reference of the terms is identical), but they do signify two different ways of viewing this referent.

Overview and evaluation of the two inoues

Both Inoue Enryō and Inoue Tetsujirō expound theories identifying phenomena and reality, where the notion of reality is fused with the notion of unity while the notion of phenomena is fused with that of diversity. This view relies on the assumption that the interrelationships between conceptual schemes, that is to say, that an adequate view of experience, can be had only by displaying the relationships between conceptual schemes and not by reducing one to the other.

What does this mean? Ordinarily if one were to ask, "What is a snow-flake?" an appropriate answer would be "frozen water." Similarly, if one were to say, "This seemingly solid desk is really a rather loose configuration of atoms," no one would give the answer a second thought. Both of the Inoues would agree, but they would also insist that in each of these cases, the referent did not change. It might be objected that there is indeed a change of reference, from desks to atoms, and that this is not merely a change of viewpoint, since the status of the categories is quite different. It

might be argued, further, that while the desk cannot help but be constituted of atoms, atoms need not form a desk. Indeed, Enryō's example of
the snowflake and water makes just this point.

The two Inoues are not likely to be dismayed by this comment, since
they could reply that the point they wanted to make is not that once the
snowflake is seen to be composed of water, there can be no difference at all
between it and any other body composed of water, but only that it can be
seen as an instance of a particular type and, thus, part of a unity. But then
again, the snowflake can also be seen in its "bare particularity" as an individual object among a myriad of other individual objects. Neither of these
descriptions has absolute priority over the other; neither view can stand by
itself. But why should one be tempted to think that it could? If the Inoues
are merely trying to say that the move to viewing particulars in the context
of some unity is the core of explanation and, further, that for there to be an
explanation there must be both the *explicans* and the *explicandum,* then one
might readily agree to the truth of this statement and yet insist on its trivi-
ality.

The Inoues can be viewed as engaging in what they believe to be conceptual housecleaning, a sort of conceptual analysis whose main point is to
argue that the distinctions of the one and many, reality and phenomena,
objective and subjective have in fact been widely misunderstood by
philosophers. A proper analysis, they might claim, would show that these
distinctions are relative in the sense that they are properly applied within
the context of some reference. Thus the objects appearing in the dream or a
hallucination are merely phenomenal or unreal in the sense that they are
not physical objects, even though, of course, this is not to deny their being
actual elements of experience. Physical objects themselves can be seen as
constructions from sense data, while it is equally possible to consider the
sense data as being mere images of physical objects. The very awareness of
diversity implies the conception of a unity underlying that diversity, but
that unity cannot then be taken to be something independent of the diversity. If it were, one could merely have added one more element to the
diversity and this, in turn, would imply the postulation of another unity
and so on, ad infinitum.

A similar point can be made concerning the objective and the subjective.
While our experiences can be cut up and organized in various ways, with
the world viewed either objectively or subjectively, the dichotomy is found
in the manner of organization and not in some ontological priority. The
distinction of objective and subjective is a distinction made within the con-

text of a unity, and this unity is not identical with either element of the distinction exclusively. Furthermore, the unity is not something over and above the distinction; it is explained by the distinction and cannot be gotten at except through this distinction. The attempt to "explain" one aspect of the distinction in terms of the other is to make the fundamental error of taking the supposed *explicans* to be the unity that underlies the distinction. This would be to attempt to make it serve two different and antagonistic functions at the same time. According to the Inoues this is precisely the mistake that both the materialists and the idealists make. Each tries to explain the other in terms of itself; each tries to make its segment of the dichotomy the ontologically significant one, the *explicans*.

At the same time it is clear that the Inoues are not merely engaging in conceptual clarification with no reference to ontology. They are doing metaphysics but a special sort of metaphysics. They are not engaged in a search for a realm beyond phenomena, a world that gives rise to the phenomenal world but is essentially independent of it, a world forever just beyond our grasp. The real world is the world we live in; it can be viewed subjectively or objectively and the fact that it can be viewed in both ways is precisely its reality. We know the world only through experience and this experience can be ordered subjectively and objectively. There is no special mode of seeing the world other than through experience.

Yet, at the same time, Inoue Tetsujirō will make statements such as "Reality is neither subjective nor objective," or "... reality is not an object of cognition."[33] This would seem to be nothing more than a paraphrase of the statement that neither *subjective* nor *objective* is a term that can be applied exclusively to the ground of the subjective-objective distinction. That reality cannot be an object of cognition would seem to mean only that it is not an object, that it is not a delimited particular but the ground of all determinations. To say it is the ground of all determinations does not mean that this reality is separate from the determinations or that there must be some special mystical way of coming in contact with it aside from cognition. To see that objective and subjective are both applicable, equally appropriately or equally inappropriately, is to have intuited the nature of reality, but not as something apart from the subjective and objective ordering of experience.

The Buddhist influence on the writings of both the Inoues is apparent. In Enryō, the vocabulary is similar to that of Māhāyana Buddhism, especially of the Madhyamika school, while in Tetsujirō the vocabulary is not quite so obviously Buddhistic. Nonetheless, it is clear that his point of view can be expressed by the statement that *nirvāna* and *samsāra* are not two but one and the same. Neither Enryō nor Tetsujirō seems to place much stress on the attainment of a state of nirvana through one discipline or another; both are much more concerned with discovering the logical structure of the world. The enterprise is a philosophical one and not a religious one, although at least for Enryō there is the motivation to show that a philosophical viewpoint can be presented in a way that accords with religious insights.

The problem is that neither of them give us much more than a simple affirmation of this intuition. Both have tried to show that materialism and idealism can each elicit objections from the other view, so that neither can be adopted as a view able to satisfy our demands for a coherent and comprehensive view of the world. But "telling objections" are not met with any more than token resistance by the advocate of the position being attacked. Ryōchū, for example, capitulates rather summarily to the attacks made by Enyū to the effect that his position did not account for the fact that the dispute was in fact going on at that moment and that this differentiation was there to be accounted for whether Ryōchū liked it or not. One gets the feeling that the deck has been stacked in advance, and that the entire dialogue served only as the prelude to the propounding of the correct view by the Master. This is most unfortunate since much of the force of the "Middle Path" derives from the argued inadequacies of the extreme views presented in the dialogues.

For Inoue Tetsujirō, the difficulty resides in a facile identification of the reality concept, which he "proves" subjectively and which he "proves" objectively. Even if one grants that he has indeed shown that each of these orderings of experience necessarily implies some concept of an underlying reality that provides the unity for the ordering, he has done no more than claim that the concepts of reality implied are in fact identical. If he had not expended so much effort to show that the concept of an individual self must itself be derived from some deeper notion of reality, some such claim would have been necessary to prevent his subjective proof from falling into the pit of solipsism. The individual self (the empirical ego) must be seen as an object constructed within the realm of mental phenomena and not as the foundation or ground of that realm. Yet he notes that different people will express this reality differently and, thus, that it is necessary to give an objective proof. This would seem to indicate that while solipsism is not a problem, there is most definitely a problem of "individual realities" as well as an awareness that the relationship between these could be expressed only by an objective approach to the concept. It would thus seem clear that an ultimate identification of the concepts is required, but Tetsurō does little more than state the fact, noting that each is an ordering of experience.

Enryō and Tetsujirō seem quite ready to accept criticisms of certain views, especially idealist views, that are based on scientific discoveries rather than on philosophical argumentation. This makes it seem as if neither of them really took the idealist stances seriously, an impression reinforced by statements made elsewhere in their writings. Earlier I referred to Tetsujirō's observations to the effect that extreme forms of idealism were not only wrong, but downright sick and perverted. There is nothing to object in such criticism as such, except that the views seems to be given rather shorter shrift than they deserve.

Both the Inoues are realists in the sense that neither would allow for individual consciousness, or even some general consciousness, to supply the content of the world. At the same time neither are they what we might call transcendent realists. The term "descriptive metaphysics" can, I believe, be applied to their philosophies without stretching the term too far. Reality is never defined in terms of an enumeration of its basic characteristics but only as that which can be viewed both subjectively and objectively, in idealist terms and in materialist terms. This is not unlike saying that the world is what is the case without making any further elaboration. In the *Tractatus* the early Wittgenstein attempts to outline the logical structure of the world in this way, although he also states that an understanding of his attempt will inevitably lead to the rejection of his description of that structure. The Inoues seem to be lifting themselves by their own bootstraps in the same manner. The crucial difference is that while Wittgenstein actually attempted to display this logical structure, Enryō and Tetsujirō are content to say that its structure is such that it can have two different frameworks imposed on it. What one would expect is a further specification of the interrelationships between these differening structures, but this is precisely what they do not do, and this I reckon to be the most glaring defect in their views.

Funayama has suggested that the Inoues expounded an "identity logic" (a logic of reality-phenomena), but it seems to me that they suffer rather from a lack of a logic. If Funayama means merely that what they were concerned with showing that the traditional structures used to describe reality are fundamentally and necessarily inadequate, and that the proper view is not the erection of some new structure in contrast to these but rather an awareness of their inadequacy, then one could accept his judgment. Still, the designation of this as "logic" strikes one as odd to say the least, and while I would like to postpone discussion of the problem of logic and what it excludes until we have addressed Nishida's concept of predicate logic, it seems useful to consider the grounds for Funayama's use of the term in reference to the two Inoues.

The aim of the dialectic used by Inoue Enryō, for example, is not merely to dismiss each of two opposing viewpoints but to show that each of them is necessarily inadequate because of what they purport to do. It is not that the particular "axioms" of a given view are wrong, but that the whole notion of trying to characterize reality in some specific fashion is doomed to failure by the very nature of what it means to characterize. Characterization in a certain fashion presupposes an opposition, and this opposition in turn presupposes a unity within which the dichotomy is set. To equate the unity with the dichotomy that is grounds is presumably the first step in generating the "identity logic" of which Funayama speaks. The same insight is crucial to the development of Nishida's thought, but in the work of both Inoues it does not develop beyond an embryonic state.

The claim that the world of reality for the idealist, where being or substantiality is invested in the conscious subject, and the world of reality for the materialist, where being or "thinghood" is accorded to physical objects, are in opposition on one level and not on another is also crucial in Nishida, for whom existence or reality is relative to the nature of the world in question, to the "point of view" on which the world is founded.[34] What is necessary, however is to show, in detail, how these "worlds of reality" are related, and this is precisely what the Inoues do not do.

The examination of a number of other philosophers (for example, Miyake Yūjirō, 1860–1945) or religious thinkers (like Tsunajima Ryōsen, 1873–1907) could more fully document the extent and nature of the philosophical tendencies that formed the backdrop for Nishida's thought. Since such an examination is not likely to advance our understanding of Nishida's thought significantly, we may exclude them from the present discussion.[35]

CONCLUSION

Taken as a whole, the philosophical position enunciated by the two Inoues can only be labeled syncretic. They both perceived that the traditional problems arising from the dichotomies of the one and the many, phenomena and reality, subjectivity and objectivity, could not be explained adequately by an attempt to reduce one aspect of the dichotomy to the other or to display a one-way dependency. They also saw that any attempt to represent the dichotomies themselves as specious would be defeat themselves by introducing a new dichotomy. In short, both realized that the problem lay in the sorts of questions being asked, and therefore that a totally new approach would have to be taken. The issue hinged on clarifying the nature and origin of these dichotomies.

Both Inoues felt that the Middle Path of Buddhism held the answer. This was their positive legacy to Nishida. Unfortunately, their appeals to Buddhist principles amounted to little more than a casual gesture. Their views on the character of the epistemological framework and the interrelation of principles were overly simplistic. The intuition of a dynamic unity, they were convinced, solved everything. They were wrong. What was needed was a working out of the intuition, a mechanism or principle that would show precisely how this dynamic unity functioned. In this sense, one may say that the philosophical writings of Nishida are the record of an attempt to clarify this principle.

2

The First Attempts:
Radical Empiricism and Voluntarism

IN THIS CHAPTER we will consider the two works of Nishida that are essential to an understanding of the development of his logic of basho: *An Inquiry into the Good* and *Intuition and Reflection in Self-Consciousness*. In them Nishida is trying to do what the two Inoues had failed to do, namely to find a principle that would explain the dynamic unity of subject and object. This is not to say that Nishida explicitly addresses himself to their writings, but the direction of his argument is much clearer set against the background of their thought.

If the subject-object distinction does not represent a fundamental cleavage in the structure of the world, and if one side of the distinction is not reducible to the other, then, as the Inoues had recognized, it is necessary to find a principle that would account for the distinction. The principle would have to show how it is that we can, even must, assume the various points of view that we do. Nishida's first attempt at locating such a principle centers around the notion of "pure experience" in *An Inquiry into the Good*. When this notion proves inadequate to the task he reassesses the problem, and after a frustratingly arduous inquiry, arrives at the notion of "absolutely free will" in *Intuition and Reflection in Self-Consciousness*. Although neither of these attempts is totally successful, they both represent crucial stages in the growth and development of the basic insight of the dynamic unity of subject and object.

AN INQUIRY INTO THE GOOD

Nishida's maiden work, *An Inquiry into the Good* (1911), belies its name inasmuch as it is not primarily a work whose main theme is ethics at all. It runs a broad gamut of philosophical concerns from epistemology to religion. The central purpose of the work is no less than an attempt to provide a coherent and comprehensive view of reality. The title of the work reflects Nishida's concern with the human individual and the human situation. Nishida is always a "philosopher of life," as he himself puts it, in the sense that his motivation is not merely intellectual exercise but an attempt to solve the basic problems of human existence. Philosophy must provide a solution for our problems — the problems we encounters every day. It is not like chess, a complex and exacting activity that is at bottom merely a form of amusement, nor is it the mere proclamation of an ethical stand or the utterance of a *kōan*. Rather it is a rational inquiry into the nature and structure of reality itself. Without an understanding of this ultimate structure of reality, no ethical stand can have any foundation.

Nishida's main concerns are evident in this work as are the germinal indications of the nature of solutions he will propose later, but the articulation of insights is more in the nature of claims, analogies, promptings, and the like rather than philosophical analysis proper. It is clear that Nishida sees the blind assumption of the subject-object distinction to be the cause of most philosophical errors and paradoxes. It is also clear that he envisages the world as seen through the eyes of the physicist, the biologist, the psychologist, the artist, and the mystic to be different worlds, ordered into a hierarchy with the most abstract being that of the physicist. All of these worlds are seen as abstractions (even that of the artist, although it is less abstract than that of the physicist) of a reality that itself cannot be viewed as a world. If this reality were viewed as a world, then it would be viewed as an object and the subject-object distinction would thereby be applicable to it, making it less than the reality that engenders all these various worlds. The subject-object distinction is drawn within this ultimate reality; it is a fragment of it. Because of this distinction the various abstract worlds are possible, but what Nishida calls reality lies beyond this distinction; it encompasses and generates the distinction. Thus, it is clear that Nishida does not mean to opt for a materialistic position or even an idealistic position that is simply on a par with but opposed to materialism. In this respect, his orientation is identical with that of the two Inoues, as we were at pains to show in Chapter 1. But there is a difference. Nishida attempts to get at this reality by a more direct means than the dialectical arguments employed by either Inoue Enryō or Inoue Tetsujirō. The mechanism he uses is the concept of pure experience.

Of the four parts of the book—entitled respectively Pure Experience, Reality, The Good, and Religion—we shall consider here only the first two. While the religious concepts that Nishida employs are fundamental to a total understanding of his thought, my primary interest lies in his logic and concepts that led to the development of that logic. It should be noted here that logic for Nishida is not divorced from metaphysics but inextricably bound to it. Precisely what this means will, I hope, be made clear as our study progresses.

The Concept of Pure Experience

The term *pure experience* was borrowed from William James, whose influence on Nishida does not seem stop there. Not without good reason Nishida's position has been termed a form of "radical empiricism." At first it would seem that Nishida is emulating the good Bishop Berkeley, in that the first indication of what he means by pure experience is his characterization of it as direct experience.[1] Pure experience is said to be "the state of true experience itself without the addition of the least thought or discrimination."[2] The example that Nishida gives suggests an allusion to what Berkeley termed "ideas." He speaks of the instant of seeing a color or hearing a sound before there is any thought of the color or sound as being something external or as being something sensed, that is, as the instant before any judgments are made concerning the color or sound. What can this mean? At first it would seem to signify a state of blind sensation, a pre-intellectual state similar to that of a newborn child. Such a reading is soon proved erroneous when Nishida goes on to insist that even thought is a kind of pure experience; hence the association with Berkeley's ideas. The connection is lent further plausibility by the fact that one of the chapters in the section on "Reality" is entitled "Conscious Phenomena: The Only Reality." Nishida, however, explicitly rejects this interpretation. He specifically states that the atomic sensations of the psychologists are not what he is referring to when speaking of pure experience, since these atomic sensations are, as he says, only the results of analysis, no more than objects posited for the purpose of explanation.

The Berkeleyan interpretation is doomed for a more basic reason. According to Berkeley an idea necessarily implies a subject who had that idea. For Berkeley the subject-object distinction is fundamental, while for Nishida, pure experience is prior to any such dichotomy. In his words, "It is not that there is first the individual and then experience, but first there is experience and then the individual."[3]

These words are among the most frequently cited passages from *An Inquiry into the Good*, and not without reason. Marxists regard this passage as providing the grounds for their justly accusing Nishida of neglecting the individual at the expense of some "totality" (which they see as referring to the State), thus justifying their placing of his philosophy in the camp of latent fascism. Similarly, the emphasis on experience has been used to "demonstrate" Nishida's idealism. I have no desire to become enmeshed in the tangle that surrounds the political interpretations of Nishida at this point, but the charge that this passage clearly stamps Nishida as an idealist would, if it were true, be serious enough to nullify the effect of much of his writing and for that reason merits a closer look.

Nishida is forceful in insisting that he is not an idealist, and that his position locates him beyond the materialist-idealist clash. Yet, as we will see, there seems reason to argue that Nishida does in fact fall into the "idealist trap." In particular, his method of overcoming the dichotomy of subject and object is to pierce the veil of subjectivity. In other words, Nishida attempts to go beyond the distinction by pushing one aspect of the distinction to its limits until the distinction itself collapses. This procedure will be most evident in his later work where he adopts the distinction between noema and noesis and speaks of "transcending in the noetic direction,"[4] but the same move is easily recognizable already in *An Inquiry into the Good*, even if its effectiveness is much less pronounced at this early stage. In order to see how this move is made, it will be necessary to inspect the notion of *pure experience* in some detail and see how Nishida adopts it in his discussion of reality.

The approach that Nishida uses to get at the notion of pure experience is psychological; indeed, the notion as originally propounded by James seems more appropriate to psychological investigation than to philosophical inquiry. Nishida himself criticizes much of *An Inquiry into the Good* in a preface to a later edition of the work (1936) as being far too psychologically oriented. Be that as it may, after giving the capsule definition of pure experience cited above, he proceeds to examine what sort of things can be characterized as pure experience and, in so doing, turns his attention consecutively to perception, thought, will, and intellectual intuition. These categories are examined precisely because they are ordinarily thought to be disparate from one another. What Nishida attempts to show is that their distinction and seeming independence is only the result of abstraction, and that concrete experience, by its very nature, embodies the characteristics of all these categories. In so doing he lands himself in apparently contradictory claims, such as the two statements alluded to previously: "pure experience is experience itself without the least admixture of thought" and "conceptual activity is also a kind of pure experience."[5] The question is whether this pair of statements, and numerous others like it, is really inconsistent or whether there is an interpretation capable of rendering it consistent.

The first question for Nishida is whether pure experience is complex or simple. His answer is direct: "No matter how complex pure experience is, at the moment of its happening it is always one simple event."[6] The idea behind this rather odd-sounding statement is that although an examination of an event of pure experience may reveal many different things to be going on in the experience, there was a cohesive unity at the time of the actual experience. The complexity to which he refers is not merely the variations that can be seen in the perceptual field at any given time. He is not merely referring to the fact that a red patch has some shape or other, or that a tone has a number of harmonics. He wants to speak of pure experience even when the context shifts from red patches and simple tones to the experience of seeing a complex landscape with a variety of shapes, sizes, and colors in the form of mountains, clouds, sky, trees, and so forth, or in the auditory realm, to the experience of hearing a cacophony of noises produced by a variety of instruments.

That said, the complexity Nishida acknowledges is still greater than what can be seen in in such instantaneous experiences as these. For him the complexity of the pure experience extends to temporal diversity as well.[7] Consider a situation where you are riding on a train and watching the scenery slowly pass by, staring out the window in a dreamy state and not making any particular judgment about the scenery or the stiffness of the seat in your carriage. The perceptual series can continue for a considerable time without any break in its unity. The entire episode could be said to be a single event of pure experience. The example Nishida himself uses is that of a musician playing a piece he is very familiar with. The examples seem to differ radically in the sense that the first seems to refer to a thoroughly passive state where one is merely sitting and watching a flood of images wash across the visual panorama, whereas in the second the musician is actively engaged in the production of a piece of music and not merely listening to what others are playing. The difference is rather important in the sense that it is just this active-passive distinction that Nishida means to break down. To see the first example as essentially passive is to have made a distinction between an object and the subject to whom that object appears. What Nishida would stress in both cases, however, is the fact that in the experience itself there is no distinguishing the subject from the activity in which the subject is engaged or from the scene that the subject is viewing. The experience is dynamic in both instances, and it is only after the fact that we can dissect the experience in such a way as to talk of the subject as passive in one case and active in the other. The dissected or analyzed experience is not itself the pure experience but only a reconstructed model of that experience. The model has a unity, but it has this unity only by reference to the original experience; it is only with reference to the original experience that the model has any sense.

Each of the above examples displays a certain unity and therein lies the purity of the experience. Its purity does not in the least depend on the degree to which the experience is diversified or to what extent it can be dissected, analyzed, or brought into relation with other experiences. Indeed, analysis of the experience disrupts the unity. Within the experience itself there is an internal unity, a necessary progression that can be seen as the unifying activity of the experience itself. When the experience is brought into relation with other experiences this internal unity is shattered. Now what can this mean? For one thing, the internal necessity cannot be a binding force that is consciously felt; such force would be an external intrusion, a disruption of the unity of the pure experience. It is crucial to the purity of the experience that its necessity or cohesion is not brought explicitly to consciousness. The musician does not feel himself impelled by some force or constrained in some fashion; indeed, in the case envisioned by Nishida, he is not conscious of himself at all. What flows and develops is the music. Of course, his hands are moving over the keyboard, but he is not conscious of them unless something untoward should happen like striking a key that is out of tune or misfingering a passage. Barring such occurrences, Nishida would claim that the experience has a unity an internal necessity—or, if you will, a natural progression.

Given all of this, there must be a sense in which pure experience is not in time. At the very least it cannot be in the time of the physicist or even in the time of the psychologist. These times are modes of ordering, relating, and analyzing pure experience and, as such, represent a fragmentation of that pure experience. The very act of making a judgment is seen as a disruption of an event of pure experience. The judgment itself is not the mere concatenation of symbols of one sort or another but an integrated whole based on an event of pure experience. Take, for example, the statement, "This horse is white." Here there is no question of an abstract notion of horse and an abstract notion of white that are subsequently tied together by a copula to produce a judgment. What we have is rather the simple intuition of a particular white horse, which is then analyzed in the judgment. The idea here is that underlying each judgment there must be some unifying intuition and, further, that the unifying factor must be a fact of pure experience. This would mean that the unifying factor must be a specific experience and it would seem difficult to claim specificity for a mathematical intuition or an intuition of a law of logic. The term *intuition* seems to be used here in a slightly different though related sense from the sense in which one sees a particular horse. What Nishida seems to mean is that in pure experience there can be the internal necessity of movement from one judgment to another.

This last statement may strike one as slightly odd, if only because it was preceded a few lines previous by a statement that seemed to imply the very opposite. The reason for the apparent contradiction would appear to lie in the fact that the referents of the term *pure experience* were not made clear in the two statements. Let us take an example. Say that you are sitting on a fence gazing into the pasture and suddenly exclaim, "That horse is white." What would be the explanation of this event in terms of the notion of pure experience? One might say that the internal unity of the experience had been shattered by the exclamation, but just what would this amount to saying? A reasonable interpretation might be that one had not expected to see a white horse in that particular pasture, or that that particular horse was, in all respects save color, the exact duplicate of a horse well known to you, and, thus, when one encountered this white horse one uttered the statement, "That horse is white." Another possibility is that a white horse was precisely what you had been looking for and therefore made the statement once you had found it. In any case, the natural assumption is that statements, if they are truly statements, are not made without some reason, which in this case is the unexpectedness of the experience or the attainment of a goal.

The same point could be made by focusing on the thought without any stipulation that it be expressed later in verbal form. The point of saying that this thought or this judgment is a disruption of a pure experience seems to mean just that the unity and continuity of the experience is broken. But, here again, what does that mean? What could it mean but that the pure or unified experience is not taken as something to be related to other experiences, some *thing* to be treated as an object. Once it has been treated as an object, the unity of the experience is disrupted. The judgment that this horse is white adds nothing to the content of the original experience; it merely relates it to other experiences. The experience of seeing the white horse that is the foundation of this judgment is now analyzed, though obviously not completely since there is more to the original experience than the concepts "horse" and "white."

But now what are we to say of this act of making a judgment itself? Is it not also an event of pure experience? And if so, how can one say that there is not an element of discrimination in pure experience, that there is no element of thought in pure experience? If, on the other hand, judgment is to be counted an event of pure experience, then precisely what does the concept of pure experience exclude? This was in fact the objection, though in slightly different form, raised by Takahashi Satomi. The response will become apparent as the discussion progresses. Nishida's own answer is that he is not primarily interested in distinguishing pure experience from impure, but only in showing that perception, thought, will, and intellectual intuition are basically of the same form. Throughout, the crucial aspect of his discussion of the notion of pure experience is that of unity.

Thought for Nishida arises when there is a conflict; it is a reaction to conflict. Thus, in the example cited previously, the thought "That horse is white" was seen to arise in response to a problem or an unexpected turn of events (or as a goal that is hoped for, but more of this when we come to a consideration of will). The flow of the experience is interrupted and its unity shattered. In what way? Its unity is destroyed by arresting attention and fixing it on a particular aspect of the whole experience, thus dissecting the experience by thinking about it. Certain elements of the whole experience are singled out and made the object of thought because these elements "jarred" with the experience as a whole. In what way did they conflict with the experience as a whole? The first reply, that one was not expecting to see a white horse to be in that particular pasture, could be dismissed on the grounds that one's expectations are not part of the experienced scene but merely personal feelings that neither contribute to nor distract from its purity. The problem with this sort of objection is that it leaves the notion of pure experience out of the picture entirely. The objection assumes the distinction of the subjective feelings of the subject and the objectively based origin of the scene being viewed, with both the feelings and the scene being described antecedently. This is the very sort of objection Nishida is trying to sidestep with the notion of pure experience. The unity of the experience is not a unity (in this example at any rate) of the objective scene. Such unity would not be fractured let alone shattered by the kind of judgment made in the example. The unity of the experience was not some combination of antecedently given elements, namely, the objective scene and the subjective feelings, since no mention was made of any conscious sentiment of anticipation. All of this was introduced only in the attempt to give an account of the reasons for making the judgment. Viewing the original experience as pure experience,[8] as an active, dynamic flow of experience that is later analyzed as having elements of anticipation on the part of the subject, helps to make what Nishida is driving at somewhat clearer.

The same example may be used to illustrate a number of other points as well. The "intrusion of thought" shatters the pure experience, but it is not only that the judgment is based on an event of pure experience but that the act of thinking about the experience is itself an attempt to unify. The origin of thought lies in conflict and its purpose is the resolution of that conflict. This unification, when seen as the imposition of a unity on the chaotic, needs to be kept distinct from what Nishida means by pure experience, but thought is not something one engages in from a distance. It has its own internal unity and one is caught up in it. One can become engrossed in a problem to the point of "forgetting oneself," and when the problem is resolved one may feel as the problem had solved itself. The process of thought moves on its own toward a solution. This unity, or flow, can also be broken, of course, and the entire train of thought can become the object of investigation, but in respect of its unity it does not differ at all from the flow of experience we saw in our example.

Moreover, thought can be seen as essentially concerned with truth, not as a mere subjective ordering of experience or is it a mere bestowal of meaning. The whole object of knowledge is practical; it aims at the unity of pure experience. Thus Nishida says thought can be viewed as "a process in the development of a great system of consciousness."[9] It is at this point that he makes reference to Hegel's notion of thought being concrete and goes on to state that if one speaks of thought in this sense, it would be possible to say that pure experience is thought:

> Seen from concrete thought, the generality of a concept is not, as is usually said, that which is abstracted from similar characteristics, but is rather the unifying power of concrete events.[10]

It is this notion of dynamic unity that is seen to operate in thought as well. The orientation of thought is toward an ever greater unity, a unity that will encompass everything. In this sense thought moves beyond the individual, as indeed it must if one is to speak of it as pure experience.

Self-conscious awareness is what brings about the disruption, but Nishida never explicitly says as much. This in itself, is a bit disconcerting considering that his approach is—as he himself later acknowledged—psychologically oriented. As we shall see when we consider Nishida's later work, this concept of self-consciousness, together with the concepts of nothingness and "predicate logic," becomes pivotal in his philosophy. The Inoues did not refer specifically to self-consciousness either in order to explain their views, although it is hinted at in the work of Tetsujirō in terms reminiscent of Nishida's own intimations.

In the light of the foregoing, the idea of pure experience as prior to the intrusion of any thought whatsoever and the classification of thought as pure experience do not seem quite as paradoxical as they had at first. To be sure, this does not make the notion totally clear and distinct. We have still to consider the emphasis on the notion of activity and on the will before accurately assessing the significance of the concept of pure experience.

Having pointed to the fact that thought has essentially a practical basis, that is, a foundation in the will, Nishida then goes on to speak of the will and attempts to discover what differentiates it from thought. Once again he begins in an essentially Berkeleyan manner, but he uses this approach only as a stepping-stone to a quite different view. His own view is one in which differences of inner and outer, of subjective and objective, and the like, lie not in the different content of the "ideas" but rather in a difference of relationship. In other words, by discovering into what coordinate frame the terms are placed, their distinctness turns out to be only apparent.

Nishida analyzes will to be an "idea of movement"[11] and a feeling of anticipation. This is a traditional phenomenalist tact and is taken for the same reason: to show that there is no need to appeal to a will over and above the phenomena of consciousness. The difference between will and knowledge is simply that, in the case of the former, the "idea of movement" tends to dominate consciousness. Nishida's wording is confusing here, but fortunately he adds a number of examples to clarify what he mans. His analysis centers around the fact that in order to desire something, it must be singled out and chosen, but at the same time, in order to do so, one's attention must already be turned toward it. Desire involves some structuring, some thought. One cannot be said to desire unless there has been a cognitive (not necessarily conscious) process of singling out the object. As he had noted earlier, however, this cognitive structuring is basically practical and has an inextricable relation to the will. One can differentiate the two by saying that with the intellect subjectivity seeks accord with objectivity, whereas with the will the reverse is the case. But this only indicates a difference in emphasis and not a dichotomy, for some of each occurs in what we would characterize as intellect as well as what we would characterize as will (for instance, one cannot will the impossible). Thus, an experience can later be analyzed as intellectual or volitional, but this characterization at best designates an emphasis, not the essence of the experience. Looked at purely in terms of conscious events, there is no way to make any absolute distinction between the intellect and the will. Even if one introduces the notion of free will, it is not sufficient to establish such a dichotomy, since we decide and act because of demands and these demands are "given," not freely established.

In most of his arguments and analogies Nishida seems bent on showing that given any concrete experience, it is impossible to find either element lacking. There are no purely volitional events; nor are there any purely intellectual events. The difficulty with his examples is that they lead the reader to want to know how, even if any experience will have all these features, one can thereby conclude that intellect and will are identical? It is like saying that hue and intensity are not distinct simply because one cannot find any color that does not have both. But clearly Nishida does not want to say that intellect and will have nothing to differentiate them. He merely wants to show that they are interdependent and, thus, not "building blocks" for one another.

The distinction between subject and object, fact and ideal, arises from the conflict of experiential unities (systems), and attempts to resolve this conflict are made by moving toward a high unity. The unity he has in mind here, whether in knowledge or the ideal of truth, is not the arrival at an abstract common denominator but something that more closely approximates concrete experience. "Perfect truth is individual and real."[12] That is to say, truth is not an abstraction but a union, in some sense, with fact. The upshot would seem to be that it is only when the subject-object distinction vanishes that such perfect truth can be realized. The variety of attempts at scientific explanation approach the truth, but in the end they are doomed never to attain "perfect truth" because of their basic adherence to the subject-object dichotomy and the bias toward the objective dimension of reality.[13]

Will is also seen by Nishida as basically an attempt to arrive at a state of internal unity. If one thinks of will purely in terms of desire, then one seems to be constrained to speak of an individual; consequently, all talk of unity will only be a subjective form of unity. Nishida finds this approach mistaken for the simple reason that desires signify a disparity, a clash of will with facts; desire implies that the will is obstructed. The demand for ideals that go beyond the realm of the individual is crucial here. This demand is seen not as the conscious establishment of ideals as yet unrealized and in conflict with the reality of present circumstances; it is rather like the guidance of ideals that function without one's being conscious of them. In fact, the ideals could not function if they were conscious. If the ideals are made the object of investigation, as such they cannot any longer operate directly to guide inquiry. An example may help. Consider an artist painting a portrait. When fully absorbed in his work, there is no consciousness of painting an object; it is almost as if the painting were painting itself. The painting is a directed, but not consciously directed, activity that Nishida speaks of in terms of a unity of consciousness, a unity of the will. The direction is guided by an ideal of beauty, not an ideal that is in some abstract sense consciously in the artist's mind, but, rather, an ideal that guides her fingers, her eyes, her whole body; it is an ideal that realizes itself in the painting and that is developed and enriched through the painting. The attempt of the art critic to rationalize the event, to characterize the underlying ideal, forsakes the idea that moves the artist for another. The critic attempts to unite the painting systematically to other events, outside the actual composition of the work. When Nishida states that "at the basis of all reason and law there is operating the unifying activity of the will,"[14] he is not referring, then, to will in the sense of conscious will (which he has already analyzed in phenomenalistic terms) but to the unifying power of ideals outside the conscius sphere. He suggests that these be considered as the realization of the will of reality itself.

Nishida's discussion of intellectual intuition builds on these concepts, typically taking them to refer to the intuitions of artists, mystics, and so forth. He rejects the notion that it is some special sort of seeing or a completely new type of experience. He talks, rather, in terms of the scope of the unity that is introduced and that maintains the initial intellectual intuition. A deepening and enlarging of experience is achieved by bringing a greater range of experience into the unity. This does not mean that it is purely an intellectual exercise; it is rather something like the "perception" of the ideal that permits the artist to paint in the first place. It is the seeing of an ideal and the attempt to realize it concretely. The point is that all systems, intellectual or otherwise, are systems by virtue of their unification. Their unity derives from their being based on an intuition of an "ideal," and the system itself is the attempt to express or realize itself. The system is the development of the ideal or the intuition. This last point is important because it helps to explain what Nishida means when he argues that one differentiates intuition from imagination on the basis of a difference in the scope of their unity. Whether what feels that an intuition is an intuition or not depends simply on whether the claim to unity is valid or not. One might use the example of scientific theories and say that what makes one better than another is not some purely internal difference, but whether or not the theories do, in fact, explain the facts they purport to. Deciding between theories is a question of determining which ties together more of the fabric of experience in a coherent way.

The notion of pure experience presented in this first section can be linked to the problem of the given. There is a sense, Nishida claims, in which the whole notion of an absolute given is a completely misguided notion.[15] The reason is that anything "describably given" is already "thing laden." To talk of red color patches, sounds, and so forth, as the given is putting the cart before the horse. These "givens" are arrived at only after a lengthy analysis beginning with the assumption of a subject-object distinction. Even Kant's solution is inadequate, according to Nishida, since the given content that is structured by the forms of intuition and the categories is, in some sense, independent of the structuring self. This is the very point that Nishida will take up later in his *Reflection and Intuition in Self-Consciousness*.

The first section of *An Inquiry into the Good*, which deals explicitly with pure experience, was written after the section on "Reality" and was intended as an explication of the concept used in that earlier section. For this reason he states in the preface that it is not necessary to read the sections in order; in fact, if one has difficulty in following the line of reasoning in this first section, it would be perfectly feasible to skip it and begin with the second. This may be due to the way he introduced the concept of the "given" in the first section, namely, with its strong psychological overtones. Nishida tries to lead one into "seeing" pure experience rather than elaborate or logically demonstrate its relations with other more familiar notions. In this respect he differs dramatically from the Inoues in the sense that their "identity logic" never involved this dissection of the various types of mental phenomena with an eye to piercing the veil of the subjective-objective distinction. Instead, it consisted in moving back and forth between a subjectivist and an objectivist point of view, remarking on the inadequacies of each. Tetsujirō, it is true, does seem to move in a direction similar to that taken later by Nishida, but he does so in what we can only call an offhand manner. When he notes, for example, that we are aware of things only through phenomena and that we encounter and know phenomena only directly, his "proofs" are not restricted to any sort of phenomenological analysis. While the Inoues are pulling themselves out of the swamp by their own pigtails, Nishida attempts to reach the same position by pushing in one direction of the dichotomy to such an extent that he breaks through the walls erected by that dichotomy. This pursuit of the path of pure subjectivity, as distinct from a subjectivity that is opposed to objectivity, characterized Nishida throughout his career.

At this point it may seem that the concept of pure experience is of no help whatsoever in discovering a new philosophical position or sorting out an important philosophical issue, since all Nishida appears to have told us is that what we experience is richer than the content of our dissection of that experience. If that were in fact the case, there would be nothing very remarkable in the notion. On the contrary, it would even seem to be wrong. One need only think to those occasions when something previously experienced is amplified by the awareness of some detail that had so far gone unnoticed. The idea of a pure experience richer than our thoughts about it seems perfectly plausible when one thinks of the difficulty of communicating one's feelings on parting with one's beloved or when one recalls the way she looked at the parting, rare though such events may be. Is it not the case that we can be corrected with respect to judgments we make about our experience? Someone may say to me, "But you did see that boat; you were looking right at it." Is this not just what happens when a master teaches an apprentice the art of seeing things that are normally overlooked?

Nishida was not unaware of this sort of question, but he insisted that noticing elements in experience not previously attended to does not imply any addition to the experience by means of later judgments. In fact, the very assumption that there are discrete parts in an original experience that are later brought to attention is precisely what he is challenging. His position would be equally untenable if understood to claim that an experience cannot be meaningfully explained, as any number of examples would prove. But he is not saying this either. What he does claim is that, while experience can be explained, such explanations add nothing to the experience itself; they do not render the original experience any fuller. On the face of it, this seems absurd, for surely noticing something that had gone unnoticed must be considered an enrichment of the experience in some sense. To notice something like this and single it out as the object of a judgment may relate this experience to other experiences, and indeed this is precisely what Nishida says it means to give meaning—but it does not touch the original experience. Relating one experience to others is an attempt to widen the scope of that experience and effect a greater unity, which would seem to enrich the original experience by locating it within a higher unity.

The difficulty presented here, namely, that one talks of the "purity" of the experience as being destroyed while at the same time affirming its placement in a higher unity of experience, seems to stem from the attempt to view the notion of pure experience in terms of discrete segments. One wants to talk of this or that example of pure experience and contrast it with examples of impure experience, but according to Nishida this is precisely what one cannot do, since to make an object of pure experience is to shatter its unity as pure experience and to devitalize it. The basic characteristic of pure experience is activity, a dynamic with an internal (not conscious) necessity.[16] The activity is lost when the experience is taken as an object of analysis. This does not mean that all activity is lost. Pure experience, Nishida would say, develops, and one form of the development is for part of experience to be taken as an object. Taking an experience as an object is nothing other than the development of that experience. Here Nishida points to, but does not elaborate, a position we will see him take in his later work. This mechanism of development is self-consciousness, but no allusion to self-consciousness as such is made at this point.

Reality

Nishida tries to develop a view of reality based on his notion of pure experience. The view is stated in terms of consciousness as the only reality, but consciousness needs to be undestood here as pure experience and not as part of the subject-object opposition.[17] Crucial to this step is a kind of Cartesian doubt, in the sense that what Nishida seeks is a standpoint free of presuppositions, a radical empiricist standpoint where no appeal is made to dogmatic assumptions of any kind. For Nishida, Descartes' *cogito* is to be rejected as an inference but can be accepted if undestood as the expression of an intuitive certainty joined to reality.[18] He will make frequent reference to Descartes' *cogito, ergo sum* in subsequent works, always on this same point.[19] One may well compare Nishida's assessment with certain modern critiques of the Cartesian statement, such as those based on the discinction between performatives and deductions. What Nishida appears to find objectionable in the deduction interpretation is the fact that it presupposes the "ownership" theory, or simply the subject-object distinction, or again the thinker-thought distinction. It is just this no-ownership view that separates him from Berkeley. At the same time, it does not force Nishida into a Humean stand, although there are passages that suggest this, such as the following:

> To say that consciousness must of necessity be somebody's consciousness means merely that there must necessarily be unity in consciousness. It is clearly dogma if it is thought that beyond this there must be an owner."[20]

This Humean quality is especially prominent when one looks at the following discussion in which it is argued that there is, from the viewpoint of pure experience, no absolute distinction between "I" and another, but only a different grouping of experience. This begins to sound very much like Hume and one would expect the same difficulties found in Hume when he attempts to give an account of the unity or groupings we encounter. But this is where Nishida turns the tables upside down. Where Hume would attempt to analyze the notion of activity, Nishida takes activity to be immediate. To attempt to analyze activity, he insists, is to enervate it. It is this activity that is the core of reality, or in other words, the development of pure experience.

Thus, while using Berkeleyan arguments to reject the notion of matter existing beyond the phenomena of consciousness, Nishida also avoids the pitfall of solipsism in a more convincing way than the good Bishop had. Rather than invoking God to rescue one from solipsism, Nishida simply points out that the solipsistic stand requires the prior distinction of subject and object. The solipsist must hold an ownership view for his position to have any meaning. He must claim something to the effect that the world is nothing more than a creation of his own mind. Technically, this sounds correct, but one wonders whether it is not possible to construct a solipsism that did not hold this "dogma." Such a view would have to be something like the claim that only one individual self could be abstracted from the flow of pure experience, a view that seems not only less forceful than the former but also much more difficult to argue.

Nishida argues for the consideration of experiences purely in terms of content; as such it makes no sense to talk of my experience except as unified in a certain way, that is, as located in a certain nexus. The content, he claims, is perfectly general and, indeed, it is possible to communicate not only thoughts but also emotions. He wants to argue that reality cannot be merely the object of the intellect but must be a pure experience where there is no prior distinction of subject and object, nor of intellect, emotion, and will. This is not to say that experience is merely general or abstract. In fact, Nishida specifically states, immediately after pointing out that emotion and will must both be seen as having transindividual elements, that true reality can never be communicated. At this point one becomes aware of a frustrating polarity in the work. On one hand, Nishida wants to maintain that consciousness is the only reality and that the individual is created from experience, as opposed to maintaining that the individual is ontologically prior to experience. On the other hand, he wants to talk about an individual stamp imprinted on reality that seems to lead to a notion of individual realities. In other words, he would both affirm and deny a unity to pure experience.

The apparent contradiction allows Nishida's central point to rise to the surface. There is not just one unity. There is the unity of individual consciousness and the unity of the objective world. This latter is established when, according to Nishida "the phenomena are universal, that is, when they maintain a unity beyond small individual consciousnesses."[21] Here again he appeals to the notion of a norm or an intuition to serve as the bridge to a communal and not merely solipsistic world. The flower seen by the physicist does not occupy the same status it does for the botanist and the poet. Each of them sees a different reality, or perhaps we might say there are three different realities, three unities, each of which has the same form if they are truly unities. Each is the explication of a point of view (a term to be understood without reference to the notion of an individual and subjective point of view), but there is an implicit whole prior to these points of view, a whole that becomes explicit through the differentiation of content. Each is a unity grounded in an intuition, or a norm, or an ideal, in the sense previously discussed, but the scope of their unity is quite different. The physicist's unity pales beside that of the artist's simply because it leaves out so much—the beauty of the flower, for example. Yet even the artist's expression of the flower pales beside the reality of the flower itself— not the flower as a physical object, but the flower as an event of pure experience.

At this point, Nishida begins to resemble the Inoues in that he begins to discuss the notion of dynamic unity that he had been employing with reference to reality, i.e., pure experience. At the outset it makes the same point as the Inoues and Hegel, to the effect that unity is inconceivable without opposition and vice versa. The unity underlying the natural world is force while the unity underlying the world of mental phenomena is the unifying power of consciousness. But these two worlds must be further unified, and the fact that they are so unified is attested to by the fact that mathematics and logic present us with principles that are applicable to the objective world. In fact, Nishida says in a much later work, logic is reality's form of self-expression.[22] This latter statement will take more than a little unpacking, but we will set it aside until the notion of predicate logic has been taken up.

The example Nishida gives of a tree that "exists through the opposition and unity of its parts"[23] might have been given by either of the Inoues, but his explication goes far beyond theirs. Both the Inoues stop with "points of view" united into a whole, whereas Nishida goes on to stress the dynamic nature of the unity and the form of its development. It is one thing to say reality maintains distinctions in the midst of unity (a purely static view), and quite another to speak of the manner in which the single system that constitutes reality develops.

Nishida also makes considerable use of the same kind of arguments used by the Inoues when he talks of reality as identical to phenomena, but he leans more heavily on the notion of living things containing unlimited opposition and their capacity for unlimited change. His language is hyperbolic, but the meaning is clear. The idea of unity he seeks is not a static or artificial unity, but a dynamic, active unity, a unity that develops of itself and that brings forth oppositions from itself. Reality could not derive its unity from anything other than itself for the simple reason that there *is* nothing else. If we look at the unity of consciousness, for example, it is natural to think of the elements of consciousness as disparate and independent, and from there to suppose that any unity that exists is an imposed unity. Yesterday's consciousness and today's consciousness are separated by a space of time and are independent entities within the fabric of time, or so the view goes. Nishida argues, however, that the notion of time itself is established only within the flow of experience as a means of ordering experience, which is to say that time itself is not ultimate but rather depends on a unity that in some sense lies behind it. Time can be seen as the objectification of the flow of experience, but as an objectification of that flow time does not itself determine the flow but is rather something that is determined by it.

Basically the unity of which Nishida speaks is present immediately before one as a fact. This is not to say that it is presented as an object, but rather that there is a direction to the flow of experience. Each and every unity, be it a unity of the individual self, the objective world of the scientist, or the world of consciousness, has the same form. At this point Nishida tries to impart a vision rather than to give a strict argument, and he does so by speaking of a "law" in accordance with which all things in the universe are established. The law is not seen as an abstraction of the relationship of individual items in the universe but as the rule of development that results in the postulation of matter and spirit. At first glance, he seems to be reverting to a position that Inoue Enryō had rejected as "archism." Not so. Nishida nowhere makes the claim that his law is anything more than a mere unifying principle that cannot be considered apart from the unified elements. It is never the object of consciousness for the simple reason that making it so would destroy its unifying power.

It is this notion of power that Nishida refers to when attempting to explicate the meaning of true activity. He does not want to say that activity is merely a change in physical relations or a passing from one state of consciousness to another. These are the results of activity. What he is after is the unifying powers that allow this change. This ultimate unifying factor is found in a strict subjectivity that, as was stated previously, is to be contrasted with a subjectivity that is opposed to objectivity. This is reality, or pure experience.

Following the formula given by the Inoues, Nishida talks of this reality as open to any number of perspectives. One can think of the natural world as pure experience without the unifying function. This is the world of the physicist. Here the unity is not an internal unity but merely a relation in space and time. Explanations turn out to be no more than certain regular associations, a type of explanation that Nishida discards as totally inadequate. Why so? What other kind of explanation can there be? The answer lie in something like "organic unity" or "purposive unity." Nishida takes as an example a bronze statue that obeys all the laws of chemistry and physics that one can apply to such an object: dimensions, weight, chemical composition, and the like. As such, the statue fits into the scheme of laws devised for a purely material, technical explanation. But it is more than a heap of bronze; it is a creative work of art that expresses human ideals.[24] There must be some unifying force beyond the purely mechanistic one to account for this fact.

This unifying force, the force of our ideals, is directly encountered in pure experience. The object is no longer merely something unified from without as is the object as seen from the point of view of mechanics. It has a purpose, a significance, and even a self (in a very broad sense of the term). The unifying power does not reside outside the object but constitutes its very nature. This unifying force behind nature is not something "beyond the pale," as it were; it is nothing other than the unifying power of consciousness itself. Furthermore, descriptions in terms of the expression of ideals and mechanical explanations do not as such contradict one another. They are more like the overlaying of the object with different coordinate grids. Thus Nishida concludes:

> Therefore our understanding of nature's significance and purpose is based on the subjective unity of the self's ideals, emotions, and will.... As our ideals and emotions become deeper and broader, we are more able to understand the true meaning of nature. In short, our subjective unity and nature's objective unifying force are basically identical.[25]

The words seem altogether incomprehensible, since he appears to be saying that this unity is internal to nature and yet, at the same time, that it is due to consciousness. Even if one can accept the statue as having a unity over and above its unity as a purely physical object, it strikes one as odd to say that this unity is internal and at the same time is the unifying power of consciousness. In his defense Nishida asserts that such objections are based on the prior assumption of the subject-object distinction, a distinction that is absent in pure experience. His "explanation" does little initially to allay the confusion, given that the notion of pure experience itself is already fraught with difficulties and unclarities. But what he wants to say is not so complicated: nature cannot be conceived without reference to consciousness.[26] The unity apprehended must be related to consciousness since this unity is directly apprehended in direct experience and is not inferred. The unity itself can be viewed objectively as the internal unity of the object or subjectively as the unity of our ideals. Viewing it in one way or the other is possible only once the subject-object distinction has been made, and for this reason both perspectives are abstractions from the concrete fact of pure experience.

That said, the mode of viewing this object in terms of purpose and the like can be said, objectively, to have a higher status than viewing it in a purely mechanical way since this latter captures less of the experience than the former does. "Consciousness" does not refer to individual consciousness but to the unity of pure experience. Individual consciousness is but one more of the myriad of "fragmented unities," not the whole of reality. Put this way, the assertion that subjective unity and the unifying force of nature are basically the same does not sound quite as self-contradictory; both are taken to be polarizations of the same thing, of pure experience. The deepening and enriching of our ideals and emotions does not take place in a vacuum; as Nishida reiterates again and again, there is no subjectivity without objectivity. The enhancement of our ideals and emotions is also a deepening and enriching of experience itself; it belongs to the story of the development of pure experience.

However, just as nature cannot be considered without reference to subjectivity, spirit (or mind) cannot be considered without reference to matter. To speak of subjective mind or spirit apart from matter is to speak in abstractions. One can speak of a unifier only in the context of something unified. Yet again Nishida argues from the coordinate nature of the concepts. The very distinction between mind and matter arises from conflicts within experience itself. It is only when two unities come in conflict that the notion of spirit comes into being. What is more, Nishida sees the notion of spirit as dependent on the notion of ideals. Ideals take shape by contrast with actual fact. One does not become conscious of one's desires and motives until they have in some degree been frustrated. The conflict of these various unities is inherent to the nature of reality; it represents a mode of development and is the key to the generation of spirit (or mind). These entities are, of course, unities of events of pure experience; they are not themselves dichotomized into subjective and objective aspects until such time as there is a conflict that involves them, that moves in their "direction," as it were.

From this conflict emerge mind and matter. Nishida is not so willing to accord equal status to spirit and nature, since he places the unity of spirit higher than that of nature by virtue of the fact that it can see and make its own unity. In other words, spirit is conscious of its own unity; it is self-conscious and that is what enables it to develop its unity to a greater degree than nature is able to do. Self-consciousness is a concept that Nishida will explore in his later work and elevate to one of the core notions of his entire system, but at present he simply does not have the mechanisms to deal with it adequately. To say that the unity of self-consciousness is greater than the unity of nature does not mean that heightened self-consciousness is to be pursued as an ultimate goal. In fact, heightened self-consciousness and the elevation of the individual ego constitute a barrier to "seeing things as they are." This is why he speaks already at this early stage of knowing in the sense of becoming one with the object: "When one sees a flower, this means that the self becomes the flower."[27] Not that one is consciously transformed into a flower and begins to feel the itch of insects crawling around on one's petals. It is only that in the apprehension of the flower there is no consciousness intrusion of an individual self. If the individual self is located in consciousness, then one might say that one was apprehending a relation between the flower and the self. In that case, one would be centered not on the flower but on some fact concerning one's relation to the flower, which is something quite different. "Truth is obtained by submerging the subjective self and becoming objective."[28] Here again we see the link of the subjective to the objective, clarifying and reinforcing Nishida's claim that he is searching for an ultimate objectivity that can be achieved only by adopting a viewpoint of strict subjectivity.

Criticism

Critics like Komatsu Setsurō[29] contend that this talk of strict subjectivity and of a transcendence beyond the confines of either materialism or idealism is merely a dodge, and that ultimately Nishida is a dyed-in-the-wool idealist. This seem a reasonable enough conclusion so long as one restricts one's view to Nishida's talk of the phenomena of consciousness as the only reality.[30] It becomes harder to defend when one takes into account the distinction of the subjective and objective that Nishida goes on to make. Objections like that of Komatsu are typically based on the first steps of Nishida's argument, confusing starting point with conclusion. Little is accomplished if one is not prepared to meet Nishida on common ground, and in fact the results are all but completely predictable. Such prejudicial reading has debilitated many a wholesale rejection of Nishida's work. Reading him with even a modicum of openness allays any suspicion that he is a materialist, let alone some kind of subjective idealist. There is certainly a tendency to move in the direction of what might be called idealism in the latter stages of his section on reality, but the label is not much help. Even to call him an objective idealist would require defining that term in a way peculiar to Nishida's case.

Shimomura Toratarō raises a more serious question when he states that *An Inquiry into the Good* does not distinguish clearly enough between "not yet differentiated" and "no longer differentiated."[31] This ties in with an objection raised by Takahashi Satomi concerning the supposed levels of unity and the distinction between thought and intellectual intuition.[32]

Concerning Shimomura's point, we may say Nishida seems to be trying to express much the same notion we find in the celebrated Zen saying:

> At first mountains are mountains and rivers are rivers. After one has meditated a bit, mountains are no longer mountains and rivers are no longer rivers. Upon reaching enlightenment, mountains are mountains and rivers are rivers.

Given Nishida's strong interest in Zen Buddhism, one is inclined to read him in the light of sayings like this. Nishida has not, Shimomura insists, clarified the relation between one who has attained this level of intellectual intuition and one who has yet to make the subject-object distinction. Surely there is a difference between a child who has not yet developed a strong sense of individual ego and a musician who navigates an intricate composition without making a distinction between "I" and "the music I am playing," and this kind of difference needs clarifying. But this is too weak a response. It is not merely that Nishida presents us with a hierarchy that progresses from no distinction, through distinction, to the obliteration of that distinction. If this were what he was doing, there would be very little difficulty in explaining process. As Shimomura points out, the "first" and "last" stage or the "lowest" and the "highest" stage are not merely identical, but are dialectically identical. They are identities in difference. He does not, unfortunately, clarify that statement, but it is this very point that Nishida will seize on in the development of the notion of basho.

Moreover, as was mentioned previously, even this differentiated, self-conscious state can be seen as an event of pure experience. This is the gist of one of the criticisms made by Takahashi. That Nishida intends to distinguish different levels of unity is abundantly clear from his discussion of intellectual intuition, but, Takahashi asks, if there are such differences, how is it possible to speak of directness? If one wants to maintain that there are degrees of unity while maintaining that each is pure experience, then it would seem to land us in a contradiction. Takahashi sees the contradiction surface in the following statement of Nishida: "When any conscious state is unified it is pure experience, i.e., simply fact; meaning and judgment arise only when this unity is shattered."[33] If every degree of unity is pure experience, and, thus, "simply fact," then one could not distinguish meaning from fact. If everything can be said to be fact, then it could equally be said to be meaning.

Nishida acknowledges Takahashi's point but does not see it as a difficulty. Any experience can be seen either way, depending on one's point of view.

Meaning and fact are no more than two aspects of the same conscious state, and each and every conscious state has aspects of both unity and diversity. This seems to amount to saying that any conscious state can be made an object of inquiry and thus lose its status as pure experience.

In fact, the question goes a deeper, since the whole notion of pure experience is built around the idea of unity. Each of the unities in question is an "oriented" unity; if this were not the case, it would make no sense to speak of them coming into conflict. And that would be disastrous for Nishida's position, since it is only through the conflict of these unities that the concepts of self, objects, and so forth are engendered. But how do conflicting "lesser unities" arise? If the unities are part of the fact of pure experience, as Nishida says, then how can meaning be explained? Nishida's only reply is that the "facts" contained in pure experience are not in opposition to meaning but rather must be seen as meaning. As explanations go, this does not seem very helpful. Nor does the example he gives, similiar to the earlier example of the tree, to show that no meaning is introduced that was not there at the beginning, but that when one aspect of the experience comes to be emphasized or clearly cognized, others are obscured. The problem remains, and will in fact become the principal focus of *Intuition and Reflection in Self-Consciousness*. In a word, the failure to explain the precise relation of meaning to fact is one of the most compelling reasons for saying that Nishida has given us at best a psychology of pure experience but is yet to offer a logical analysis.

Two further criticisms of Takahashi are most instructive because of Nishida's replies. First, he argues that Nishida wants to speak of pure experience as the spontaneous autonomous development of a "self moving" universal, but this presents the problem that pure experience itself must be located at some level or stage of that development. That being so, the experience is merely part of the development and not all experience can be said to be pure experience. If one takes the opposite view and conceives of pure experience as the whole process, then there seems to be no way we could possibly know it completely.

Nishida immediately rejects the notion of pure experience as being only part of the development, since this would be to speak of an analyzed, objectified experience, and not pure experience itself. The response is in keeping with his earlier remarks about the difference between pure experience and the analyzed experiences spoken of by psychologists.

Nishida's reply to the second alternative is more interesting. He agrees that if one is going to attempt to characterize pure experience at all, it must be as the whole ongoing process, but he objects to the idea that this means that we cannot know it. Takahashi's point is that if this is a process with infinite variation, as Nishida indicates, it would seem absurd to speak of knowing the whole of this infinitely developing reality within the context of finite experience. Nishida's reply is that knowing this totality does not merely mean linking all the various levels at all possible points into some exhaustive scheme of classification. It means knowing the internal movement of the development. This suggests something like a direct awareness of the generative form or motivating force of the development. Nishida does not get more specific; spelling out the point will be left to later works. Suffice it at this point to note that his position has certain affinities to Hegel's statement that understanding how the dialectics works does not imply the ability to deduce Professor Krug's pen.

It is worth remarking here that Nishida's resemblances to Hegel continue throughout his career, but, as will become apparent when we examine Nishida's logic, their views are far from coincident. In a later essay entitled "Hegel's Dialectic from My Point of View,"[34] Nishida observes that Hegel's dialectic requires the Absolute be treated as an object, which sets it fundamentally apart from his own view. The differences will become clearer as we follow the development of the idea pure experience.

The second of Takahashi's criticisms I wish to single out is that in expounding the developmental aspect of the notion of pure experience, Nishida sees it not as an opposition of subject versus object or of unity versus opposition, but an opposition between these distinctions and that which allows them, or between these distinctions and the unifying power of the whole. In other words, Takahashi is claiming that Nishida has fallen into a position similar to that rejected by Inoue Enryō as "archism." Nishida acknowledges that he has not made himself sufficiently clear on this point, but rejects the interpretation of pure experience as a unity apart from opposition. There is, he claims, a unity in oppositions.

This is very much like the position he will pursue in later works, with the difference that he will first erect a logical scaffolding to give his claims a more solid footing. Nishida had not developed at this time the concepts of basho and nothingness that he would later use to meet this type of objection. Nishida treated pure experience in categories similar to those with which he treated those aspects of experience that he wanted to contrast with pure experience. This elicited a variety of criticisms from various quarters and continues to annoy the reader in search of an inner consistency to the text. Simply put, the concept of pure experience is not sufficiently sophisticated to do the job it must do. It represents an insight, but the insight has yet to be given a firmly developed structure.[35]

Conclusion

As noted previously, *An Inquiry into the Good* lays out the core intuitions of Nishida's philospohical outlook: the attempt to get beyond the subject-object distinction, and to do this by "pushing" in the direction of strict subjectivity by means of an emphasis on the dynamic nature of the development[36] and on the intuitions underlying the various unities or points of view, taking a strong anti-metaphysical stance with respect to the "news-from-nowhere" metaphysics, and with a commitment to a holistic approach that does full justice to all aspects of human experience. At the same time, the work fails to answer certain crucial questions for want of a sufficiently rigorous logical framework.

Nishida's book may be placed in the tradition of the Inoues, going them one better in its attempt to provide a method for presenting the Middle Path of which they have spoken. Like their work, however, it fails to penetrate deeply enough into the relationships between the diverse parts of experience. The work is more full of puzzles than the articles written by the Inoues. This seems to be a result of Nishida's attempt to argue from one base, although there are places in the section on "Reality" where he appears to shift his argument from an individual to a universal perspective, though without providing proper justification for the move.

Nishida also means to reject the Kantian notion that there is a fundamental dichotomy between form and content. This contrasts strongly with the view expressed by Inoue Tetsujirō, who takes a correspondence theory of truth. This rejection of a correspondence theory, it should be added, also leads Nishida to deny the possibility of absolute truth, since he is persuaded that truth can be spoken of only in terms of some point of view. In pure experience it makes no sense to talk of truth or falsehood, as this would imply a specific conscious standard or perspective, which, in turn, would imply that the unity of the pure experience had been shattered.

The shortcomings of Nishida's first book are painfully apparent. Aside from the large number of arguments that are in effect nothing more than analogies or at best broad logical leaps,[37] there are the difficulties pointed out above concerning to the relation of meaning to fact, the relation of intuitions to elements united by those intuitions, the precise way in which these unities are related to each other and to the whole of experience, and the lack of precise structures that allow one to speak of pure experience without becoming inextricably entangled in paradox. These defects seem so great that I would venture to say that if Nishida had died after having written only this work, he would not have had the stature that he enjoys today in modern Japanese philosophy. This work contains the seed of a mature philosophy, but without a great deal more patient nurturing there would have been no such thing as "Nishida philosophy."

THE VOLUNTARISM OF *INTUITION AND REFLECTION IN SELF-CONSCIOUSNESS*

Although Nishida produced a number of articles between *An Inquiry into the Good* and *Intuition and Reflection in Self-Consciousness*, it is only with the publication of this latter work that he effectively comes to grips with the problems with which his maiden work could not adequately deal. Although *Intuition* is much longer than *An Inquiry into the Good* and the arguments it contains are much more detailed, we shall devote much less space to it than was spent on the earlier work, and that for three reasons. First, the space required for a detailed treatment is is well beyond the scope of the present study. Second, this work does not follow in any sense a neat progression of ideas forming a unified structure. As Nishida himself put it in hindsight, it is "a document of the bitter struggles and agonizing conflicts in my thought."[38] Third, Nishida himself admits in the preface to the second edition that the work ended with the problems intact, which is to say, unsolved.[39]

Intuition represents a reassessment of the notion of pure experience and an attempt to articulate a mechanism for solving the problem of standpoints. In it Nishida seeks to provide the epistemological foundation that was lacking in the first work. In his own words:

> The purpose of writing these essays is to think of all reality in the form of what I call a self-conscious system, and by this means to attempt to explain the union of value and existence, and of meaning and fact, which together constitute an important problem in contemporary philosophy. Of course, what I call "self-consciousness" is not the so-called self-consciousness of the psychologist; it is the self-consciousness of the transcendental ego. It is something like Fichte's *Tathandlung*. I believe this was suggested to me by the appendix to Volume 1 of Royce's *The World and the Individual*. I had this concept already in mind when I wrote the

article "The Understanding of Logic and the Understanding of Mathematics" for my *Contemplation and Experience*. This work is the result of my attempt to pursue this idea as thoroughly and completely as possible. If I have succeeded in this purpose, then I think it will be possible to give a firmly based synthesis of the present-day Neo-Kantians and Bergson by giving a new meaning to Fichte.[40]

At least implicitly Nishida had been dealing with self-consciousness in his exposition of the concept of pure experience, but he had not really delved deeply enough into its nature. He admits in effect that Takahashi's criticisms of his notion are fundamentally correct and he sets forth to meet these objections with the aid of a view of self-consciousness provided by Royce.[41] Since the emphasis throughout the work is on self-conscious activity, it is not altogether surprising that the end result is a mysticism presented in terms of the absolute will, a will that is the ultimate ground of unity for the worlds that he views as being created by the various epistemic standpoints such as the physical world, the historical world, the world of art, and the world of mathematics. All of these are said to be interpretations or rationalizations of ultimate reality, the world of the absolute will.

Nishida begins his inquiry with an investigation into the judgment of identity. Although this is purely a logical judgment, he believes that he can show the opposition of meaning and existence even on this level. Furthermore, he believes that he can show the relation between the two to be one of internal necessity founded on the act of judgment itself. While he is in sympathy with the Kantian analysis of judgment and readily admits the necessity of a transcendental synthesis for there to be judgment at all, he argues that the synthesis and the result of that synthesis are one. As he sees it, there is no opposition between a content given from without and a form supplied by the subject. Both the form and the content are given immediately in experience. Given a judgment of the form "A is A," there is a tendency to make a distinction of the conscious content, A, and the synthesis of this as an object, and then to regard the content and the synthesis as independent of each other. But if one carefully reflects on the judgment "A is A," one realizes that the content and the synthesis are not independent but are only different ways of taking the same concrete experience. In viewing the concrete experience statically, the notion of an unchanging object arises; whereas if the experience is viewed dynamically, it becomes the act of judging or the synthesis. Consequently, in order to take something as an object one must first understand it as self-identical.

This last statement, which is intended to be something in the way of an explanation, seems to be at least as cryptic as the original statement. The difficulty lies in the fact that the term "something" used in the explication has the same logical status as the term "A" in the original statement. One must speak of a something (object) when one tries to say that it becomes an object through synthesis. Less cryptically, it means that in order to think of an object, an object of a certain sort must exist. To have an object at all one must, at the very least, think of it as self-identical. One must be prepared to say "A is A." By the same token, to say "A is A" meaningfully, one must be thinking of something named by "A," an object. There is then an equivalence between saying "A is A" meaningfully, as a judgment, and saying "A is."

The notion of any object, "A," and the idea that "A is A" expresses a necessary condition for objecthood are merely different ways of viewing the same concrete experience. To say that the concrete experience is merely the apprehension of a content or that it is merely the awareness of the necessity of the law of identity is to make a fundamental error. One cannot have one without the other. Furthermore, there is no agent-subject involved in this taking of "A" as referring to an object or in the setting forth of the conditions of objecthood. There is no agent-subject in the concrete experience of making the judgment; there is at most pure activity. "There is only the spontaneous fact (*Tathandlung*) 'A is A' as the concrete total experience, i.e., as the true reality."[42]

Thus, even at the basis of purely logical judgments there is self-consciousness; concrete experience is basically self-conscious in character.

> We say that "A is A" is our reflecting on "A," but seen from "A" itself, it is the "A" consciousness returning to itself, in other words reflecting on "A" is to intuit a unifying "A," which is at its foundation. To reflect on that which is independent is to reflect on that which unifies. In such a case, my activity is the activity of a higher unity. Reflection is the intuition of a greater unity; it is the development of a still greater life. What is objectively the development of a greater reality is subjectively the deepening of reflection; reflection is the process of the development of reality.[43]

In this way there is constituted a self-conscious system. This self-conscious system is, however, a most abstract one in the sense that the objects are merely logical objects and the unifying idea or a priori, as Nishida refers to it, is merely a logical principle. One might say that he has demonstrated how the system of logic is a self-conscious system, but the question that then remains is how to proceed. He states that his purpose is to view all reality in the form of a self-conscious system, and this obliges him to apply the model to all aspects of experience. He must make the "transition from a system of thought to a system of experience."

Nishida goes on to interpret various systems of experience—such as the the perceptual system—as self-conscious systems. He has to show not only that there are a number of self-conscious systems, but also that they are interconnected and related in such a way that they form one coherent, all-embracing system. The different standpoints or the a prioris that determine them will have to be shown to have a necessary relation to one another, for example, the relation of logic to mathematics and the relation of mathematics and perception. Failing to do this, he will be unable to show the essential identity of the subjective and objective realms. He tries various approaches, only to land himself in difficulties similar to those of *An Inquiry into the Good.*

Most of the examples used in these attempts are drawn from mathematics, especially conic sections, analysis, and Cantor's set theory. He places particular emphasis on the examination of the notion of a limit in mathematics. This seems to be the mechanism that will permit him to explain the relationships between the various a prioris. Thus, he speaks of a limit as being a higher standpoint, a more concrete standpoint than that of which it is the limit. No collection of points is ever capable of giving a continuous line and no collection of polygons can yield a circle. But a continuous line is the limit of a collection of points, just as the circle is the limit of a series of polygons. To see the limit as a limit, however, requires a new intuition. This is just to say that in order to take "s" as the limit of a collection of "t"s one needs more than just the idea of "t," one needs an intuition of "s." Nishida concludes:

> Our concrete experience cannot be satisfied from the standpoint of an abstract system. The concrete experience, i.e., our life itself, demands a still more concrete position, and, thus, our thought ever progresses towards concreteness.[44]

From there he attempts to account for the relationship of the various a prioris. In each case there is an appeal to a concrete consciousness that lies in the background. Thus, it is not that logic demands mathematics, but that the foundation of logic is also the foundation of mathematics. It is demanded by logic plus mathematics. The example of analytic geometry is clearer. It is not just a happy accident, he argues, that algebra and geometry can be brought together. It is rather the result of what one might call a "transcendental sensation."[45] The creation of analytic geometry is not the joining of two disparate fields but a returning to a more concrete system. This more concrete system is not the outcome but the foundation. Knowledge moves from the abstract to the concrete, the goal being to return to concrete experience. Reflection is the generative principle of that development: reflection on a standpoint is the intuition of a new standpoint that is more concrete and includes the former standpoint. Each of these standpoints will be a self-conscious, self-developing system. When we reflect on any such system, we can do so from within, as it were, and so view it in its primal form. But it is also possible to view it from a still larger, more concrete position that lies in its background, and so view the more concrete as the limit of the less concrete. In terms of physical science this is simply the difference between a mechanistic and a teleological conception of the development of the physical world.[46] In similar fashion Nishida goes on to speak of the relation between body and mind, arguing that the mind is the body's concrete ground, or again that the body is the mind's means while the mind is the body's goal. Finally, a self-conscious system is formed that encompasses worlds of varying degrees of concreteness tied together by teleological relationships. This self-conscious system is concrete reality.

Now these various worlds can also be seen as independent worlds, and viewed in this way, they can be said to make contact in the present. This is not the static point instant of the physicist, but rather a focal point on which the whole of reality is projected. It is what Bergson called the leading edge of the *élan vital*, the leading edge of the development of reality. It would seem that Nishida has accomplished his aim, but as he pursues his investigation he comes upon a contradiction that forces him to retreat into mysticism. The present is both the leading edge of creative development and the point of reflection on the past; but it is impossible for us to return to the past, even for a split second. The resolution of the paradox can be found only in the will, for it is the will that is the true source of unity for the various a prioris, and the will cannot be the object of knowledge:

> We transcend the present self in memory and, thereby, unify the whole individual self; we transcend the individual self in thought and unify the whole transcendental self; but in the will we transcend the world of cognition and unify the whole of reality.[47]

The difficulty that Nishida encounters here is that cognitive structures cannot encompass all of reality for the simple reason that every cognitive structure is essentially a viewpoint, and this, he argues, implies a distinction of the knower and the known. The knower and the known are not immediately united in knowledge. It is not so much that the intellect cannot return to the past as that it cannot encompass the present. Whatever is the object of knowledge must be limited, specified, and determined, and a limited present is not the actual present. The active present is the reality that cannot be reached by thought; it is the limit of thought. It is the will. Thus he remarks that Scotus Eriugena's denial of even an internal necessity in the will of God holds a profound meaning.[48] The transition to a complete mysticism is now complete. Reality is ineffable; it can be characterized only in a negative or an analogical way. In this context Nishida refers to a number of medieval mystics such as Dionysius and Eriugena, citing the latter's characterization of God as the identity of *natura creans et non creata* and *natura nec creata nec creans*.[49] It is the world of religion, a world open to mystical insight, but not to the intellect. If it has to be characterized philosophically, it must be called the absolutely free will.

It is only by a move in this direction that Nishida is able to secure a mechanism for uniting the various a prioris. He accepts the Kantian view that it is a matter of unifying experience from a particular point of view. True subjectivity is not the subjectivity of our mind, which stands in contrast to the objects of the external world, since such subjectivity is the object of introspection and as such is on a par with the objects of the external world. This is to say, the empirical ego is not true subjectivity. True subjectivity must be that which constitutes the objective world. Knowing is here understood by Nishida to be a constitutive act. Pure subjectivity constitutes a world of objects but it can never be made an object itself. Accordingly, various worlds—for example, the world of mathematical objects, the world of artistic objects, the world of history, and so forth—are constituted according to various a prioris. But all these are particular points of view; they are, if you will, particular interpretations of experience. The world prior to all these constructions must be a position of no positions, a standpointless standpoint. It is the world of direct experience, the world of pure experience, the world of absolute free will.

Nishida characterizes true reality as being both infinite development and infinite return, both *egressus* and *regressus*. From one point of view, true reality is the infinite progression of fact that is at once value, while from another it is the "eternal present" that can freely return to its origin. He alludes to terminology of the Neo-Platonic tradition to characterize the absolute, speaking of the Plotinian One that must be recognized before the

Ideas of Plato, but feels that their characterization is couched in overly intellectual terms. For his part, he prefers Origin's characterization of "creative will."[50]

We are in contact with this world of the absolute will, or rather partake of it, in each act of will. The immediate object world from the standpoint of the absolute will must be a world of free will, a world of independent activity. This is a world where everything is a symbol. Even the material world is nothing more than a kind of symbol.[51] The symbols are not all on the same level, however. The two most direct and concrete systems are the world of religion and art, while the natural world occupies a place much farther down in rank.[52] At any rate, we are members of a large number of different worlds and it is the will that permits us to move freely from one to the other. In moving toward the more concrete we are going toward our fundamental ground, epistemologically, ontologically, and ethically. Pursuing this train of thought, the concluding last section of *Intuition* presents a splendid, mystical vision that can hardly leave the reader unmoved. Unfortunately, it is precisely that: a vision.

This sketch of Nishida's second attempt to solve the problem of standpoints is far too brief to indicate the complexity and the subtlety of the reasoning involved, but even this glimpse at of the bare bones of the argument is sufficient to indicate why the attempt failed. Nishida himself, as we have noted, freely admitted that it was a failure. The employment of a Fichtean notion of self-consciousness as the basis for building a structure to resolve the subject-object dichotomy led necessarily to a form of mysticism. Although infinitely more sophisticated than the solution put forth by Inoue Enryō, seen as a whole, Nishida's attempt suffers from the same defect as that of his predecessor: his solution is no solution at all. Still, the effort was not in vain in that it had provided him the occasion to attack meticulously, even brilliantly, some of the most difficult problems of philosophy, and in so doing had led him to forge the intellectual tools that would turn him into a first-rate philosopher.

Summary and conclusion

In this chapter we have examined the first two attempts made by Nishida to solve the problem of standpoints. Both of them, as we have seen, were unsuccessful. But there is a basic difference in the way they were unsuccessful. Briefly put, *An Inquiry into the Good* failed because it lacked a rigorous structural foundation, while *Intuition* failed because of a retreat into mysticism resulting from an over-emphasis on the notion of activity. Although neither managed to solve the problem philosophically, taken together they represent a vast improvement on the simplistic solutions offered by the Inoues. What is more important is that they helped to lay the groundwork for the further development of Nishida's thought.

In *An Inquiry into the Good*, Nishida's solution to the problem of standpoints is presented by means of the concept of pure experience. Epistemologically viewed, pure experience is a state of direct awareness of things as they are, a state of immediate apprehension in which there is no distinction drawn between the content of the experience and the act of experiencing that content. It is a state in which there is no differentiation of thought, will, and emotion. Pure experience is an absolute and simple unity that is both the ground and the goal of all partial, conceptual unities. It is not merely a particular psychological state of an individual, since the individual is constituted in experience. Ontologically, pure experience is a self-consciously, spontaneously developing unity that constitutes the whole of reality. It is the ground of the physical and the mental worlds that are but partial and abstract constructions produced from the infinite richness of pure experience. All attempts to delineate the nature of reality are doomed to failure. Although there is a hierarchy of increasing adequacy from the physical to the artistic, it is only through religious experience that we can come into immediate contact with the whole of this reality.

The exposition of the concept of pure experience in *An Inquiry into the Good* already displays a number of ideas that will be central to Nishida's later work, among them the rejection of the subject-object dichotomy, the emphasis on utter subjectivity, the centrality of self-consciousness, the notion of a hierarchy of worlds, and the importance of the religious dimension. The defects of the work stem primarily from an insufficient epistemological grounding for the notion of pure experience. The relationship between the various levels of experience and pure experience is not made sufficiently clear. Various inconsistencies appear in his characterization of pure experience for which he cannot fully account. The work is less a presentation of a string of philosophical arguments than a weaving of a vision. He has tried to present a unified principle to account for the dynamic unity of standpoints, but he had not worked out the principle with sufficient vigor.

The absence of detailed argument is most definitely not a characteristic of Nishida's second attempt to present a principle for the solution of the problem. *Intuition and Reflection in Self-Consciousness* is a tortured account of detailed arguments based on an interpretation of self-consciousness not unlike Fichte's *Tathandlung*. The interrelationships between the various worlds (each of which is a self-conscious system based on a particular a priori or unifying intuition) are spelled out in detail. The final self-referential unity, however, cannot be established until Nishida resorts to a mystical resolution in terms of the self-consciousness of an absolutely free will. There seems little doubt that the move to this form of voluntarism amounts to a retreat into mysticism.

Nishida acknowledged his defeat: "I may not escape the censure of having broken my sword, expended my arrows, and finally surrendered to the camp of mysticism."[53] This admission is of great importance for understanding the development of his philosophy. Many commentators consider the statement uttered in jest, because, they argue, Nishida's long training in Zen could not possibly have allowed him to place mysticism in the enemy camp. I think them mistaken and see no reason not to take his words at face value. Nishida was profoundly religious, but this does not mean that he regarded mysticism as a suitable replacement for philosophical argument. The task of philosophy is to show structure and to do so rigorously; to resort to mystical explanations when caught in a philosophical predicament is to relinquish that responsibility. If this were not the case, there would have been no need for him to continue to revise, refine, and rework his approach. In the case of *Intuition*, it is precisely because of his recognition of his capitulation to mysticism that he turned to a reassessment of the problems of consciousness to discover the cause. He found the cause in his attempt to interpret knowing as an activity. It is the rejection of the emphasis on activity that marks the transition to the concept of basho.

3

Consciousness and the
Mystical Foundations of Realism

AFTER "HAVING capitulated to the enemy camp of mysticism" at the end of *Intuition and Reflection in Self-Consciousness*, Nishida made a number of attempts to clarify his thought and deliver himself from defeat. In this spirit he turned to the fields of art and morality.[1] This, however, provided no significant breakthrough and only served to intensify the feelings expressed in earlier works: artistic intuitions were more concrete and accurate modes of perceiving the nature of the world than those of the natural sciences. The problem remained: How, without resorting to blatantly mystical language, does one explain why artistic intuition occupies such a position? It would mean unraveling the whole knot of epistemological problems. But such a reexamination could not be conducted without guidelines. It was clear that the move made toward voluntarism in *Intuition* had not been successful; still, the attempt had shown that the role of self-consciousness in the knowing process did indeed hold the key to some solution.

Nishida's insistence on the importance of self-consciousness was accompanied by an equally strong insistence on the notion of a hierarchy of worlds—each based on some fundamental intuition (or a priori, one of his favorite terms in *Intuition*). Together with a delineation of the relations between these worlds, this hierarchy gave each world its distinctive quality. By speaking of an a priori of a prioris (which he took to be the "absolutely free will") he hoped not only to specify the relationships between these worlds, but also to show how it was possible to negotiate one's way from one to the other. As I have tried to show in the preceding chapter, this explanation in terms of the absolutely free will is what he finally dismissed as a "capitulation to the enemy camp of mysticism." At the same time, Nishida will felt that a hierarchy of worlds or "viewpoints," related internally or organically, would be absolutely essential. He did not want to adopt a materialist or an idealist stand, nor did he want to compromise with some sort of dualism. Rather, he wanted to develop a position showing that these were both partial and limited views, views that could not give an adequate description of the whole of experience. The philosophical position sought would not be a mere rejection of these limited views nor a nihilistic sigh that no adequate account could be given.[2] It would have to be a systematic and coherent position that would subsume these positions. In his essay "Basho"[3] we find an initial development of this position; the present chapter will be concerned with the transition to it.

As Nishida himself states, the development of his thought from *Intuition* to the position expounded in "Basho" can be best described as a transition from voluntarism to a form of intuitionism.[4] These terms, especially the latter, are in need of an explication. Suffice it for now to characterize the move in his own words as a shift from a "position that was quite akin to Fichte" to one whose central concept was that of "seeing all that acts and all that exists as a projection of that which reflects itself in itself while making itself to be nothing."[5] Unpacking of this last phrase will require more than a few pages. In a sense it will the remainder of this book. For now, we may understand it basically as a rejection of the view that self-consciousness is an activity.

In general terms, the transition consists of a move away from the interpretation of self-consciousness in terms of structure. Since this transition is marked by a basic reconsideration of the nature of consciousness, we will give some indication of the results of that investigation before attempting to characterize the concept of basho.

The reexamination of the nature of consciousness through a consideration of the analysis of consciousness offered by various schools of psychology that Nishida undertakes in *The Problems of Consciousness* resulted in a clear rejection of atomistic psychology and a decided preference for a gestalt orientation. This alone was not enough to provide Nishida with the appropriate mechanisms for escaping from the appeal to mysticism. He still leaned in the direction of treating consciousness as an activity, the very thing that explains his failure in *Intuition and Reflection in Self-Consciousness* to develop an adequate answer to the problem of standpoints.

The introduction and development of the concept of basho as a mechanism to solve the problem of standpoints is not explicable merely in terms of Nishida's rejection of atomistic psychology or his frustration with the results of interpreting consciousness as an activity. Indeed, as I have indicated in the introduction, the modifications of Nishida's thought are not mere rejections of previous standpoints in favor of some totally new position woven out of whole cloth, but are better viewed as a series of related attempts to develop a technical mechanism for expressing insights gained through meditation. There is a tension in Nishida's thought between the desire to express religious intuition and the desire to make this expression one that has its own philosophic and logical integrity. The key to understanding the rhythm of his thought is to bear in mind the strength of these basic impulses.

Attention to Nishida's religious experience will assist us in understanding the transition from voluntarism to intuitionism. More specifically, the concept of basho, which Nishida will present as the mechanism for solving the problem of standpoints, becomes intimately related to the concept of nothingness. The concept of basho is to be taken here as a technical philosophical concept and not primarily a religious concept, but it is only by virtue of its interrelationship with the concept of nothingness that it can serve as the mechanism Nishida is seeking. It is not only that basho is a complex of logical, epistemological, and ontological characteristics. Already earlier Nishida had endowed the concept of "pure experience" and even that of the "absolute will" with a similar set of complex characteristics, although, as we have seen, they failed to perform the task expected of them. What gives the concept of basho the likelihood of performing this function is that it serves as the basis for a logic of basho that is fundamentally a logic of nothingness. It is only the characterization of basho as nothingness that gives it the force that it has.

The concept of nothingness is one of the central concepts, if not in some sense *the* central concept, in Zen Buddhist thought. And since it was essentially his Zen experience that laid the foundations of Nishida's philosophy, it is not surprising that it should come to play such an important role in the formal structure of his metaphysics. That said, the notion of nothingness appears explicitly as a formal element of the system only after Nishida has introduced the concept of basho and attempts to derive a "new logic" to serve as a grounding for his metaphysical system. The concept of nothingness is the key to understanding the Zen experience and it is also the key to understanding Nishida's metaphysics in general and the concept of basho in particular. It will thus be necessary to inquire into the nature of Zen nothingness in order to provide the background for an exposition of basho.

I do not mean to suggest that the concept of nothingness was not present in Nishida's philosophy prior to the article "Basho," but this is the first time that he expressly employs it as a structural element in his philosophy. One might even say that his escape from mysticism was brought about by tools provided by mysticism, such as the concept of nothingness, and that it was only after his defeat at the hands of mysticism that he turned to a structural interpretation of nothingness as the only possible path to pursue. This chapter will thus be devoted to a brief assessment of Nishida's re-examination of consciousness and a clarification of the traditional concept of nothingness in Zen. The emphasis in the latter exposition will fall on the intertwining of the logical, ontological, and psychological features of the concept, and on the various metaphors that have been used to illustrate these features. This is particularly crucial, since Nishida makes use of many of these metaphors in the exposition of his concept of basho.

THE RE-EXAMINATION OF CONSCIOUSNESS

In the 1920 work *Problems of Consciousness*, Nishida takes up again some of the problems that had been at the core of *Intuition*. In the preface he admits that, despite some interesting points, he has not arrived at a solution. The end result has been only to raise more questions. In general his arguments are concerned with an examination of consciousness and particular modes of consciousness such as sensation, feeling, and will. He refers particularly to claims made by the school of experimental psychology in its attempt to analyze consciousness without reference to introspection. While there is no need to go into detail here, it is useful to consider an example of the position he develops in order to appreciate the continuity of his thought.

Nishida's essay on feeling is a case in point. In it the main tendencies of his thought come vividly to the fore through his general pattern of reasoning. To begin with, he attempts to characterize feeling as distinct from sensation. The characteristic that most broadly distinguishes feeling is its "subjectivity." This is not only to say that sensation represents what has been objectively given by some stimulus, while feeling represents the individual response or the "something extra" introduced by the subject. To characterize the difference this way would be to place sensation and feeling on the same level and to trace their differences to their respective origins, internal or external. Nishida has no interest in this sort of "objectivized subjectivity." He is after something much more concrete. To say that feeling is more subjective than sensation, he argues, is to say that it lies in a deeper level of consciousness, that it represents a higher degree of unity than sensation does. Accordingly, if one can conceive of sensations as representations standing in discriminate relationships, then feeling is the consciousness of that which establishes these relationships.[6] From the shallower standpoint, feeling is seen as "irrational" or "subjective," and when any attempt is made to analyze what is at the higher level, the analysis cannot be effected except in terms of the elements of the lower level. Thus, empirical psychology "reduces" feelings to organic sensations of some sort. But to do this is to destroy the unity that is characteristic of feeling. This amounts to saying that an analyzed feeling is not a feeling since an analyzed feeling does not have the power to unify experience. This, in turn, means that an analyzed experience is not a felt experience.

In this way Nishida's attempt to distinguish sensation and feeling nudges him toward a distinction that reflects the unifying power of subjectivity. He feels that the reductionist tendencies in experimental psychology reflect a fundamental misconception of the nature of consciousness and the unity of experience. The reductionist view, though perhaps useful in some sense, is rejected because it does not do justice to the radical shifts in perspective that are possible in consciousness. Nishida is more concerned with the radical, qualitative difference between the experiences of, for example, seeing a book and wanting to read a book. He would vigorously deny that these are experiences of the same sort, differing only in the number of atomic elements that make up the experience. He would deny that an adequate analysis of the experience of desiring to read a particular book can be gotten from speaking of a visual sense datum attended by a cluster of other sense data. The difference between these experiences can be described only if one conceives of consciousness as a "multi-leveled system."

For Nishida, then, the general nature of consciousness is such that various standpoints are possible within it, and these standpoints in turn are interrelated in such a way that the lower standpoint is the more restricted or circumscribed. It is narrower than the higher standpoint and subsumed by it. From the point of view of the lower, the higher standpoint is always indeterminate and, thus, in a sense, free. There are, for example, various levels of intellectual activities, such as sensation, representation, and memory, but feeling is beyond any intellectual determination. It is, he says, "what is left over after all content of consciousness has been intellectually objectified."[7] The content of feeling can never be completely expressed in intellectual terms but only through some means such as art. This is not to say that feeling is something added to intellection, but rather that feeling represents a dynamic unity of consciousness, a unity of various intellectual activities and is thus, in his terminology, an a priori of a prioris. This is the reason that the content of feeling cannot be expressed merely on the intellectual level, for "concrete feeling is at a deeper level of consciousness than knowledge and expresses a still deeper reality than the objects of cognition."[8] Nonetheless, we are, in fact, conscious of feeling, and if the content of what we feel is not exhausted in intellectual terms, there must be a higher standpoint from which feeling is seen to be objective. This higher viewpoint is the will. Feeling is the content of the will, and will is the activity of activities. The will is the highest level of consciousness, and, as the phrase "activity of activities" suggests, Nishida remains committed to developing his position in essentially dynamic terms. Any number of summary statements—for instance, "Feeling is the consciousness of the unity of activity"[9]—confirm the point.

Of what value is all this talk of "higher" or "deeper" levels of consciousness? Nishida's point seems to be the same as that in his previous works, namely to claim in effect that the richness of our experience cannot be accounted for by a simple arithmetic summing of disparate elements. The supposed simple elements resulting from analysis, even when combined in an extremely complex way, do not yield an explanation of the unity of the experience. His framework sees consciousness as organized into various levels of experience, ranging from the abstract to the concrete. Feeling is on a deeper level of consciousness than sensation because the analysis of feeling must take into account a unity of consciousness not derivable merely from an analysis of sensation. This view stems from the commonplace observation that one can never completely objectify feelings and moods. It means little more than that the felt quality of an experience is lost when the experience is subjected to analysis. What is significant for Nishida in all of this is that felt quality that is lost is not merely another element of objective experience, nor is it simply some non-essential subjective overlay to the concrete elements of objective experience. Rather, it is an essential part of all conscious experience.

Feelings can become objects of analysis but only when they no longer function as feelings. Once again, this is a truism, but it is significant precisely because, in acknowledging it, we are, Nishida says, admitting three things: (1) that feelings can become objects of knowledge; (2) that when they do, feelings cease to function as feelings, in that they no longer serve to unify or "color" experience; and (3) that the fact that we know that the situations described in these two statements occur implies that an adequate description of consciousness cannot be given in terms of the nature of objects of knowledge.[10]

In short, Nishida is once again saying what he had said about the structure of consciousness in *An Inquiry into the Good* and *Intuition and Reflection in Self-Consciousness*. There is a hierarchy of realms of consciousness, the lowest being the intellect and the highest the concrete realm of the will. The height of the realm (or standpoint) is determined by the degree of concreteness of the experience, or rather, since Nishida does not want to discriminate experiences in terms of concreteness, the height of the realm is determined by the degree of the concreteness of the elements of analysis of the experience. This degree of concreteness is precisely the degree to which the elements of the analysis resemble the actual felt experience. This is an exact reversal of the reductionist's claim. Nishida is arguing that the realm of the intellect (the objects of knowledge) can be arrived at by abstracting from the more concrete level of feeling or will, but that it is not possible (as the reductionist position would claim) to arrive at the level of feeling or will if one starts from the level of intellect.

Here again, it should be emphasized that Nishida does not want to talk as if there were disparate realms of consciousness. But while consciousness remains a unity, we can discriminate levels of richness and, moreover, move from one level to another. I can be looking at my beloved and decide to shift my perspective to see merely a person before me, shift again to see a mere physical object, and even shift to seeing no more than a mass of visual sense data of a particular shape and coloration. If one were to adopt the sense data level as the basic level, then the notion of a physical body could only be regarded as a fiction, as a "subjective construction." So, too, if one were to adopt the stance that admits organic bodies as "proper elements" or objective elements of experience, then the feelings involved while viewing one's beloved would be "subjective additions" or "irrational elements." What is seen to be subjective is the unity recognized on a different level of analysis.

The thrust of Nishida's inquiry into the problems of consciousness is therefore consistent with his previous attempts, even as progressively more attention is paid to the role of self-consciousness in the determining of the objects of experience. Still, he has yet to effect a breakthrough. His analysis continues to turns on the notion of intuitions determining the standpoint and the realm of objects, and his primary emphasis remains on the interpretation of the intuition of unity as an activity. This tendency to stress the personal nature of the deeper levels of consciousness and the concrete world will prove to be a constant feature of Nishida's outlook.

The second point that we should note is Nishida's fondness for a particular kind of mathematical examples:

> Just as infinite numbers, which cannot but be seen merely negatively in the standpoint of finite numbers, can be thought of positively from a higher standpoint such as that of set theory, so, too, feeling can determine a positive content from the standpoint of the will, even though it is thought to be undetermined from the standpoint of the intellect.[11]

The fondness he displays for such examples is not motivated by any desire to bind his investigations to some revered discipline by means of vague analogies or to make his discussions sound more authoritative. But neither is it mere coincidence that so many examples should be drawn from the field of mathematics. The debt he owed to certain mathematical considerations in *Intuition* is, I think, clear from the sketch given in the previous chapter. What we need to note here is that the influence of mathematics did not stop there but remained an abiding presence in his work.

The nature of this influence, as well as the significance of the above analogy, will become clear when we discuss the notion of "topos" or "basho." We need only remark at this point Nishida's interest in logic is largely motivated by the feeling that any philosophical view of the world that did not have a "logical foundation" could not, in fact, lay claim to being "philosophical." As noted earlier, Nishida's sense of failure at the ultimate surrender to mysticism in *Intuition* was genuine, but this does not mean that he rejected mysticism completely. Indeed, the passage from the preface of *From the Acting to the Seeing* cited above (pages 2–3) states quite explicitly that he is seeking to provide a logical foundation for the mystical insights of the Japanese, and especially Buddhist, tradition. And he is attempting to do so in a coherent philosophical structure.

But what precisely are these "mystical insights," or better, what is this outlook for which he is attempting to find a logical foundation? One can, of course, simply say that it is the position of Zen, but this would need to be spelled out in greater detail. The concept of "nothingness" (*mu*) is at the core of Zen thought and also plays a central role in the development of what Nishida calls predicate logic. Without some brief discussion of the traditional understanding of this concept, it will be difficult to advance to the core of Nishida's philosophy.

THE CONCEPT OF NOTHINGNESS

Examining the concept of nothingness in Zen tradition not only will put us in a better position to assess the use that Nishida makes of it in developing his logic of basho; it is essential for understanding his thought as a whole in that the Zen experience remained a continuing source of inspiration for his philosophical reflections. In retrospect, such an examination will also help to throw further light on his earlier attempts to solve the problem of standpoints. In particular, it will help clarify the shift of emphasis from activity to intuition.

Noda Matao, in his illuminating article "East-West Synthesis in Kitarō Nishida," speaks of the concept of nothingness in connection with its implications for egocentricity. He remarks that the cultures of the East tend to give high value to nothingness not only in an ethical sense but also in a more fundamental, ontological sense. The remark is suggestive enough, and our appetite is further whetted by a quotation from Hōshaku, "All our doings are like brandishing a sword in the air [void]."[12] His failure to say more on the subject is not surprising. Indeed, it may well be that anything like an "adequate understanding" of the idea of nothingness is impossible in intellectual terms.

This, at least, would seem to be the gist of comments made by innumerable Zen masters who, when queried by their disciples on the ultimate nature of reality, reply in unexpected and seemingly irrational ways: beating the student over the head, remarking on the price of a robe, laughing, and the like. This pattern of reply belongs to the genre of the kōan, whose importance in Zen tradition is based on the conviction that intellectual discourse can never fully explain the nature of ultimate reality. One can experience ultimate reality, but not dissect or analyze it. Thus, we have examples of a monk asking, "What is Zen?" and receiving the reply, "Brick is stone." When the monk responds with another question, "What is the Tao?" the master replies "A block of wood."[13] One's initial reaction to this might well be an attempt to find some "hidden meaning" in the exchange, something symbolic in the notions of brick, stone, or wood, or even in material objects in general. It would be absurd, of course, to take the words at face value and argue that the monk was advocating some brand of materialism. In fact, all interpretations seem equally doomed to the charge of absurdity, particularly if one attempts to find a rational order in the vast number of kōan that have been handed down. A more plausible explanation is that the answer suggests the question is absurd; but even this cannot be the case, for discovering the Tao is, admittedly, the aim of the religious training that the master has undergone.

Let us take a clear example of the function of the kōan in general:

> The master asked Pai-chang, one of his chief disciples: "How would you teach others?" Pai-chang raised his staff. The master remarked, "Is that all? No other way?" Pai-chang threw down the staff.[14]

The message of this kōan seems to be that there is no unique way to impart teaching to others, but beyond that, and more significantly, it indicates that there is no rational, discursive method of communicating that message. This did not preclude some masters from attempting to give a more cerebral or academic orientation to their teachings, but never without a warning that the exposition was at best partial and ultimately meaningless.

There is an interesting parallel between this attitude of the Zen masters and Ludwig Wittgenstein in the *Tractatus Logico-Philosophicus* (6.54), where he writes:

> My propositions serve as elucidations in the following way: anyone who understands me eventually recognizes them as nonsensical, when he has used them—as steps—to climb up beyond them. (He must, so to speak, throw away the ladder after he has climbed up it.)[15]

As a matter of fact, the passage highlights a point of similarity (but not identity) between Wittgenstein and Nishida that we will turn to later in the book.

The Poetic or Direct Characterization of Nothingness

What then are these characterizations of nothingness? In *The Zen Doctrine of No-Mind* D. T. Suzuki claims that the characteristic emphasis of Zen was given by Hui-neng, the sixth patriarch, with the words "From the first not a thing is."[16] If this statement, which Suzuki regards as of such great importance, is not to be taken merely as a callow sort of nihilism or a desperate cry of despair, it must be carefully unpacked and seen in relation to similar claims about the nature of the world.

As Suzuki and others relate,[17] Hui-neng and Shen-hsiu were the two outstanding disciples of the fifth patriarch Hung-jen, and, due to the different interpretations that they placed on the teachings of their master, there arose in seventh-century China a split into the Northern and Southern schools of Zen.[18] The difference of views held by the two is shown in two poems they purportedly submitted to the Fifth Patriarch, Hung-jen. The first poem is by Shen-hsiu:

> This body is the Bodhi-tree
> The mind is like a mirror bright;
> Take heed to keep it always clean
> And let not dust collect upon it.[19]

The second is by Hui-neng :

> There is no Bodhi-tree
> Nor stand of mirror-bright.
> Since all is void,
> Where can the dust alight.[20]

At first glance, we have, on the one hand, a sincere and scholarly attempt to encapsulate in a terse poem the depths of a religious vision and a guide to the attainment of that vision; and, on the other, what appears to be a puerile quip that dismisses the whole enterprise. But then how can one explain that for well over a thousand years so many Zen scholars and religious men have revered Hui-neng over Shen-hsiu?

If Hui-neng's poem and Hōshaku's saying cited in the previous section earlier are not to be interpreted as facile and empty word play, then just how are they to be interpreted? The poem of Shen-hsiu might be taken to mean that physical things provide the occasion for attaining enlightenment. The Bodhi-tree sheltered the meditating Gautama on the occasion of his enlightenment, although it did not in any way directly contribute to the process of enlightenment. The mind must return to its pure, undefiled state, which is likened to that of a mirror that reflects totally without distortion. The mind, in its pure state, reflects things as they are and makes no attempt to alter them. This means that "the true state" of the mind is not to cleave to any particular orientation or mode of interpretation. Rather one should be utterly free of any limited orientation that would structure the given or categorize it. And just as it is quite easy for dust to collect on a mirror, so the mind quite readily adopts particularistic points of view. Human beings are prone to many and widely varied desires, just as mirrors can be covered with dust in an infinite variety of patterns. As the reflective properties of a mirror will be different depending on the nature, amount, and pattern of the dust, so, too, will the mind differ depending on the nature, number, and form of its desires. If one had only the reflections to go on, one would conceive the nature of what was reflected quite differently depending on the reflective properties. Furthermore, if one had never seen the reflections given by a mirror that is utterly free of any dust, one might never understand the true nature of what was being reflected, especially if one were unable to look in more than one mirror at any given time. The different mirrors would be seen to be intrinsically different in character. If one were to consider the matter carefully, however, one would see that the only way to get at a true reflection would be to clean the mirror of its dust. It is not possible to get a true reflection by searching among the various patterns of dust for the most "adequate," since none can be taken to be truly correct. In addition, once polished, the mirrors would all be seen to be of the same exact nature. Thus, to understand the true nature of the world, to perceive reality properly, we must free ourselves of all limiting schema. We must free ourselves of all desires so that we can come in contact with the world-as-it-is. This can be accomplished by meditation, the process by which one constantly strives to rid oneself of "worldly preoccupations" and the even more subtle forms of "attachment." Having done this, one would see the self-same Buddha nature that in all things is one.

I have given this rather lengthy extension of the poem's metaphor, in part because it naturally lends itself to such extension, but primarily because Nishida makes prolific use of this very metaphor when expounding his "new logic." Here again we find additional evidence, if any be needed, of the influence of Zen on Nishida's thinking.

In replying that there is no mirror and that "all is void," Hui-neng is essentially saying that the view represented by Shen-hsiu's poem is an instance of the subtlest form of clinging—attachment to the liberated mind.[21] Hui-neng seems to say that Shen-hsiu's analysis of the situation is accurate enough as far as it goes, but it stops one step short of giving the true picture, a step that makes all the difference in the world. Practically speaking, he is implying that preoccupation with making progress in meditation, emptying one's mind of particular considerations, might result in meditation becoming an end in itself. Thus, one might lift weights to develop muscles in order to improve one's overall physical well-being, but in single-mindedly emphasizing weight lifting, the activity can become the center of one's attention to the exclusion of the original purpose, the enhancment of one's general physical condition. One might well end up too muscle-bound to do anything but lift weights. The process that was intended to improve one's well-being results in worsening it. So, too, excessive emphasis on a single path of meditation may lead to an inability to see the true nature of the world.

Such unhappy consequences are the result, Hui-neng seems to be saying, of Shen-hsiu's retaining a radical dichotomy between the mirror and the dust. To keep the mirror in its original condition seems to imply that it has an original condition that is intrinsically different from what it is reflecting, and from the dust that chances to gather on it. As is the case in the traditional mainstream of European philosophy, this amounts, in a subtle sense, to treating the mind as a substance apart from its attributes. In claiming that "all is void" Hui-neng is attempting to clear away the last obstacle to seeing the world as it is, but his conclusion seems a little drastic in taking the world away as well. While it is clear what view he intends to refute, does his refutation not throw the baby out with the bath water? This is the case if we take him to understand "void" or "nothingness" in the simple sense of non-being. If he means something else, it is not immediately apparent what that might be.

NOTHINGNESS AS A *VIA NEGATIVA*

A good deal of light can be shed on this matter by examining the analysis of "Oriental Nothingness"[22] given by Hisamatsu Shin'ichi.[23] He begins by distinguishing what he calls a negative delineation of the concept from a positive one. His negative delineation consists of five senses of "nothingness"[24] (non-being, negation), each of which can be shown to differ from the notion of Oriental Nothingness. The five are are: (1) nothingness as the negation of being, (2) nothingness as a predicative negation, (3) nothingness as an abstract concept, (4) nothingness as a conjecture, and (5) nothingness in the sense of absence of consciousness.

There are certain confusing features about Hisamatsu's breakdown. The first sense is clearly the denial of existence for a particular thing, a class of objects or even for all objects. One would expect such examples as "There are no unicorns," or even "There is nothing at all." But one of the examples he give is puzzling: "There is not this desk." The use of the demonstrative in this example seems to be so totally at odds with the use of the negative term (not to mention English usage) that I can only assume that Hisamatsu simply wanted to illustrate the negation of a particular existence (for example, "Pegasus did not exist") and either he or his translator bungled the phrase. This example might also give rise to certain objections, but these would be easily disposed of by treating proper names as definite descriptions, as Quine suggests in "On What There Is." In the case of Hisamatsu's example, he probably intended the demonstrative to eliminate the need for a more cumbersome way of describing a particular item that is said not to exist. In any case, we have no evidence that he was even aware of such problems.

Our suspicions are reincorced when we examine his second sense of nothingness, that of predicative negation. Not only does he fail to make the distinction of the "is" of identity and the "is" of predication, but he also goes on to cite examples like "That isn't anything whatever." The former difficulty can be overcome by construing this sense of negation to be that which denies the applicability of a certain predicate or relation (identity as a relation would then be covered), but this would not resolve the difficulties attending the instances of "total negation" that he cites in his examples. Here again, the difficulty stems primarily from the use of the demonstrative in statements which, if taken literally, would be patently nonsensical.

It is also clear that he is not using the example to mean anything at all like "That is meaningless," "That is insignificant," or the like. He clearly intends to establish a parallel with the first sense of "nothingness," where he spoke of both the denial of the existence of a particular object and the universal denial of the existence of any objects. Thus, he gives examples of the denial of a particular predicate, as well as examples of the universal denial of the applicability of predicates. This leads him into the difficulty of having to deal with an example such as "That isn't anything whatever." This he says is a total negation, but one that does not entirely deny the possibility of predication. At a later stage in the paper he goes on to say that the predication "…isn't anything whatever," when applied to a particular subject, yields a statement to the effect that that subject is just what it is and nothing else, since, if it has been delimited as a subject—for instance, this desk, that book, and so on—it cannot be totally without properties. I fail to find even a modicum of meaning in his analysis. It seems to be saying that to claim something is nothing is to claim that the thing is self-identical, and this seems to me absurd.

Hisamatsu does, however, allow for a second possibility of total negation, and this one seems to be more plausible. On this interpretation, when one says that something isn't anything whatever, one means it is beyond all predication. As he later notes, this is the sense of "nothing" used in the Christian tradition when it is said that God is beyond all predication, that he is "no-thing." The difficulty with this reading is that Hisamatsu restricts it to "infinite" subjects like God, Buddha-nature, *nirvāna*, and so forth, while one is tempted to interject that it is precisely such uses that account for our calling them "infinite" in the first place.

At any rate, Hisamatsu denies that Oriental Nothingness is nothingness in either of the first two senses. That he would not equate it with negation of either the existential type or the predicative type is, of course, not surprising. Nor is it surprising that he wants to distinguish it from universal existential negation, or nihilism. Further, one has no difficulty in accepting his citations that such an interpretation has always been regarded as overly literal and simple. What occasions surprise is the statement that Oriental Nothingness is not to be equated with what he calls "total predicative negation," that is, the sense of being beyond all predication. This sense of nothing merely means "is not any-thing within all that is." In effect the he is merely denying that what is referred to as Oriental Nothingness can be the equivalent of any finite thing whatever.

He goes on to state that Oriental Nothingness cannot be equated with the abstract notion of nothingness or non-being as a logical category. To this end he cites the *Nirvāna sūtra*: "Buddha nature is not being and is not non-being," and the *Sata sastra*: "Being and non-being are both (originally and fundamentally) Non-Being."[25] His point is that Oriental Nothingness cannot itself be taken as a category, because it is that which grounds all categories, including the categories of being and non-being. In other words, being and non-being are coordinate concepts and Oriental Nothingness is more fundamental and not on a par with either. It is the Non-Being, Hisamatsu asserts, that transcends both being and non-being.[26] (We may note here Nishida shows a particular fondness for phrasing of this sort, though, happily, he is more careful in his elaborations.)

Hisamatsu introduces the fourth and fifth senses of nothingness to point out that Oriental Nothingness cannot be construed merely as some particular subjective state of contemplation wherein one imagines all things to be empty. Nor is it to be construed simply as the cessation of conscious activity. Were this the case, it would be nothing more than a surrogate for death. At this point he notes that Oriental Nothingness is perfectly lucid and clear in its meaning "that awareness of Oneself in which subject and object of awareness are one and not two." In other words, Oriental Nothingness as "No-Mind" is clearer and more penetrating than any other state could possibly be.

Taken by itself, this negative characterization of what Hisamatsu calls Oriental Nothingness can only lead to confusion. One has the sense of being dragged back and forth between ontology, logic, and psychology, only to end up with something like the following: *Nothingness* is a term that has a long tradition of use in Zen Buddhism to refer to both the ultimate nature of reality and to the religious experience of intuiting that reality. Whatever its positive significance, it most definitely does not mean a mere nihilistic denial of all existence or a claim that the basic nature of the world is beyond description. Furthermore, the term does not refer to a particular category or abstract concept, to any particular conscious state, or to an absence or cessation of consciousness. The reason for the apparent diversity would seem to lie in the occurrence of *mu* in "all is *śūnya* [*mu*]"[27] as well as injunctions concerning the attainment of the state of No-mind (*mushin*). Thus, one can see the true nature of the world only when one reaches this state of no-mind. In this state, it does not make any sense to speak of a subject seeing (or contemplating) an object since there is no distinction between subject and object; there are no minds and no things. The reason one has difficulty dealing with the notion is that one wants to separate some objective component from the act of contemplation, whereas the basic character of the notion militates against any such separation.

While none of the above senses of negation or nothingness can be said to be equivalent to the Oriental Nothingness of which Hisamatsu speaks, neither they are they very far divorced from it. After walking the *via negativa*, Hisamatsu sets out on a more descriptive path.

The Analogical Characterization of Nothingness

In his positive characterization, Hisamatsu concerns himself with six characteristics, some of which, it will be noted, resemble mental properties. Once again, as with the discussion of negative characteristics, he is not concerned with analyzing either of the two aspects of Oriental Nothingness, the ontological character or our awareness of this character. His aim is rather to to point to something that is both immediate and beyond conceptual discrimination.

The first characteristic he calls the "Not-a-Single-Thing" nature of Oriental Nothingness. In his words, this "Oriental Nothingness is the Nothingness-state of Myself that is, it is no other than Myself being Nothing-ness."[28] He takes pains at this point to make clear that he does not mean to describe some internal state that is in contrast with an external world. This "Myself" is said to go beyond the internal-external distinction. He speaks of an "I" that is shackled or captured, an "I" that is limited by objects, as opposed to an "I" that is unfettered and not conceivable in terms of *noema-noesis*. The former is equated with the changing ego, the ego that develops and changes in accord with the objects that hold it captive. These objects are of the most variegated sort: wealth, fame, the Buddha, and even "nothing whatever, wherever." In contrast, the latter "I" is not dependent on any object; it has no object.

The former "I" looks to be the equivalent of the empirical ego as it is defined and delimited in terms of objects of consciousness and their relations; the latter, having no relation to objects whatever, seems to be beyond definition. Not only is it indefinable, it is free and unbounded in the sense that it is not "captured" by any object, and in this sense lies beyond the distinction between internal and the external. Even referring to it as "it" is to totter on the brink of misconception. In this connection Hisamatsu alludes to Hui-neng's poem:

> The Mind of "not a single thing" alone is the mind which is not cap-tured. If it is this Mind which in its nature is not a single thing, there is no way for it even to attract dust.[29]

Such a mind is beyond good and evil in the sense that it is libereated from such categories. Hisamatsu cites Takuan:

> Again the mind is an actor which performs every role.... The Mind being left with no role is called Emptiness.... Not being restricted to any one role is called Emptiness.[30]

Here again we see that by emptiness he does not mean something like a vacuum or the mere absence of an object; nor does he merely mean that the mind is a blank. This is seen in a passage drawn from the writings of D. T. Suzuki:

> A monk asked him [T'ou-tzu]: "How about a thought not yet arising?" This refers to a state of consciousness in which all thoughts have been wiped out and there prevails an emptiness; and here the monk wants to know if this points to the Zen experience; probably he thinks he has come to the realization itself. But the master's reply was: "This is really nonsensical!" There was another monk who came to another master and

asked the same question, and the master's answer was: "Of what use can it be?"[31]

The metaphor of "roles" that Suzuki cites is valuable. It is reminiscent of the statements made by the two Inoues' talk of the "Middle Path" and of Nishida's talk of an "a priori of a prioris"—that is, of a a position that has no particular postulates to determine its coordinate system but embraces all positions that do have determinate coordinate systems. This "Mind" has no role not because it is a particularly useless consciousness, but because it is not the sort of thing that could have a role. In this state, it makes no sense to speak of a role, because it makes no sense to speak of a mind distinct from its object. In the same way the "Middle Path" for Enryō is not just one more point of view on a par with materialism or idealism, differing only in the sense of being less specific about its assumptions than either. It is a deeper path, which by its very nature forbids such a determinate structure.

Hisamatsu uses analogy to present the character of being-like-empty-space as a characteristic of Oriental Nothingness. He then offers ten characteristics of empty space to describe the properties of Oriental Nothingness. Most of them are what one would expect. "Without obstruction," "impartial," "formless," "pure," and "voiding of being" are mentioned to bolster the notion that Oriental Nothingness cannot be categorized in any delimited fashion, that it cannot be ascribed to any specific characteristic or distinguishing set of features. Furthermore, Nothingness is said to be omnipresent in the sense that it permeates or underlies all phenomena, material and mental. And just as empty space accommodates any sort of configuration, so too Nothingness "accepts equally the pure and the defiled... it treats in the same way good and evil."[32] It is a repository of form but has no form itself. For Oriental Nothingness, the stability of empty space—the fact that it does not suffer generation or destruction—is taken to mean that it goes beyond the categories of space and time, enfolding both within itself. Finally, Nothingness is "the voiding of voidness," which Hisamatsu interprets to mean that Nothingness is beyond the distinction between something and nothing:

> Since it is Nothing as Non-Abiding-Subjectivity, which is completely beyond all determination, it neither abides in something nor does it abide in no-thing.[33]

This latter characteristic is particularly intriguing since the characteristic of empty space that provides the analogy is one of "voiding voidness," which appears to mean "that empty space is not attached to its voidness."[34] I confess to finding it difficult to make sense of this. If anything, the analogy seems to have been turned around in the opposite direction. The notion of attachment seems basically to refer to consciousness and to the will, but not to space. If, on the other hand, attachment can be taken to mean "characterized by," then the explanation would be more plausible.

Be that as it may, the simile of empty space is rather prominent in Nishida's work, as well as in the Zen tradition, while the notion of a negation of negation is downright fundamental. The reason it is so important is that the nothingness he has in mind is not to be interpreted as merely the absence of objects. In contrast, when Hisamatsu alludes to the characteristics of empty space, one has the sense that the analogy is forced. If empty space is not the absence of objects, one would have to posit something like an absolute space; but even though Hisamatsu uses the term "absolute" when speaking of his Oriental Nothingness, it seems quite clear he has no intention of using absolute space as an analog. This would be in his terms a species of being and not true Nothingness. We shall see presently how Nishida handles this simile.

Hisamatsu goes on to emphasize the "Mind-like" character of Nothingness. This is necessary, he argues, because of a misconception that might arise from the use of the simile of empty space that emphasizes its static structure or its objective aspect. The dynamic, living, conscious character of Nothingness is not, however, to be interpreted as meaning that it is the very same thing we ordinarily refer to as "mind." The reference to mind and mental characteristics is simply one more analogy. One is tempted to think that this analogy is the more fundamental, given the countless phrases that seem to pair the ultimate with mind. Some of those cited by Hisamatsu (many more could be found throughout the literature) are: "Mind-in-itself is Buddha," "There is no Dharma outside of Mind," "Pure Mind," "Mind Source," and "Mind Itself." Indeed, throughout his essay Hisamatsu seems to favor phrasing that stresses this particular aspect, as, for instance, where he speaks in a general context of "Mind" where we would otherwise expect "Nothingness." Too heavy a reliance on this metaphor alone risks the collpase into a form of idealism. Indeed, it may be said that Nishida succumbed to that very temptation in *An Inquiry into the Good*.

The distinction between Nothingness and mind as we ordinarily conceive it must be preserved. Fundamental though it be, in the end it is still only an analogy. Hisamatsu notes this by stating that what is ordinarily called mind does not have those characteristics of empty space that he previously discusses as belonging to Nothingness. He summarizes:

> The True Buddha is not without mind, but possesses Mind which is "without mind and without thought," not without self-awareness, but possesses Awareness which is "without awareness."[35]

It is, therefore, "an egoless ego." It possesses consciousness, but not in the sense of a delimited consciousness. It is "Mind like empty space."

Lest one be tempted to objectify this "Mind" as some transcendent "Other," Hisamatsu says, "This Mind is not the mind that is seen but the Mind that sees."[36] He speaks of it as utterly subjective in order to indicate that in it there is no duality whatsoever of subject and object. By stressing its utter subjectivity, he forestalls any superficial tendency to reject the duality and then covertly reintroduces a more sophisticated duality by regarding that which has gone beyond this distinction as somehow being objective.[37] The "Buddha is I, Myself" and not some external controlling force; it is a pure, absolute subject in the sense that it can never be objectified. Therefore, this ultimate subject cannot be identified with the empirical ego or with any objectified notion of the Buddha or God. "Your own Self-Mind is Buddha"—it is beginning to sound as if the other is being told, "You are the the whole of reality." One is tempted to ask what that makes the one who is uttering the statement. The point is of course, that when Hui-neng says, "Your own Self-Mind is Buddha," he is saying that one's empirical ego does not define the bound of reality. In fact, it makes no sense to speak of "your self-mind" being independent of or standing opposed to "my self-mind," since this would relegate the notion of self-mind to the status of mind in the ordinary sense. It would make it an object.

It is this feature of nothingness that gives rise to the incoherent mixture of ontological and epistemological principles one encounters in Zen writings. One wants clean distinctions among terms like *nirvāna*, "reality," "the Buddha," and the states of being to which they correspond. But this is the sort of distinction that Zen masters find incompatible with the state of highest wisdom. The injunction is not to "know the Buddha" so much as to "become the Buddha" or to "become *nirvāna*." Precisely what this means, assuming that it is not simply a state of blank consciousness, is stated only in highly allegorical language. A discursive explanation, it is said, cannot be given; full understanding can only come with the attainment of the state itself.

These characteristics suggest to Hisamatsu two other traits pertinent to a discussion of Nothingness: freedom and creativity. The notion of freedom, he argues, is inextricably bound to that of Nothingness and, like it, lies beyond all constraint and delimitation. Hence, as noted earlier, "It is not bound up with the way of thinking in terms of good and evil." It is not that "True Nature"[38] spontaneously follows a set of fundamental rules. If that were the case, it would be relative and no longer lie beyond all characterization and attachment, including the attachment to *nirvāna*.

Speaking of the creative character of Nothingness, Hisamatsu makes reference to two metaphors helpful for our study of Nishida and the Inoues: the image of waves and water and the image of the mirror. The former already showed up in our discussion of Inoue Enryō, and Hisamatsu's use of it is remarkably similar.[39] He sees the import of the metaphor in the unchanging stability of the water as compared to the ephemeral nature of the waves. The water is not changed in its essential features by the presence or absence of waves and yet it is the source of the waves, that to which they return. Thus, he says, "Oriental Nothingness is this Mind which is to be likened to the water as subject."[40] The phenomenal forms that appear in Oriental Nothingness arise from it and return to it, but do not affect it in any way. Nothingness is the ultimate ground and, as "True Self," can be seen as opposed to the ordinary self. In this sense it can be likened to the substantializing of the waves that appear for a short time only to return to their source. The empirical self is a wave on the ocean of Nothingness. To assert that this self, or indeed anything, is ultimately nothingness is only to say that waves cannot exist apart from water. The language is, admittedly, metaphorical, but Hisamatsu seems to consider it more suitable than that of the mirror, which he describes in these terms:

> In Buddhism on the contrary, that which is reflected in the mirror is not something that comes from outside the mirror, but is something which is produced from within the mirror. It is produced from within the mirror, is expressed by being reflected in the mirror, passes away in the mirror and, passing away, does not leave any trace in the mirror.[41]

Unlike the image of the water and waves, there is no actual instance of a mirror with the properties suggested, which limits its function as a metaphor. Its importance for us lies in Nishida's extensive use of the notion of "reflection." Both of these metaphors are misleading in one very important respect: they suggest a substantialization of nothingness. Like most metaphors they serve to emphasize one aspect of the concept they are used to elucidate, but there is a strong danger of the analogy being extended to aspects that extend beyond the original intention. Indeed, it is just this sort of "substantialization" that Inoue Enryō constantly argues against when discussing his notion of the "Middle Path" or the "Enryō Path" and against which Hui-neng argues in his poem.

CONCLUSION

This concludes our cursory survey of the concept of nothingness as interpreted in the Zen tradition. It remains for us to indicate how the concept fits into the development of Nishida's thought. Our exposition is not, and was not, intended to be an exhaustive analysis. Perhaps, as Hisamatsu admits, the idea by nature prohibits precise rational description. In any case, the broad contours of the term should be clear enough, as should be its traditional function among Zen masters whose aim is not to teach their disciples to weave elaborate intellectual embroideries with assorted concepts, but to bring them to the point of experiencing for themselves the Buddha, *nirvāna,* or nothingness. This is essentially a religious aim and excessive intellectual acrobatics easily distract from it. They may even be an impediment to attainment of the goal of Zen practice. Thus although attempts have been made explain truth by the use of analogy or systematic negation, the Zen masters typically have come to rely on the kōan as a means effectively and dramatically to put an end to the intellectual speculation that impedes the progress toward the attainment of real insight.

For all this, humans are, by nature, doomed to rationality. To condemn empty, fruitless speculation is one thing; to condemn all intellectual inquiry is something else. Zen masters condemn theorizing not because of what it is, but because too often it comes to take the place of the experience that is the ultimate aim and that theory is supposed to serve. To be sure, certain statements of the masters can be interpreted only as maintaining that all philosophical speculation is useless, but they overlook the fact that Zen can also be served by disciples obsessed by the desire to think things through until they reach conceptual clarity. If there is truth in the Zen perspective, there is no reason it should be impossible to find an intellectual model more or less suited to reflect its structure. Nishida was just one of those persons and the constant reworking of his philosophical position attests to the fact.

In Nishida the passion of philosophical inquiry was interwoven with a passion for religious insight. During the period of his intense engagement in Zen meditation Nishida's diary is filled with references both to the philosophical works he was reading and to the practice of *zazen*. He came to feel that only by the attainment of enlightenment could he philosophize in more than a sterile fashion.[42] He did achieve enlightenment and he did philosophize.

Nishida's greatness as a philosopher rests on both the depths of his spiritual insight and the strength of his intellectual integrity. He would not and could not resort to the facile mysticism of the two Inoues. When his solution to the problem of standpoints failed, he recognized his failure and sought a better solution. There are two distinct, basic impulses in Nishida and the interplay between them helps to account for the development of his thought. Only a combination of deep mystical insight and passion for rational structure could possibly give rise to a formation such as the logic of basho.

We may, I think, apply the metaphors used to explicate the concept of nothingness to Nishida's thought itself. It is almost as if his philosophical output expressed the attempt to work out in detail one or more of these metaphors in the hope of achieving a sound philosophical view. I do not mean that he took a one-sided view of nothingness but only that the metaphors served him as an alternative approach. This seems to be the case particularly during the period in which he was developing his logic of basho. In *An Inquiry into the Good* the ideas of immediacy, unity, omni-comprehension, and non-characterizability were prominent. In *Intuition* there is a shift of focus to creativity in the sense of activity. During the basho period, however, the image of the mirror image and analogies of space, neither prominent in the earlier works, appear with greater frequency. Nothingness understood as as no-mind also receives greater attention. The emphasis on activity as the pivot of analysis is gone and in its place we see a new stress on structure. As we progress through a consideration of Nishida's logic of basho and its development, it will become apparent how the characteristics that Hisamatsu ascribes to Oriental Nothingness make their appearance, not as randomly cited analogies but as elements of a coherent philosophical structure.

4

The Concept of Basho

IN THIS CHAPTER, I would like to give a preliminary account of the notion of basho[1] as Nishida develops it in his effort to solve the problem of standpoints. Since a proper analysis of the concept, however, will emerge only in the exposition of his system as a whole, it is fitting that we begin with an overview of that system.

The development of the concept of basho, as we observed at the end of the previous chapter, marks a discard of the attempt to interpret the knowing process and self-consciousness in terms of activity. The rejection of activity in his philosophical stance assumes particular significance in light of the discussion of the poems submitted to the fifth patriarch. There, too, the emphasis on activity was rejected in favor of nothingness. In fact, although I would not claim that there is any causal relationship between the two, I think it of great significance that nothingness is chosen to replace activity as an explanatory device. As I have been insisting all along, Nishida's deep involvement with Zen is crucial to interpreting his philosophical views and the changes they underwent. The examination of nothingness in the previous chapter provided a general backdrop against which to describe just what Nishida is trying to do with his concept of basho. With that in mind, we may now consider some of its more specific traits.

We may start with a brief account of what occasioned the concept of basho and from there attempt to locate that concept in modern logic. Our discussion will then turn to examples of basho in order to bring out the various dimensions of the concept, especially as its relates to judgments. Next, in order to show the various dimenions of the idea, it will be necessary to examine in some detail the problem to which Nishida is responding. By showing how the problem, as he sees it, manifests itself in slightly different forms in different fields from formal logic to metaphysics, and why alternative solutions are unsatisfactory, we will be in a better position to unravel the complex nature of basho.

These defining characteristics of basho will be seen to overlap at several points with the characteristics of nothingness discussed by Hisamatsu. In particular, the complex interweaving of structural, ontological, and epistemological characteristics evident in Hisamatsu's analysis will be found to apply to basho as well. More importantly, the fusion of objective and subjective characteristics that proved so puzzling in the case of Hisamatsu's discussion of nothingness will reappear in Nishida's concept of basho. At the same time, a strong contrast betwen the two will emerge, a contrast not in content but in structure. Nishida's concept of basho will be seen to have a unified structure, such that the various characteristics will be integrated much more precisely than they are in Hisamatsu's discussion.

Finally, a brief sketch of the general structure of Nishida's philosophical system will be given to display the interrelationship of the various characteristics of basho. This will prove particularly useful in relating the structural aspects of basho to self-consciousness, which is critical for an assessment of Nishida's status as a philosopher. The Zen monk's main task may be to arrive at a personal realization of nothingness, but the metaphysician's or philosopher's is to display and explain the structure of experience. Nothingness may be the culmination of religious insight, but it becomes part of a philosophical analysis only when its relation to more "ordinary concepts" is displayed in a detailed and structured fashion. The fact that Nishida even attempted this task is itself a novelty in the history of ideas and reason enough to ensure his status as a philosopher.

Although it is clear that the concept of basho is rooted in Nishida's Zen background, just how it is rooted will, I hope, become more apparent as we progress. This of itself, however, is not enough to account for the appearance of the concept at this particular point in his career, if only for the reason that Zen was not the only interest that formally engaged him at the time. Although I have the impression that the Zen outlook permeated all his activities, he needed something more to focus his philosophic attention on the concept of basho.[2]

THE NON-BUDDHIST ORIGINS OF BASHO

Nishida indicates that the concept of basho owes something to
Plato's notion of the receptacle or space as expounded in the *Timeaus*.
Kōsaka Masaaki tells us that Nishida had been using the works of Plato
and Aristotle for his seminars in the period just prior to and during the
publication of the essays that make up the volume *From the Acting to the
Seeing*.[3] The significance of this piece of information is not immediately
apparent until one recalls that the seminars, although ostensibly dealing
with an historical philosopher, were not so much historical in nature as
problem oriented. Since the dominant trend at that time was to give
courses using the works of one or another of the nineteenth-century German idealists, the choice of texts made by Nishida seemed out of step to
most students. It represented, as Kōsaka remarks, a move from idealism to
a position better characterized as realism.[4] While Nishida's earlier works
lend themselves to being interpreted as a form of idealism, as I have
remarked earlier in connection with *An Inquiry into the Good* and *Intuition*,
he himself realized that idealism could give at best only a limited and partial description of reality.[5]

The debt Nishida owes to Aristotle is even more marked than his debt to
Plato. It was to Aristotle that Nishida owed the problem he hoped to solve
by the concept of basho. This is not to say that Nishida thought he was
answering a problem left over from the writings of Aristotle. Rather, he
seems to trace the origin of the problems that concern him to the way in
which Aristotle developed his metaphysics and applied his logic to metaphysical questions. In short, Nishida was stimulated by Aristotle's discussion of primary substance and considered it a fruitful starting point for his
analysis. Nishida was conscious that his attempts to build on the insights
of other thinkers (James in *An Inquiry into the Good*, Fichte and Bergson in
Intuition) had failed to produce an adequate solution to what I have called
the problem of standpoints, and that the reason for the failure was that he
himself had not adequately come to terms with the roots of the problem.
The precise relationship of Aristotle's definition of primary substance and
Nishida's system will be discussed later in this chapter and more fully in the
next, but at least some indication of the relationship is called for here.

Aristotle defines primary substance as that which can be subject but
never predicate. In so doing he posits an intimate connection between
logic and metaphysics,[6] but at the same time he creates the problem of
finding an appropriate principle of individuation. Since an individual con-

crete thing is an existent, or being, in the most fundamental sense, and since knowledge is always knowledge of the universal, it would seem that we can never have knowledge of particulars. For no matter how one specifies a universal, even if one reaches the *infima species*, one still has a universal and not a particular. Universals, such as whiteness, then, do not contain their own principle of individuation. Aristotle took matter as his principle of individuation. Nishida, in contrast, drew on the notion of basho to provide a universal that would contain its own principle of individuation.

An important clue to Nishida's strategy is provided by Noda Matao:

> Nishida, while seeking the principle of individuation in the universal, conceives the latter as a sort of material field wherein forms emerge, so to speak.[7]

The difficulty is that it very nearly accords with the notion of the "receptacle" given by Plato in the *Timeaus,* to which Nishida acknowledged a debt while insisting that it was not what he meant by basho.

Another clue is the fact that Nishida constantly uses the term *concrete universal* in his discussion of the problem of individuation, arguing that concrete universals are universal in the true sense, unlike abstract universals, which are mere abstract concepts. Precisely what this means is not at all clear. What is clear is that Nishida thinks that there is an intimate connection between his concept of basho and Hegel's concept of the concrete universal, crucial differences notwithstanding. One hesitates to ignore these remarks entirely, but there is little doubt that the sum of Nishida's references to Hegel's concept do little to help us understand what he meant by basho. For this we need to appreciate the structure of Nishida's system as a whole. In any case, we left with the fact that the concept of basho is somehow related to Plato's concept of the "receptacle" and that it is intended to provide a solution to the problem of specifying a principle of individuation or, in other words, a solution to the problem of the relation of the particulars to the universal. As for Hegel's notion of the concrete universal, it failed as an attempt to provide a universal with its own principle of individuation because Hegel could not free himself from the objective-subjective distinction.

The reason for reverting to Aristotle is that his discussion of prime substance seems to have served as a springboard for Nishida's investigations, focusing his attention on two issues: (1) the interconnection of logic and metaphysics involved in the specification of particulars, and (2) the manner in which one can specify a principle of individuation.

A LOGICAL INTERPRETATION

I should like now to turn to a number of ideas similar to Nishida's concept of basho, which are, in a broad sense of the term, logical. This will put us in a better position to articulate what sets Nishida's idea apart. A comparison of Nishida's concept of basho with concepts used in formal logic is necessary for two reasons: first, because Nishida intends his concept of basho serve as a structural element in his system; and second, because, although he does not understand the concept of basho to be identical with any of the concepts of formal logic, neither does he want it to be in conflict with them. At first glance this latter motive seems paradoxical. On the one hand, Nishida does not envisage his logic of basho as an alternative logic to formal logic in the sense that one would be forced to choose one and reject the other. On the other, he sees himself delineating a logic that encompasses formal logic,[8] which he considers an abstraction from and a simplification of his logic of basho.[9] It is therefore useful to see how the concept of basho compares with key concepts in formal logic, especially since Nishida's concern is the result of the application of logic in the formulation of theories about the structure of reality. On this point, we shall see, he argues that formal Aristotelian logic, and even modern mathematical logic, when used as an instrument for doing ontology, places an almost exclusive emphasis on the subject-place of judgments. This entails a corresponding emphasis on objects in the metaphysical theories developed. Here we have the root of what I have called in previous chapters the problem of standpoints and what presently will be discussed as the problem of completeness.

What is more, the concept of basho is intrinsically bound up with the notion of nothingness, which, as we have seen, is one of the most significant features of Nishida's philosophy and a basic structural element in his system. Because nothingness is usually thought to be a "mystical" and religious idea, it will be incumbent to show that it is not completely unrelated to concepts that are of a strictly logical character. Only by showing that there is a plausible, albeit partial, interpretation of the concept of nothingness in the realm of logic can Nishida claim to have developed a plausible logical grounding for the "insights of religious experience."

A number of the statements made by Nishida concerning the characteristics of basho are reminiscent of the notion of domains of discourse in logic. Consider a domain of discourse whose elements are particular colors. One might make a number of observations about what things one could and could not say in such a domain. For example, what would one want to say about a statement such as "Red is a color"? In ordinary discourse, a statement such as this would cause no great consternation, though one would hardly expect to be greeted with it in the morning. In ordinary discourse the statement seems odd, as it is difficult to think of an occasion for uttering it, except perhaps as a philosophical example. Not only is it analytic, it is patently so. What happens when our domain of discourse is restricted to color? Given that we consistently remain within the prescribed domain, the oddity of the statement seems to be much greater than it would be in ordinary language. In the domain of colors, the statement "Red is a color" seems to be the equivalent of "Red exists." This sounds stranger still. What could "Red exists" possibly mean? Following the Russellian method, we would have paraphrase it to read: "There is something that is red." But of course, this maneuver will not work if we observe the restriction of our domain of discourse to color, where the individuals are the individual colors themselves. In this domain of discourse the particular colors are not predicates, but the suggested interpretation requires that they be so. One could, of course, dispense entirely with individual constants, but then the notion of domain of discourse would be undermined. The point is that given that the domain of discourse is color, the two statements come to the same thing. They merely state that red is a member of the domain of discourse in question.

This is the very point that Nishida wants to establish with respect to his concept of basho. He will repeatedly say that to claim that something exists is just to say it is located in a basho and that the meaning of existence changes as the basho changes. The distinction of the two senses of "is," identity and predication, is a fundamental point of analysis in the history of philosophy. Nishida does not want to claim that there is no distinction, but only that the utter separation of the two senses is unwarranted. He thus claims that there is a distinct link between the two senses and, further, that this link is clarified by the notion of basho. Basically, his idea is that a basho determines a domain of discourse and that to be in a domain of discourse is to be or to exist.[10]

The idea that existence is tied up with being in a basho leads to another point of similarity between the notions of basho and domain of discourse. Nishida makes the claim that basho is essentially non-being or nothingness with respect to that which is located within it. He takes great pains to show that this nothingness or non-being is not merely a non-being-relative-to-being. The claim is a formidable one, and reminds us of statements made by Hisamatsu in his discussion of Oriental Nothingness. At first hearing, one is tempted to dismiss it as so much gibberish. I would suggest that it is possible to clarify this statement in terms of domains of discourse.

Let us return to the domain of discourse we were just speaking of: color. While red, yellow, blue, purple, and green would be individual members of this domain of discourse, color itself would not be an element in the domain. This is merely to affirm that the domain would not be a member of itself. If existence is taken to mean being in the domain, then the domain could be said not to exist. But what does it mean to say that this domain does not exist? One might define a color, call it "rerple," that satisfied certain properties. One could then attempt to demonstrate either that such a color existed or that it did not. Whether or not rerple was shown to exist, the question as to whether it did exist would be a meaningful or well-formed question in the confines of the domain of discourse. However, the question as to whether color existed or not would not be an admissible question within the domain of discourse; to claim that either color did exist or that it did not would be equally meaningless. The problem could not even be formulated within the confines of the domain. Of course, it is possible to define a new domain of discourse, such that the domain specified above would be a member of this new domain. In this case color could be said to "exist" in the sense that it is a member of this new domain. It could then be said that one's ontological commitment depends solely on the domain of discourse one has opted to use.[11]

This feature of the notion of a domain of discourse also serves to give a clearer, although still partial, interpretation of what Nishida calls in *Intuition and Reflection in Self-Consciousness* an "a priori," and what he refers to in *The Self-Conscious System of the Universal* as an "intuition." It can now be seen that these terms mean something like the principle of determination of a domain of discourse.[12]

While the discussion thus far has given some indication of the way in which Nishida's concept of basho resembles the notion of a domain of discourse, it has also provided an initial interpretation of what the notion means:

1. Existence is determined by being located in a basho.
2. The meaning of existence changes with a change of basho.
3. The basho is utter nothingness with respect to the elements located in it.

Yet if all Nishida meant by the term basho were a domain of discourse, why did he not just use that concept instead of inventing a new technical philosophical expression and surrounding it with such obscure and complicated argumentation? If one could show that Nishida was unfamiliar with modern logic, this might explain matters. Indeed, when one casually pages through much of his work one finds that the references are overwhelmingly references to syllogistic logic. The fact is, however, Nishida was rather familiar with the developments in modern logic and mathematics.[13] The concept of basho cannot, therefore, be reduced to the notion of a domain of discourse, however many traits the two have in common.

Precisely how does the concept of basho differ? First, it seems to function as an ontological principle in a much stronger sense than does the notion of a domain of discourse. According to Nishida, the exposition of the relationships obtaining among the various basho and the clarification of the nature of these basho constitute a presentation of the very structure of reality and not merely a presentation of the structure of some conceptual scheme.

Second, Nishida makes constant use of the term *concrete universals* in treating basho, a term that seems to have very little to do with the notion of a domain of discourse. Further, domains of discourse are determined, sometimes quite arbitrarily it seems, by something or someone outside the domain, whereas Nishida speaks of the "self-determination of basho" in locutions such as "basho sees itself in itself" and "basho determines itself in itself." These phrases do, indeed, show that basho is not merely reducible to the notion of domain of discourse, but at the same time we should not forget that a domain of discourse displays the "purely logical" characteristics of basho.

It is this self-determining aspect of basho with which we must now concern ourselves. This will involve an inquiry into Nishida's treatment of the problem of what it means to know. This, in turn, will involve an examination of the nature of self-consciousness, for he says both "knowing is basho determining itself" and "the fundamental form of knowing is self-consciousness." It is precisely because the notion of basho has these ontological, epistemological, and logical characteristics that it can serve as the mechanism Nishida needs to make the crucial move in the development of his all-encompassing structure. This move will allows him to examine the relationship between the subject of a judgment and its predicate, and then to connect that relationships to the relationship between a particular and a universal. Finally, both relationships will have to be connected to that between the knowing subject and the known object.

EXAMPLES OF BASHO

In order to clarify the various dimensions of the concept of basho, it will be helpful to examine some of the examples that Nishida gives and his comments on them. The examples are cited with two purposes in mind: first, in order gradually, but concretely, to illustrate the complexity of the concept; and second, in order to indicate how the ontological characteristics of the Zen concept of nothingness are woven into a unified whole by the concept of basho. Concerning the first, the examples have been chosen to emphasize, in turn, the logical, ontological, and epistemological characteristics of the concept. Moreover, the progression of examples will also serve to illustrate the contrast of the objective and subjective features of the concept. The fact that each example is not, indeed could not be, a "pure example" of a particular characteristic, either logical ontological, or epistemological, is further indication of Nishida's basic view that these categories are not ultimate but only matters of emphasis.[14]

We begin with the example of color. In section two of the essay "Basho" Nishida writes:

> That which is, i.e., being (Japanese *arumono*), must be thought of as being located in (Japanese *oite aru*) something.[15]

He insists that *aru* (to be) is to be taken in the broadest possible sense and not merely in the sense of *sonzai suru* (to exist). It would seem that he wishes to reserve the latter term for a specific meaning and to use "to be" (*aru*) in a relatively neutral sense. In particular, he does not appear to want to restrict in any way the application of *aru mono* (a being), a term that can apply to anything that could become the subject of a judgment, anything that could be specified in some way or other. If this is the case, then there is no immediate conflict with either the interpretation of basho in terms of a domain of discourse or the subsequent comments on the relation between the "is" of existence and the "is" of predication. He goes on:

> For example, I think of the various colors as being located in the general concept of color; the general concept of color is the basho wherein the various colors are located.[16]

The various relationships that obtain among colors are established by the system of color, and the subject of color judgments is color itself. To ward off objection to this way to speaking, he adds that although universals are considered to be subjective in nature, it is equally true that the so-called *individuum* is an object of thought. Consequently, universals and *individua* are alike in this respect. That is to say, insofar as one is acquainted with an individual directly, that individual is known by means of its properties. We do not confront "bare particulars" but only "clothed" ones.

As Nishida has not yet clarified the meaning of "being located in" in this context, he goes on to say that he does not mean that color in general can be said to have color, since it is not the sort of thing that can have color. But neither can one regard the various colors as functions of color itself; that is, one cannot regard them as the activity of color itself, since to do so would mean introducing the concept of time, a factor that is not included in the concept of color. All one has in this situation is the notion of "including" or, from the point of view of the particular, a "being located in." He notes that this has the same relation as "the form being the shadow of the formless."

Just what does this mean? Nishida is careful to note that at this point the meaning of basho is still rather limited in that the example refers only to logical structure. Before we move on to more useful notions, it is necessary to come to some kind of understanding of this "simple example" of color versus particular colors. At one point Nishida says that the particular is not to be seen as an effect of the universal, nor as something possessed by the universal, but rather more like a part of the universal, a projection of the universal.[17] What he seems to mean by this is that the relationship of a particular to a universal is not the same as the relationship between two particulars. Accordingly, even when we speak of the relationship between the particular and the universal, we must not suppose that we are looking for some third thing to do the relating. To do so would land us in the kind of infinite regress made famous by Bradley. It is for this reason that Nishida insists on the universal being nothingness with respect to the particular in a sense similar to that outlined in the discussion of domains of discourse.

This still does not explain his use of the term *part of.* Clearly the relation between particular and universal is meant to be taken in the sense of particularization of the universal, not in the sense of adding something but of losing something. The initial confusion clears up on a closer reading of the text.

At first glance, one might reckon a given subsumptive judgment of the form "A is B" to mean that the subject of the judgment has a greater intensional complexity than the predicate. If the judgment in question is "Red is a color," this amounts to saying that the subject concept is more determinate than the predicate concept and that its extension is, therefore, proportionately smaller. If one can speak at all here of "being a part of," the natural tendency would be to conclude that the concept of color was *part of* the concept of red, rather than the other way around, as Nishida seems to suggest.

One takes the concept of color to be more abstract than that of red, and it seems to make no sense to speak of the particular color "red" being part of color in general. Nishida's perspective is slightly different: to say that red is a color is not to establish some relation between two utterly independent concepts; it is rather to take it as a specification, or determination, of the concept of color in general. A specific color is part of the total system of colors and this is the "true universal." This seems to be at least partially what he means by a "concrete universal."

What is the "system of colors"? Is it an extended particular or is it an organizing concept? The question is precisely to the point, and the answer is that it can be either. This may not suffice as a description of what a "concrete universal" is, but it points us in the right direction. What Nishida wants to say is that one does not first come into contact with specific colors and then abstract from them an abstract notion of color. In order to see a specific color such as red as a color, it is necessary already to have in one's consciousness a notion of color in general. Statements about the particular colors and their interrelations are statements that make explicit the character of color in general. Here the universal is not merely an abstract concept, but an entity that contains its specific differences within it.

Noda's earlier remark (page 93) to the effect that Nishida's basho is akin to a material field from which forms emerge can be better understood through the example of color given above. In that example, the material field is taken as the system of color, or, if you will, color space. Yet to say that "color sees itself" still strikes us as peculiar, even if one is willing to see color judgments as having color itself as their true subject. Nishida is speaking of color space with its particular colors occupying certain locations, or better, existing as certain locations in that space. When he talks of "color itself" the expression "part of" becomes more understandable. It also helps one to get at the notion of the way in which he wants to talk of this as a concrete universal; space is given as an example of what he means by a concrete universal.

Alluding to Aristotle's notion of pure form, Nishida writes:

> This form must be universal (general) and, at the same time, must be something that is always subject, but never predicate, that is, it must be a concrete universal. We see an example of this also in something like

space. The various particular spaces, as space, are universal (general) and, at the same time, since the individual spaces are determined, they are always subject and never predicate.[18]

In a sense, the explanation is more confusing than than the explicandum; it appears as if we have just referted to Inoue Enryō's talk about water. Of course space can be taken in either a universal or particular sense, but what does that show? Merely to note that there are particular and individual spaces and that as such they cannot be predicated as a character of anything (although there are, indeed, things that have the characteristic of spatiality) is to state the obvious. There does not seem to be any new insight here. Nishida might reply in terms like these:

> What prompts such an objection is the structuring of the situation in terms of objectively given individual spaces from which is abstracted a common element that is then taken to be the universal quality. The individual spaces are regarded as objective particulars while the universal is regarded as subjective, that is, as an abstract concept. It is precisely this assumption of the subjective-objective dichotomy that is at the root of all the difficulty. The notion of a concrete universal, which provides the foundation for judgment by determining itself, must be investigated without a prior assumption concerning subjective and objective states.

This is far from a definitive answer, but it does give us an initial interpretation of what Nishida means by the term "concrete universal." It is neither a particular nor a universal; it is not part of a judgment but the ground or source of judgments; the total system of colors is an example of a concrete universal and, as such, it is contrasted with the abstract concepts of color. In addition to delving deeper into the notion of a concrete universal, we will also want to know more of what is involved in understanding a simple proposition of the form "A is B." This question will be taken up in due course.

The first example of basho, that of the color system, is intended to illustrate primarily, though not exclusively, the logical character of the concept of basho. It may help to press on to a slightly more complicated example, one that would emphasize other characteristics of the concept. This is not to say that these further examples will not illustrate the logical character of basho. They do, and they must if Nishida's claim to have developed a logic of basho is to have any hope of being substantiated. What they will do is locate the logical characteriics in a broader frame of reference.

The second example of basho to be taken up is that of a force field or field of energy. Here, it would appear, we are more concerned with the ontological characteristics of the notion of basho than was the case with color. As numerous commentators have pointed out, including Noda, Yanagida Kenjūrō, and Kōsaka, Nishida was impressed by the development of field theory in physics. Briefly put, physical objects are said to be related to each other in space, but the relation between physical objects and space in the Newtonian sense is merely that of "being in." There is no sense in saying that the relations of the objects are established and determined by physical space. Merely to say that the physical objects are spatial says nothing more than that objects are in space. But, if the relation of the objects and space is now made tighter than this, if the objects are to be seen as determinations of the place in which they exist, there must be a re-interpretation of the nature of the objects. The substantiality of the objects is transferred to the field in which they lie and the objects are thus "reduced" to energy. The objects are now seen as accumulations of energy related not in space, but in the energy field of which they are a part.

The objects, thus reduced to energy concentrations, are related to each other as elements of the total energy field in which they are located and of which they are a part. The total field is expressed in these concentrations and their distribution, with each of the "objects" seen as a determination of the field as a whole. The field is not merely the sum of relationships of the particular accumulations, since this would leave the relation open-ended. The concentrations of energy are not antecedently independent entities that are then conceived as being related in some fashion. It is rather that the relations are established by the field in which the relationships hold. The relations are thus said to be "internal" to the field, and since the field is itself not just the point of view of any particular concentration, it provides the unity of the various concentrations of energy. But, as was the case with the notion of the domain of discourse, this does not mean that the field is the mere absence of particular concentrations. It means that the field is the ground of the various relations. As a result, if one were restricted to the field, one would encounter only particular concentrations and there would be no particular concentration that one could call the field.

Further, if one were to take the entire field as the subject of judgment, then the various patterns of energy distribution would become modes of the field, and what was previously an independent entity (an object) would now become a mode of the field. Thus when the basho becomes subject, what were seen as the entities occupying the basho come to be viewed as its modifications and thus lose their status as individuals.

This example shows better than the example of color what Nishida meant by the particular being *part of* the universal and what it means to say that the things that are in a basho are determinations of that basho. Note that Nishida does refer to the basho as a universal. Such a way of speaking may seem out of place in the case of a field of force, but it cannot therefore be dismissed as mere analogy: the field of force is intended by Nishida as an example of basho. What is important here is the transition from the field as determining the elements in it, to the field as an object in which the field itself is a particular that no longer determines entities but is said only to possess characteristics.

The example of the field of force, useful as it is, is not much help in clarifying the language of "reflecting" that Nishida constantly uses in connection with the notion of basho.[19] The examples given thus far give what might be called the "objective aspect" of the notion of basho. The allusion to an objective aspect, while intended to explain the subject-object dichotomy, should not be taken to imply that there are objective basho and subjective basho. It is just that the examples given thus far do not include an explanation of the claim that the "basho sees itself in itself."

At the risk of belaboring the point, I reiterate the importance of the parallels between Nishida's exposition of basho (the examples, let it be realled, are Nishida's and not mine) and Hisamatsu's exposition of nothingness. The two examples given thus far illustrate the logical and ontological features of the concept of basho, in much the same way that Hisamatsu used the concept of space to illustrate what might be termed the ontological character of the concept of nothingness. That said, it should not be overlooked what while Hisamatsu speaks of nothingness only analogically, Nishida presents actual examples of basho.

To probe the complexity of the idea of basho still further, let us take one one more example illustrating the psychological, epistemological, or "subjective" character of the concept. Much still remains to be said, but at least the example will show in the concrete how the concept of basho unifies the previous various examples in a way that Hisamatsu's exposition of the concept of nothingness does not. At the very beginning of his essay on "Basho," Nishida suggests viewing the field of consciousness as a basho:

> When we think of a thing, there must be something like a basho that reflects that thing. We can think of basho as being the field of con-

sciousness. In order for us to be conscious of something that thing must be reflected in the field of consciousness."[20]

Things like chairs, desks, and telephones are not *in* consciousness in the sense that concepts, sensations, and feeling can be said to be. Objects are taken to be external to consciousness and only reflected in it. Whatever resides in the field of consciousness is only a pale image of an external object. With respect to the phenomena of consciousness, the field of consciousness has a negative sense in that it is not one of the phenomena of consciousness. Yet neither is it merely an absence of phenomena. One can distinguish the field of consciousness from the various phenomena that come into being and pass away as the unchanging field in which these changes occur.

One might object at this point that Nishida is unnecessarily multiplying entities by distinguishing the field of consciousness from the individual phenomena in the field. A Humean objection of this sort would be appropriate if Nishida were proposing a new entity, but this is the very thing he is trying to avoid with the notion of basho. Hume is right that no inspection of the phenomena of consciousness will yield something that one would want to call the field of consciousness or the self. One can, of course, find an objectified self or an objectified field of consciousness, since it is possible to reflect on one's experiences and consider these experiences as constituting a whole to be inspected, but this whole would leave out the act of inspection that was being then undertaken. This is all quite familiar terrain and Nishida would agree with it as far as it goes. He is clear on the point that we cannot speak of the self as a metaphysical entity: "I think that even calling the self a metaphysical entity contradicts the awareness of self-consciousness."[21] The sentence is not a simple one, and we shall have to return to it later. For now, let it show that Nishida had no intention of putting forth the self as some metaphysical entity hiding behind the phenomena of consciousness. The basis for this refusal is based on the nature of self-consciousness. This point is particularly significant, since it is just this reference to self-consciousness that is most often used to "prove" the existence of such an entity. This gives us a further indication of just how radical Nishida's treatment of self-consciousness will be.

Nishida's point in referring to the field of consciousness as a basho is to bring into relief the fact that the field is an absolute nothing in relation to the elements in the field. It is not the sort of thing that could be said to either exist or not exist, and yet at the same time it is precisely the field that provides unity to the conscious phenomena. Indeed, it is only because these phenomena are located in this field that they are phenomena of consciousness. The field provides the defining characteristic whereby these phenomena are seen as individual elements of a certain type being related in certain ways. It provides this unity not in the sense of something latent among previously given entities and subsequently uncovered. It provides the unity by providing the given. It is what allows the discovery of a unity among the entities. The distinction between the content of consciousness and the general characteristic of consciousness that applies to that content is given within the field; the distinction is an abstract partitioning of the original unity, which is the field. Consciousness develops and determines itself within itself in that it specifies individual conscious phenomena related to each other in specific ways in the field of consciousness. This is not to say that the field is given the status of an entity with respect to the elements in the field. If one were to take the field as a subject of judgment, it would then be necessary to speak of the basho in which it was located; or, in the language used at the beginning of this section, one would have to have moved to a new domain of discourse.

The three examples of basho given here highlight the complexity of the concept by emphasizing various facets of it, logical, ontological, epistemological, psychological. In addition, the examples display a common logical structure so that, while each example brings into relief a particular feature of basho, it also possesses the features illuminated by the other examples.

A REEXAMINATION OF THE PROBLEM

If these examples have helped to give some idea of what Nishida is talking about with his idea of "basho," there are still cardinal features we have not yet touched on. For this we turn to a reexamination of the problem Nishida was addressing. We have seen the two Inoues confronted with what I called the the "problem of standpoints" and have followed Nishida in this first two attempts to find an adequate solution to it. In noting his failure to do so, we pointed to his over-emphasis on the interpretation of consciousness as activity. The label "the problem of standpoints" turned out to be particularly appropriate because of the essentially psychological and epistemological character of the way in which the problem had been framed, and the psychological and voluntaristic character of the proposed solution.[22]

As Nishida shifted directions, we followed him by renaming his problem the "completeness problem." I do not mean to give the impression that Nishida has left the problem of *An Inquiry into the Good* and *Intuition* behind and taken up another. Rather, his way of framing the question had changed and, as a result, so did the nature of his solution. I am suggesting that the concept of basho was developed as a response to the completeness problem because Nishida's focus has become primarily logical in character. It cannot be stressed enough: this turn marks a milestone in the development of his thought.

Before proceeding, let me sound a note of caution concerning the problem of completeness. There is a sense in which Nishida was not confronted by a single, definable problem but a cluster of problems with a common core. He himself thought as much, that he was getting to the root of a whole series of questions, and it is this that I have chosen to speak of as the "problem of completeness." He was convinced that this was the case, and that never before in the history of philosophy had the matter been viewed this way. Be that as it may, the basic reason for the complex nature of the concept of basho is that it is meant to solve a range of problems at one and the same time.

In approaching the core problem, I begin with the following observations. Basho is a technical concept with a logical aspect, while at the same time having ontological and epistemological aspects. The logical aspect has been discussed to some extent in terms of the notion of a domain of discourse, but as we saw, this does not cover basho in its entirety. The relation between "that which is located within" and the basho in which it is located must be explainable in purely logical terms if Nishida is to achieve his aim of providing a logical foundation for the "demand to see the form of the formless." But this logical structuring would be deemed insufficient if it were merely a formal and abstract logical structuring. There must be a "looping" in the completed system. In other words, it must be able to explain the possibility of its own existence.

This looping feature lies at the core of the problem of completeness. Simply put, it comes to this: any theoretical structure that purports to give an account of the whole of experience must somehow also be able to account for the possibility of its own construction. Thus, if one were to encounter a particular theory of such a kind that by adhering to it strictly one could not show how the theory itself was possible, then one would be forced to say that the theory was incomplete because it did not account for itself. This, in a nutshell, is my rationale for the term "the problem of completeness." Nishida is not concerned with the construction of an abstract structure that is then applied to a given content lying outside of the structure. Such a scaffolding, however elaborately designed, would leave the opposition of content and form intact, and, what is more, would be incapable of explaining how we are aware of that opposition.

To clarify still further, let us take three examples of the emergence of this problem in the history of philosophy. Although the problem is not manifested in exactly the same manner in all three cases, it is enough that they show the same core that Nishida was after. The three examples are Kant's critical philosophy, Wittgenstein's *Tractatus Logico-Philosophicus,* and Russell's theory of types. The first two examples are much too complex to be dealt with in any more than a cursory fashion here. Nonetheless, even a brief look should be enough to show their relationshiop to the problem of completeness. Russell's theory of types will be particularly useful as an example because of its relative simplicity and narrowness of scope. It will be possible to give a detailed account of the manner in which the problem of completeness manifests itself there, and this in turn will enable us to present a clearer picture of the essential structure of the problem.

It might be said that Kant both did and did not see the problem. He saw it in the sense that his first critique is an attack on the pretense of philosophers who speak as if they had knowledge of a realm that, in principle, could not be part of experience but was supposedly the ground of experience. Kant believed he had demonstrated that traditional metaphysics as a science was impossible. But this did not mean that no explication of the whole of experience was possible. What one *could* do, he argued, was elicit the formal structures that were the conditions under which we have the experience we do have. This was possible because these conditions were inherent in our nature as rational human beings. This is what he gave us in the forms of intuition and the categories of thought supplied by the knowing subject. When these forms were combined with the matter given from the outside, the objects of experience were constituted.

This is an over-simplification of Kant's view, of course, but sufficient to lead us to the question his solution raised, namely, "If Kant's theory is correct, how can we ever know it to be so?" The theory accounts for how we constitute the objects of experience, but not for how we know that this is how we constitute them. Nishida himself had made this point as early as *Intuition*: that the mechanisms that Kant displays to account for the structuring of experience do not account for our capacity to become aware of those mechanisms. Put another way, there remains in Kant's thought an ultimate dichotomy between the form supplied by the knowing mind and the matter supplied from without. If this dichotomy were, in fact, ultimate, Nishida maintains, there would be no possibility of the interaction needed to constitute the objects of experience. It is this tension in Kant's thought that allowed him to be the source for the later German Idealists as well as for certain twentieth-century empiricists. As the historian Frederick Copleston has remarked, "It can be argued that though the Kantian system gave rise directly to the systems of speculative idealism it is really a half-way house on the road to positivism."[23]

If one were to stay strictly within the limits of the apparatus of critical philosophy, it would be impossible to develop critical philosophy. Nishida was persuaded that his notion of basho shed light on this problem. For his part, Kant did not seem overly concerned about the point, but Wittgenstein was very much aware of it at the end of the *Tractatus*. When Wittgenstein says that anyone who has understood him will realize that all he has said is nonsense, he touched the point precisely.[24] The point is that the standpoint of the *Tractatus* itself is not encompassed within the "limits of language" it prescribed. To view the holistic structure of language and its relation to the world it describes presupposes that one can get outside the boundaries of language, but this is just what Wittgenstein denies. This does not mean the whole of the book is nothing more than a string of unconnected forms on paper, no better than the tracks a chicken might make after stepping in a mud puddle, but it does indicate a basic difficulty inherent in the theory as developed in the book.

That this is the same problem found in Kant's critical philosophy may not be readily apparent. Erik Stenius has argued for an interpretation of the *Tractatus* that sees Wittgenstein as a Kantian philosopher. In fact, he goes so far as to suggest that if one substitutes the phrase "describable in meaningful language" for "imaginable" or "intelligible" in the basic thesis of Kant's philosophy, one would get a list of basic theses held by Wittgenstein. The difference is one of "Transcendental Idealism" or "Critical Idealism" for Kant as opposed to "Transcendental Lingualism" or "Critical Lingualism" for Wittgenstein.[25]

I had no mind to get tangled in an analysis of the *Tractatus* here, but Wittgenstein's awareness of the problem posed by his own book illumines what Nishida was trying to do and how he set out to do it. Wittgenstein did no more than caution the reader that the statements made in the *Tractatus* were not "meaningful propositions" in the sense defined in the body of the text itself. He has nothing further to say of their status. Even to have attempted would have been self-contradictory since it would have meant that one could somehow go beyond language while remaining within its bounds. Nishida would grant him the point, but would disagree that this is all there is to be said. For the fact remains: Wittgenstein developed his system and that system can be understood. It is, therefore, necessary for the philosopher to explain how this is possible. Remarks made about our knowledge of the natural world are not, of course, of the same sort as particular propositions expressing such knowledge. What is required is an account of the relationship between the two, and this requirement is not met by simply rejecting the former as not being knowledge.

A consideration of how this general problem manifests itself in such a specific and technical area as Russell's theory of types will be useful in order to show the pervasiveness of the problem and also to clarify the essential structure of the problem. The theories of Kant and Wittgenstein were of comparable generality both with each other and with Nishida. Russell's theory of types, in contrast, is much more restricted in scope. Although it is true that the theory was not presented as a general metaphysical or epistemological scheme, it can be said to be a good example of the problem of completeness. Because it deals with the problem of what can be said in language, the theory of types, although specific, is general enough to generate an instance of the completeness problem. In a word, it is a linguistically expressed theory that purports to deal with the whole of language.

The question of "standpoints," originally inherited from the Inoues and the object of Nishida's concern in both *An Inquiry into the Good* and *Intuition*, remains central in the third phase of his development, which includes such works as *From the Acting to the Seeing*, *The System of Self-Consciousness of the Universal*, and *The Self-Conscious Determination of Nothingness*. There is a difference between the particular statements stemming from a given "standpoint" or a theory of interpretation and statements made about the structure of the standpoint, the theory, or its interpretation as a whole. Such a distinction between internal and external questions was formulated by Carnap[26] with the distinction between object language and meta-language in mind.

The problem of self-reference[27] is "solved" by the introduction of a scheme of levels, as we see, for example, in Russell's "beastly theory of types" as Ramsey called it. Here the problem is one of dealing with paradoxes in the foundations of set theory, but it is symptomatic of the more general problem that lies at the core of all philosophical activity. This calls for a consideration of whether these statements can be made about the general structure of our knowledge of the natural world. And if they can, they must be shown not to be in conflict with the theory being proposed. To say that the theory itself is literally nonsense because none of the sentences in the theory accords with the rules given in the theory is to say that all one has said is nonsense. And then to turn around and claim that that nonsense has resolved all the basic philosophical issues amounts to despair of knowing anything or at least a slide into mysticism.

The difficulty with respect to Russell's theory of types is not that the theory is inconsistent in the way that a system that acknowledges "p and not-p" as an axiom would be inconsistent, but, rather, that there is an inconsistency in the claim that it is able to enunciate the theory at all. To continue with the example of the theory of types without delving into all the complexities of its structure, one might say that the fundamental feature of the theory is that it presents a hierarchy of types of levels, namely, individuals, functions of individuals, functions of functions of individuals, and so forth. The theory then proposes a restriction on the formation of propositions in terms of their hierarchy. Thus, a function of type can be said to be significantly predicated only of a member of type n-1 (take individuals as being of type 0, functions of individuals as being of type 1, and so forth).[28]

The rationale for the construction of this theory rests in the desire to find a method of avoiding certain paradoxes arising from the unrestricted introduction of classes by merely appealing to a particular defining characteristic. The particular form in which the paradox is stated has to do with the notion of a class not being a member of itself. The defining property in question is, therefore, that of not being a member of itself. Thus, some classes can be said to be not members of themselves. For example, the class (set) of men is not a man. One does not say, "I count three men in this room, John, George, and Man." There is nothing untoward in pointing out that some classes are not members of themselves, and at times it is necessary, as in introductory philosophy courses, arguments concerning politics, or what have you.

This being so, it would seem possible to speak of the class of all those classes that were not members of themselves. But this is precisely where the difficulties occur, since it would not be unreasonable to ask whether this class (call it "N") is a member of itself or not. If one says that it is a member of itself, then it must have a property of not being a member of itself, since not being a member of itself is the criterion for being a member of N, and yet, if one says that N is not a member of N, then by that very fact it satisfies the criterion, and, thus, must (itself) be said to be a member of N. Thus N is a member of itself if, and only if, it is not a member of itself. Clearly this sort of contradiction cannot be allowed; if it were, all discrimination would be lost and anything would be provable.

Russell's simple theory of types is well suited to eliminating this sort of paradox.[29] The difficulty that attends to the theory of types and is of concern to us at this juncture is that in order to enunciate the theory, it is necessary to do what the theory explicitly prohibits, and that is to refer unrestrictedly to all propositions without respect to type. The theory, if it were correct, is impossible to state, for to state the theory would be to defy the prohibitions that the theory puts forth. The same sort of uneasiness accompanies Wittgenstein's views in the *Tractatus* and Kant's critical philosophy. The core problem in all of this resides in the process of knowing, and more particularly, in knowing about a particular form of knowing that purports to be all-encompassing

The three examples given here suggest that the problem they each face is so fundamental that there is a tendency for philosophers to dismiss it. To think of this problem as a problem is to involve oneself in a situation from which there is no way out. And, indeed, for Nishida this is the case — as long as one retains the distinction between subject and object as ultimate.

Clearly the difficulty is not only a function of the generality of the theory. It is perfectly appropriate to speak of a theory that deals with all material bodies, all of space-time, and so on, without becoming involved in the kinds of problems mentioned above. One finds no objection to speaking of a theory that concerns itself with all material objects because one thing that would not be required of such a theory would be the inclusion of my knowing the theory as an object referred to by the theory. And the reason is simple: my knowledge of the theory is not itself a physical object and hence not an object of the theory.[30]

When, however, the theory in question purports to speak of the limits of human knowledge or of the relation between language and the world, the theory does itself become part of the subject matter of the theory. Theories are conceptual devices whose primary purpose is to give an explanation of certain phenomena in the sense of displaying relationships, functional or otherwise. Accordingly, a theory makes statements about the way certain elements of its subject matter will affect, or be related to, certain other elements. But when it comes to discussing the structure of the theory itself, it is necessary to "step back" from the theory and view it from some point outside of the theory. The problem is, this is precisely what one cannot do if one is attempting to set forth an account of the nature and scope of human knowledge or the limits of language.

Does this then mean that every such attempt is doomed to produce nonsense? If one attempts to take this stand, could it not be objected that the claim that all such attempts are nonsense is itself subject to the same criticism? Once the merry-go-round has been set in motion, there seems to be no choice but to get dizzy or to jump off.

How did we land here? It is almost as if chaos had slipped in while we were busy with something else and turned everything upside down. If there was self-deception along the way, then we need to trace our way back and identify it as such. To take this all as no more than a cautionary tale about how contradictions arise when certain locutions are used together with a set of directions for avoiding such contradictions is hardly much comfort. Conversely, the advice that we stop cudgeling our brains with this dead-end question and get on with something constructive, that we take up problems capable of being solved, amounts to forsaking the philosophical vocation altogether.

I repeat: for Nishida this whole predicament is due to an unquestioned acceptance of the ultimacy of the subject-object distinction. His concern is therefore with the core of the problem and any specific form it takes at the periphery. His search is for an explanation that does not suffer from the defects alluded to above, one that lays bare the root cause of the dilemma. Such an explanation would have to be reflexive, but not in the sense of a vicious circle. It would have to explain its own possibility, and that means that it would have to be intimately concerned with the structure of the knowing situation and the role of self-consciousness in the knowing process. Put the other way around, a coherent and acceptable metaphysical theory of the structure of reality would necessarily involve reference to the knowing process and self-consciousness. This is the "looping" that we referred to earlier, namely, Nishida's attempt to ground his system in the notion of self-consciousness.

All of this helps us appreciate Hisamatsu's apparent vacillation when speaking of Oriental Nothingness as an ontological principle as well as an epistemological one. The essential feature of Oriental Nothingness is precisely that it functions as both simultaneously. In fact, it would not be an exaggeration to say that for Hisamatsu they are not separate functions at all, but ultimately one and the same. There seems little point to speculating how precisely the problem of "standpoint" or the "problem of completeness" presented itself to Hisamatsu, but he cannot be far removed from it.

The denial of the ultimacy of the subject-object distinction that plays such a prominent role in his exposition is directly related to Nishida's problem of completeness: if the distinction is taken to be ultimate, there is no way of avoiding the paradox that any theory of the required generality would in its very expression ensure its falsity.

Rejecting the ultimacy of the subject-object dichotomy naturally tends toward the use of terms like *nothingness*, since any objectification would introduce one side of the subject-object distinction and, hence, the other side as well. The identification of nothingness with no-mind is consistent with the fact that the problem of completeness revolves around our ability to have knowledge of the complete structure. None of this makes Hisamatsu's exposition any more acceptable as a piece of philosophical argument or excuses his lack of structure and logical rigor. But it does help us to see how the problem he was facing is closely tied to certain profound problems that have arisen in the history of European philosophy.

Nishida's way of solving this problem, as I have suggested, is what he calls "basho." Since his view is basically in harmony with that of Hisamatsu, one might well expect that basho would share many features in common with the latter's Oriental Nothingness, and, indeed, this is the case. We have already pointed to some of them, in particular, the sense in which basho is said to be nothing. But we have not inquired into the aspects of basho that would be comparable to Hisamatsu's "No-Mind". Thus far we have restricted ourselves to the formal features of basho, but this is not the whole picture.

THE ONTOLOGICAL CHARACTER OF BASHO

There is a sense in which basho can be taken as the ground for categories that define a standpoint and, thus, a particular kind of "world." Putting matters this way is convenient if somewhat obscure. Reading Nishida, one gets the impression that he is basically engaged in a phenomenological investigation, bracketing all assumptions of a subject-object dichotomy. In order to obtain an adequate analysis of knowing, Nishida feels obliged to go beyond Kant and even the Neo-Kantians who steadfastly maintained the ultimacy of the form-matter distinction. One must produce a theory that is capable of accounting for the possibility of the standpoint of Kant's critical philosophy. Epistemology, to be complete, must become one with metaphysics, but not the metaphysics of "news

from nowhere." It must be a metaphysics of experience. Such a metaphysical scheme will be developed by carrying through an analysis of knowing
that starts at the simplest and most abstract level and progresses to ever
more complex forms until the analysis not only yields an understanding of
the nature of knowing, but an ontological and axiological scheme as well.
For Nishida, such levels of being are defined in terms of levels of basho, all
of which have similar logical structures. At various times, the basho are
identified with various selves (ultimately the "true self"), or with various
levels of consciousness. This prompts him to say in the introduction to
From the Acting to the Seeing that his view could be characterized as intuitionism, although he is quick to add that his is not an intuitionism in the
traditional sense because

> it is not founded on the so-called intuition of the unity of subject and
> object but rather regards all that is and all that acts as being shadows of
> that which reflects itself in itself while making itself nothing.[31]

The opacity of statements such as this is due in part to the fact that Nishida
is straining the bounds of language in his attempt to develop a view that
will not be subject to the criticism that it fails to explain its own possibility.
But straining the limits of language is hardly sufficent warrant for uttering
gibberish, as Nishida himself was only too well aware.

In distancing his intuitionism from any intuition of the unity of subject
and object, he seems to be rejecting the view that his "intuition" is no more
than a new and mysterious mode of getting in touch with a "hidden reality." It is not a separate faculty that allows the subject to be united with its
object. It is not an intuition of the unity of the subjective and objective
orders in some Spinozian sense, nor of different orderings of the same fundamental experience in a Jamesean sense. Nishida's claims seem to be based
on the following line of reasoning: Whatever can be said to be or to exist is
delimited; it is embedded in a framework; it is locatable within the grid of
some coordinate system or other. Even though one can attempt to describe
the formal aspects of the particular object, the distinction cannot be maintained in any but a relative sense without inviting the objections about
completeness and self-reference alluded to previously. Both the form and
the content must be seen as derived from the same source, both abstractions from the same ground.

The question that immediately arises is how this abstraction occurs. Who
or what does the abstracting? To say that there is some fundamental ontological category from which the subjective and the objective aspects are

abstracted seems merely to be stating an old and already discredited solution to the problem with which Nishida is dealing. And indeed, this objection would be devastating if Nishida were assuming in his argument that
the abstractor is different from that which is known or abstracted. In point
of fact, this is precisely the assumption Nishida refuses to make. The whole
thrust of his argument is that such an assumption leads to an impasse.

It is not enough for Nishida to deny that he is invoking a fundamental
ontological category that presupposes a user. The denial can stand up only
if located in a broader context where basho holds the central place. I turn
now to a brief sketch of that system to serve as an introducion to what we
will discuss in greater detail in the following chapter.

Nishida distinguishes three basho: the basho of being, the basho of relative nothingness (non-being), and the basho of absolute nothingness.
These basho determine three distinct worlds: the natural world, the world
of consciousness, and the intelligible world. The precise nature of these
worlds and the manner in which they are related will be taken up later.
Here I would only note that the material objects, the acts of consciousness,
and the values that are the occupants of these worlds correspond to what
he calls "shadows of that which reflects itself in itself while making itself
nothing." This means that these objects are interrelated in some fundamental sense and ultimately located on the same ground. At the same time,
each of them is an object in only one of the three worlds, and indeed it
makes no sense to speak of them all without in the same breath specifying
the particular world to which they belong.

Now this relativizing of "being" to particular context or world is, by
itself, likely to provoke an objection against the systematic ambiguity of
the word "is," a point we have alluded to earlier. Still more bothersome is
Nishida's talk of something "reflecting itself in itself while making itself
nothing." Numbers are not part of the furniture of the physical world, but
neither can two desks be called numbers. One may argue, of course, that
one can construct various worlds or domains of discourse by laying down
the appropriate conditions. But what does that have to do with self-
reflection? The fact is, the notion of a domain of discourse does not coin-
cide with the notion of basho. It shares some of its characteristics, but
when all is said and done, it is too abstract an idea to handle the task
required of basho. Nishida never intended that the concept of basho be
reduced to formal logic. It was to explain how formal logic is applied without itself belonging to the structure of formal logic.

Nishida means to argue that the three worlds do not result from the action of a particular set of categories on some antecedently given matter, but rather that both the formal aspect (the universal characteristics) and the material aspect are manifest in the self-determination of the viewpoint itself. Here we strain for clarity, since it seems nonsensical to speak of a viewpoint determining itself or, indeed, of a viewpoint doing anything at all. Viewpoints do not act except in a metaphorical sense. They are taken or adopted by a conscious being. One can talk of possible viewpoints, but then one would still have to say that one was talking of viewpoints capable of being adopted by some conscious being. Nishida is barred from arguing this way because it would lead him to assert what he cannot: the objectification of both the viewpoint and the consciousness that takes it. This would amount to perpetuating at the deepest levels the very subject-object distinction he means to deny and lead him back to the paradoxes he is seeking to overcome. It is precisely to avoid all of this that Nishida speaks of the basho as determing the various object worlds in terms of consciousness.

Caution is called for at this point. Although the basho that determine the three worlds can be understood as levels of consciousness, consciousness cannot be understood in any ordinary psychological sense. To do so would entail an objectified consciousness, which would be incapable of constituting a world of any sort. To speak of "active consciousness" is to prompt the question of where this activity takes place and what its ground is. One ends up speaking of consciousness as "something that acts" in the manner of Descartes' "that which thinks." Nishida's recognition of this difficulty is one of the primary motives he entitled his fourth book *From the Acting to the Seeing*.

Here we begin to see why the notion of nothingness is so crucial to the whole discussion. The intuitions that serve as the foundations for the various worlds must be nothingness (non-being) with respect to the elements of the particular world. Insofar as they can be determined at all, they must be determined in some place and this means they cannot themselves be ultimate. Consequently, the final place, the last basho, must be absolute nothingness. The relation between the universal that determines a structured world of a particular type and consciousness is brought out in the following statement:

> When the universal becomes the basho in which all being is located, it becomes consciousness. To the extent that the universal is still determined as a universal, i.e., to the extent that it has not yet become the true basho of nothingness, substance is seen externally and universal concepts are seen internally.[32]

This distinction of external and internal occurs, therefore, in a basho that is not yet the basho of true nothingness. In other words, it is is a level of consciousness but not the deepest and most profound level. Consciousness in the deepest sense is completely undetermined and hence cannot be said to exist or not exist. This is explicitly stated by Nishida in passages like the following:

> Behind consciousness nothing at all can be thought, for if it stands on something, it is not consciousness; consciousness is everywhere immediate. Whatever is to any degree objectified is not consciousness, and the psychologist's consciousness is nothing more than something cognized (something held within consciousness).[33]

For Nishida, then, true consciousness is close to what Hisamatsu referred to as No-Mind or no-consciousness. We move from the level of the basho of being to the basho of relative non-being and, finally, to the basho of absolute non-being by moving deeper and deeper in the recesses of consciousness.

Each of the worlds spoken of in connection with the three levels of basho can be said to be founded on a clearly determined universal.[34] But these universals, since they are determined, must be grounded. Merely to call them concrete universals, however necessary, is not sufficient to give a full analysis of either the knowing process or the nature of the basic ontological structures. Nishida remarks:

> As long as what I term *basho* is thought to be a universal that is established by discursive knowledge and is thought to be a concrete universal, it is still subjective (in a grammatical sense) and thus is still an object. But, as I have said before, as long as discursive knowledge is established there must be a reflective universal behind the concrete universal.... This predicate plane, which must always underlie discursive knowledge, is what I term *basho* and it corresponds to Kant's cognizing subject with the difference that it is not a point of synthesis but an enveloping plane.[35]

Basho is therefore essentially self-reflective; it is self-consciousness in the deepest sense of embracing not only what is subjectively thought but also what is objectively given. All the various selves—the cognitive self, the willing self, the feeling self—are ultimately located in this final basho, as are the object worlds of these selves. While basho is not to be equated with the consciousness of which the psychologists speak, neither is it explicable in purely objective terms. Without stressing the subjective aspect of basho as truly subjective, that is, as opposed to an objectified aspect of basho, there would be no cause to claim novelty for the idea. Nor, Nishida would claim, would there be any way to resolve the problem of completeness.

In the next chapter, we will turn to the details of Nishida's thinking on the interrelationships between the various levels of basho, and the development of what he terms "predicate logic."

CONCLUSION

In this chapter we have considered the basic characteristics of the concept of basho, followed its development in Nishida's philosophical thought, and related it to the idea of nothingness in Zen. After a reappraisal of the nature of consciousness, the voluntarism of intuition was rejected along with its emphasis on activity. A more instructive key to the dramatic change of perspective that took place in Nishida's thinking was the exchange of poems by Shen-hsiu and Hui-neng. There we saw a rejection of an "activist" view in favor of one focused on nothingness. Despite these similarities, it cannot be said that Nishida's Zen experience has found a place in his thought as a structural element.

Hisamatsu's listing of the traits of Oriental Nothingness helps shed light on Nishida's characterization of basho. The analogies of the waves on the sea, the mirror, and space are of particular interest for understanding Nishida's statements about the character of basho. The analogy of the mirror, for instance, is alluded to directly in Nishida's works, and the analogy of the waves and the water is remarkably similar to his own example of a force field. More examples could be given.

Nevertheless, the Zen notion of nothingness cannot cover the full complexity of Nishida's notion of basho. The logical and structural aspects appear to be stimulated by his interest in mathematics and Aristotle. Basho is intended to serve as a tool to solve the problem of completeness. This problem centers on the fact that no theory attempting to give an account of the whole of experience can be complete unless it includes an exposition of its own possibility. This self-referential character of the problem makes it impossible to reach a solution in objective terms alone. The complexity of this problem and the multiplicity of forms in which it manifests itself demand that any solution possess logical, epistemological, and ontological characteristics.

The concept of basho as set forth by Nishida seems to function as a category in the general sense, but it is far more than that. Quine's remark that ontology is determined once the overall conceptual scheme has been established seems particularly close to Nishida's comments on basho's determination of being. In both of these statements there is an interpenetration of logical, epistemological, and ontological characteristics. There is a crucial difference between them, however, in that Quine would restrict himself to speaking of conceptual schemes while Nishida would not. Quine's categories are all objectified categories, and for Nishida this is not enough — there must be a move toward utter subjectivity.

The characteristics of basho that we have discussed in this chapter can then be summarized in two grops of statements. The logical characteristics that basho shares with the domains of discourse are these:

1. the "is" of existence and the "is" of predication are intimately related;
2. existence is determined by being in a basho;
3. a change of basho means a change of entities; and
4. from the point of view of elements in basho, it is nonsensical to say that basho either exists or does not exist.

The primarily epistemological and ontological characteristics are these:

5. basho determines itself;
6. basho reflects things and itself;
7. the elements in basho are a part of basho;
8. the elements in basho are images of basho;
9. there is a final basho; and
10. basho contains its own principle of individuation.

Thus, there is a sense, as Noda has suggested, in which basho can be said to be a material field, though this is only part of the concept. Self-consciousness is one of the most important features of the concept since, as we might expect, it will prove necessary to build the structure as a whole. It is critical that the notion of self-consciousness be understood in structural terms within the system. The equation of knowing and the self-determination of basho is also important, since the notion of determination is basically a structural one. Finally, it has come to appear that a coupling of the notion of nothingness and the notion of self-consciousness will be required for Nishida to effect the "looping" that is necessary to solve the problem of completeness.

The three levels of basho that have been introduced here serve to bring into relief only some of the most general features of Nishida's structure. Only with an exposition of the complete system will the characteristics of basho become fully apparent. In the following chapter this structure will be analyzed in detail to show precisely how self-consciousness is interpreted in structural terms by means of the concept of basho.

5

The Logic of Basho

THE PREVIOUS chapter presented a preliminary exposition of the concept of basho, a concept Nishida introduced in an attempt to find a mechanism for solving what I have called the "problem of completeness" of epistemological and metaphysical schemes. The complex intertwining of the logical, epistemological, and metaphysical characteristics of the concept was seen to be essential for the concept to provide a key to the solution of this problem. At the same time, we saw how the interweaving of seemingly disparate characteristics render the concept difficult to comprehend. Only by seeing the concept at work in the development of a scheme that "displays the structure of reality" can we hope to gain sufficient understanding for an evaluation of the viability of the concept.

Nishida presents his system as a completed structure. Using his concept of basho, he develops a scheme for describing the structure of reality in a series of essays that were gathered together in a work entitled *The System of Self-Consciousness of the Universal*, and it is this scheme that will be the subject of the present chapter.[1] In the "General Summary" to *The System* (an English translation of which is included as an appendix to the present volume), Nishida presents an overall view of the developed scheme. Since the summary is meant to be read only after one has worked through the other essays, by itself it tends to be more confusing than elucidating. Moreover, since Nishida is trying to clarify certain possible misunderstandings of his treatment of judgment and self-consciousness, the system, as presented in that summary, may easily give the impression of no more an intricate web of ungrounded concepts. Nowhere in it does he make explicit the necessity for building the structure itself. What is more, the full range of the effectiveness of the concept of basho is obscured by the lack of an explicit outline of its main characteristics. Thus, while the summary is of decided value as an indication of Nishida's style and the pattern of his argumentation, its role in clarifying the concept of basho is limited.

In this chapter we will consider the pattern of argumentation Nishida used to develop the structure of basho from the ground up. This will uncover the interconnectedness of the various worlds discussed briefly in the previous chapter, as well as the logical and structural functions of the concept of basho. I intend to show that there is basically one pattern of argumentation that, when successively applied, forces a move upward from a relatively simple set of categories to a richer and more complex one. The reason for this way of arguing is not just to demonstrate how a more complex categoreal structure develops, but also to show why the richer categories are not reducible to the simpler ones. In this way Nishida hopes to explain the essential dependency of the simpler categories on the more complex, that is, to show why the former can be abstracted from the latter but the latter cannot be constructed from the former. I will devote a rather large segment of the chapter to the development of the universal of judgment[2] that determines the world of nature. This is the basho of being, the "shallowest" of the three basho introduced in the foregoing pages. This development also may be seen as an uncovering of the structure that is needed to support the claims to objective knowledge.

It is helpful to comment at this point on Nishida's use of certain key terms. As we saw, he distinguishes three basho: the basho of being, the basho of relative nothingness, and the basho of absolute nothingness. These three determine the three object worlds of the world of nature, the world of self-consciousness, and the intelligible world respectively. Nishida uses the term *universal* in much of his argumentation as essentially interchangeable with the term *basho*. As the title of the work suggests, the term is central to his thought, and it is therefore important to clear up possible misunderstandings from the start. Certain of these were pointed out in the previous chapter, but it may be helpful to recapitulate here.

Nishida uses the terms *universal of judgment, universal of self-consciousness,* and *intelligible universal* as alternate expressions for the three basho indicated above. There is no radical divergence in understanding involved, but the terms do represent a shift of emphasis. Basho is a concept fitted out with an extremely complex set of properties, but we often find Nishida restricting his use of the term to those times when he wants to stress its ontological character, as when he speaks of objects located in a field or "basho." In contrast, he seems to favor the term *universal* when he is more concerned with the logical or epistemological character of basho. Thus, when he speaks of the universal of judgment, for example, he is speaking of the basho of being, but he is doing so with an emphasis on the categoreal structure of the conceptual scheme that is proper to the basho of being. This is not to say that the term *universal* is to be taken merely as referring to an abstract set of logical categories. Such a view would run counter to Nishida's intentions, which is why he continually refers to these universals as *concrete* universals. The universals, then, are the basho; and, as such, they have all the characteristics of basho. However, in order to show the interrelationship of the various basho, Nishida focuses on the categoreal structure appropriate to each, and it is to these structures that the recursive pattern of argumentation is applied.

Since this pattern is recursive, we may begin with a detailed examination of its use at the simplest level of analysis and a somewhat more general indication of the application of the argument in order to display the constitution of the more complex levels. For this reason, the examination takes as its starting point the subsumptive judgment that Nishida employs to exemplify the essential structure of knowing. A fairly detailed examination of the relation of the structure of judgments and the nature of the objects of knowledge, considered in terms of what Nishida calls predicate logic, will lay bare the basic structure of the universal of judgment. The mechanism for proceeding from the abstract to the more concrete levels of knowledge will be seen to reside in the discovery of the contradictions that appear when an abstract set of categories is applied unrestrictedly. The mechanism that displays the structure of the universal of judgment is the same mechanism that requires a transition to be made from this basho of being to the basho of relative nothingness, which supports it.

The key to uncovering the structure of the universal of judgment lies in demonstrating the dependency of our knowledge of the natural world on self-consciousness. The movement from the basho of being through the basho of relative nothingness to the basho of absolute nothingness is essentially the process of making explicit the deeper levels of self-consciousness. The basho of being resides at a level in which self-consciousness does not appear as self-consciousness; at that level there are only the relations of objects. In the basho of relative nothingness self-consciousness appears as self-consciousness, but only as an objectified self-consciousness. In the basho of absolute nothingness, self-consciousness is fully explicit. Everything that appears is seen as self-expression; in the end even the opposition of noesis and noema is dissolved. In this way, once the development of the universal of judgment has been traced out, describing the structure of the other universals can quickly be done by relating them to the structure of the universal of judgment. Not only the structure of the particular universals but also the relationship between them will be seen to be based on a single principle. Thus far, the pattern of argumentation may be seen as a series of transcendental steps based on a simple principle: where a contradiction arises when using a particular set of categories, that set of categories is not ultimate but derivative, and must therefore be gone beyond to a further set of categories. This process is applied until finally even the category distinction of subject and object is itself shown to be derivative.

Systematically showing that the subject and object distinction is itself derivative completes one part of Nishida's task. What remains is for him to show how his general structure, and the notion of basho at the heart of it, can be applied to illuminate all aspects of experience without losing sight of the problem of completeness. The remainder of this chapter will, therefore, be devoted to a view of the system "from the top." Think of climbing a mountain and drawing a map on the way up to record the path that led you to the summit but that had been been impossible to detect from below. Once at the summit, you look down the mountain and sketch a map of the mountain as a whole, showing the full panoramic view that only the summit can give. This view from the standpoint of "nothingness" will allow the concept of basho to appear in its entirety. In particular, the utter subjectivity, which Nishida speaks of as a way of going beyond the subject and object distinction, will become clear, as will the fundamental character of seeing the various worlds as expressions of the self.

The possibility of such a change in orientation to a "view from the top" of the theory's structure will vouch for Nishida's claim to have solved the completeness problem. This reorientation pivots on the concept of basho and, in particular, on its characteristic as nothingness. This latter will also render more intelligible Hisamatsu's characterization of nothingness as "No-Mind." The description of the means by which the logical structure of the system has been generated, and the overview of the completed system combine to illumine the interconnection of the various characteristics of basho. This combination gives Nishida justification for claiming to have produced a theory that covers the full range of human experience, including the construction of the theory itself.

THE JUDGMENT AND PREDICATE LOGIC

Although reference was made in the previous chapter to the question of judgment and its relation to the notion of basho, the discussion did not advance beyond an elementary stage. It was noted there that the crucial move for Nishida was displaying the connection between a pair of relations, namely, the relation between the subject and the predicate of a judgment, and the relationship between particulars and universals. This connection, we saw, is made explicit in Nishida's claim that the subsumptive judgment "A is B" simply expresses that the particular, "A," is in the universal, "B." This relation of "being in" is in turn connected with the relation of the knower and the known. It is the identification of these relationships, plus an account of the role played by self-consciousness, that allows Nishida to develop his "logic of basho."

Nishida begins his investigations with the subsumptive judgment, the simplest and most schematic level of judgment. He then proceeds to show that the categories and patterns of analysis proper to that judgment are too restricted to give rise to the concepts that we actually use. For these we need other categories not accommodated on that first level, and they must be more than a simple extension of the categories of the subsumptive judgment. A conceptual leap of some sort is required. All of this, Nishida argues, shows that the "simpler" patterns and categories are not basic but derivative, not building blocks but abstractions. In the case of the level of subsumptive judgment, the general categories are species and genus.

Of course, it might be objected, thinking and knowing are not exhausted in judging and the subsumptive judgment is not the only sort of judgment. Nevertheless, Nishida's strategy of explaining the nature of knowing in terms of this subsumptive relationship is not without reason. It is the simplest of forms and it is paradigmatic. The relationships he is seeking to illuminate are seen most clearly in this simple form, and the critical moves that relate to metaphysics can be discussed as side issues. His attention to subsumptive judgment may seem to expose him to the charge of not fully appreciating the logic of relations. I would argue not, but this is a point we cannot take up until after we have an idea of the complete structure developed on the basis of the subsumptive judgment.

The principal aim of Nishida's comments on the subsumptive relation-ship is to establish a connection between the grammatical subject and the individual or object of knowledge entailed in such a judgment, as well as the connection between the grammatical predicate and the knowing sub-ject. To this end he calls attention to Aristotle's definition of the ultimate reality (πρώτη οὐσία) as "that which is neither predicated of a subject nor present in a subject," that is, as the ultimate subject. This identification of the subject of judgment and the real in the most fundamental sense sets the stage for the problem of completeness.

As indicated in the last chapter, the difficulty that besets this orientation is finding a principle of individuation. There are two points to be noted here, both leading to a consideration of the notion of a concrete universal as a solution to the problem: the relationship between the subject and the predicate of the subsumptive judgment, and the relation of the individual to its predicates.

As we have seen, Nishida considers a subsumptive judgment of the form "A is B" to comprise three distinguishable elements: the subject or the par-ticular, the predicate or the universal, and the copula that expresses the relationship between them. What remains is to explain the nature of these elements and the way in which they constitute judgment. To avoid getting caught in Bradley's infinite regress, it is obvious that these elements must not be taken as distinct beings that then somehow have to be related one to another. Viewing the relationship as that of a particular being placed in a universal (which then is its topos), the burden of the explanation is to account for the relations between these elements without falling into the regress.

The difficulty stems from treating both the particular and the universal as beings,[3] from treating them both as objects, that is, as things capable of occupying the subject position of a judgment. Nishida's point is that if one places them both on the same level, it is possible to establish some sort of relation, but not a subsumptive one; whereas if one places them on differ-ent levels, one is faced with Bradley's regress. This is what leads him to con-clude that the universal must be nothingness in the sense described in the previous chapter. In short, for the judgment to be a judgment, the subject must be immediately *in* the universal; the universal must be the "topos" of the subject.

This may become clearer by taking the example of basho as color intro-duced earlier. In the judgment "Red is a color," one is asserting that red is an occupant of the domain of discourse of color, or more accurately, that red is part of the color system. What this means is that the universal is not merely an abstract concept, but a field that encompasses the subject. The statement is therefore partially a remark about the nature of our whole conceptual apparatus with respect to color and partially a remark about the colors and how they are actually related. Strictly in terms of the subsumptive judgment, one must have a relation of the subject and the predicate such that whatever is to be the subject of the judgment must be universal in some sense.

What does this entail for Nishida? He could possibly mean that for something to be the subject of a subsumptive judgment, it must at least be able to be characterized (even if the characterization is not actually done) in the fashion indicated by the predicate. It follows that only to the extent that something can be conceptualized is it capable of becoming the subject of judgment. Does this imply that the subject of the judgment will always be a universal? If so, it seems blatantly wrong. Or is Nishida merely saying that judgments are possible? If so, it hardly seems a very direct or profound way of saying so. If not that, what could he mean? One possible interpretation is that he wants to emphasize that insofar as a thing is to become subject of a judgment, and thereby an object of knowledge, it cannot be completely beyond the scope of all predication; there must be some essential connection between the subject and the predicate, a tie that allows the subject to be predicated. In fact, as we shall see, this is precisely why nothingness cannot become the subject of judgment.

Again, this tie cannot be between two things of the same level, or we are right back at the problem of infinite regress. We must also keep in mind that Nishida is dealing here with the subsumptive relationship — judgments of species-genus relation — which means that the subject of each such judgment will be a universal and not a particular. They are kinds, not individual instances. The problem is not new with Nishida. His point at this simple level (later to be applied to more complex examples of knowing) is that there must be a fundamental unity between the subject and the predicate for the subject to have the predication applied to it. In other words, he appears to be claiming that all judgments must be the amplification of an intuition. As early as his first work, *An Inquiry into the Good*, Nishida spoke of a judgment as the bifurcation and structuring of an intuition. The unity that ties together the subject and the predicate is not another object that could in its turn become the subject of another judgment, but must be the place that harbors the subject and makes the subject what it is, something that can be said to have that predicate predicated of it.

This unity Nishida claims is to be found in the direction of the predicate rather than in the direction of the subject of judgment. He seems to have in mind a difference like that between the statement "Green is a color" and "A-flat is a color." The first is not only a judgment, but a true one. The second is neither true nor false; it is simply nonsensical. The nonsense stems from a category mistake that can be accounted for only by assuming one of the following: (1) that the person who uttered the words did not know their meaning; (2) that she was deliberately trying to confuse the listener; (3) that she had a rather twisted sense of metaphor; or (4) that she is a philosopher giving an example of nonsense utterances. At any rate, taken literally, the sentence is no more than a string of words; it is not a judgment. To be a judgment there would have to be an intuition on which the judgment was based.

That intuition would reveal the unity of the subject and the predicate, not as previously given entities somehow brought together into a unity, but as diverging specifications or determinations of the same thing. In short, the unity would be a predicate unity. To say "Red is a color" is to say that red is a part of the total system of color that must be intuitively given in order to make a judgment in the first place. What is conceptually primary, Nishida claims, is the whole conceptual system connected with color. One does not start out with a concept of red independent of a concept of color in general.

Subsumptive judgments about color are not the result of uniting two independent concepts. On the contrary, one does not have the concept of red without having, at the same time, a concept of color. This means that both the specific color and the characteristic that makes it what it is are of the same order. In other words, the recognition of red as a color implies the recognition that it belongs to a total system of color, which implies its having a particular relationship with green, blue, black, and the like. Conceived of as a total color system, the universal is both extensionally wider and intensionally richer than the particular colors. Not only is it applicable to a wider range of objects than any particular color, but the content of the concept also includes the relations among the various colors. Furthermore, the true subject of a judgment is not the grammatical subject (hereafter simply "g"); rather, the subject matter, or the intuition, and the explication of it constitute the judgment. In the case of color judgments, this would mean the whole color system.

Or again, take the example of the field of force also discussed earlier. All judgments about the particular elements in the force field, that is, the particular accumulations of energy, are seen as judgments about the nature and structure of the field itself. The judgment can then be said to be the self-determination of the intuition that is itself universal in that it is the "location" of the subject. Intuition is that by virtue of which the grammatical subject becomes the grammatical subject. Judging simply objectifies this intuition, and that objectification is a self-objectification or a self-determination. To speak of the objectification of the intuition by something outside the intuition would necessitate treating the intuition as an object. Thus, a judgment such as "Green is a color" may be said to be the working out or specification of an intuition, but the intuition itself would play no part in the analysis of the judgment. The intuition is not part of that judgment, but its ground. The intuition itself cannot be perceived except as the object or a possible subject of a judgment; if it could it would no longer be an intuition but an object that is the result of some other intuition.

Seen in this way, judgment is the self-determination of something that itself can never be the subject (g) of a judgment. This means, of course, that the something cannot become the subject (g) of a judgment made in terms of the categories it defines. To return to the example of color, the total system of colors cannot become the subject (g) of judgments in the domain of discourse of color. This does not imply that such a something (the intuition) could not become the subject (g) of a judgment in a different domain of discourse, when different categories and, thus, different intuitions are at work. What it does mean is that the intuition can be said to be the true subject of judgment even though it is incapable of being the grammatical subject. Here Nishida is unambiguous that he means something different than a simple transfer from one domain of discourse to another.

The distinction between the "true subject of judgment" and the "grammatical subject" is critical to Nishida's argument. What he intends is clear from his remarks concerning the structure of judgment. If a judgment is the working out or determination of an intuition, this means that the intuition provides the backdrop for and subject matter of the judgment. Thus, the intuition can be said to be the subject of a judgment, even though it is not itself part of the judgment.

Basho, as we have seen, can never become a subject (g). Put another way, it has the character of nothingness. To be a being (ens) entails the possibility of becoming the grammatical subject of a judgment. This character of never becoming subject of judgment, seen in the context of the elements that go into making up a judgment, suggests that basho can also be spoken of as something that is always predicate but never subject. Indeed, this is precisely what Nishida claims about consciousness when it is viewed from the standpoint of the elements of judgment. Nishida's strategy is clear: to pursue a course the precise opposite of Aristotle's, who defined the "truly real" as that which is subject but never predicate. Nishida orients himself in the direction of nothingness, since what can never, in principle, become the subject of judgment cannot be said to be a being. Already at this stage the notion of a basho of absolute nothingness begins to make its presence felt.

The Basho of the Individuum

These considerations have led Nishida to a higher level of analysis, beyond a level of taxonomic relations between the categories of species and genus to a level of subjects (g) that are not fully comprehended by their predicates and of which incommensurable predicates are predicated. In other words, we have arrived at the level of the categories of substance and attribute. Consider the notion of an individuum (the individual object to which Aristotle refers) from the viewpoint of what are ordinarily termed universals (color, shape, size, and the like). No matter how a particular general concept, or universal, is specified or determined, the result can never be an individual. The most one can do is arrive at a complex universal that de facto could only characterize a single individual. But even in this case, a leap is required to go from the universal to the individuum. This fact presents serious problems difficulties if one is trying to make sensible statements about individua. If individua are completely beyond the reach of universals, then there is no way we could have any knowledge of them. They could not even be the subject of those subsumptive judgments that serve as paradigm cases of knowing.

There was no difficulty on the previous level where we make judgments like "Red is a color." But when we now claim that "This ball is red," we cannot possibly mean that the ball is part of the color system. The particular shade of red is part of the system of color, but the particular occurrence of that shade of red is not. Obviously not all our judgments are of the subsumptive sort. The fact is we do have knowledge of individua and make judgments about them. Analyzing the statement "This ball is red" cannot be made purely in terms of the hierarchy of abstract universal concepts.

The predicates characterize the individual; they are its properties. Yet the individual cannot "have its place in" or be located in a topos of species.

This last and somewhat obscure remark hearkens back to what has been said about basho in the previous chapter. Even in the subsumptive judgment "Red is a color" one can talk of color being the basho in which red is located, and indeed it is precisely this relation of "being located in" that characterizes the subsumptive judgment. For reasons discussed earlier, the basho here must also have the characteristic of nothingness with respect to the particulars located in it, but it is possible for color to become the subject of a further subsumptive judgment.

The phrase "having the character of nothingness with respect to the particulars located in it" is rather startling at first glance. One may take it to mean that basho is a thing that is, literally, without properties, which would be absurd. One could also take it to mean that basho has no relation whatsoever to the particulars located in it, but this sounds even more absurd. The difficulty arises from the nature of language itself. To say intelligibly what Nishida is trying to say requires taking two different viewpoints at the same time. As we have discussed in connection with the notion of the system of colors, color itself is not construed as a particular color. When we are speaking of the relationships among the particular colors, the question of the existence of color in general does not figure in the picture. One can say neither that it exists nor that it does not exist, since there is no way that "color" could be related to "red" in the way that green or black or blue is related to it. In other words, it is not a particular color but the basic category that allows one to speak of the various colors and the relationships among them.

From the viewpoint of particular colors, therefore "color" can be said to have the characteristic of nothingness in the sense that it is not itself another particular nor can it be characterized by any of the predicates that characterize the particulars. Nevertheless, we do characterize the system of colors and we find it reasonable to treat that system as an object or an extended particular. This means that its nothingness is only a relative nothingness, or to paraphrase, that the abstract universal is only a determined (specified, objectified) basho. Such a basho can serve as both subject and predicate of judgment because it does not "mediate itself." Here again, the point is that the abstract universal has become objectified and, as such, is no longer capable of functioning as the intuitional ground of judgment. Nishida's statement in this regard is turgid but unambiguous:

If for a universal concept to determine itself it must determine itself subjectively (g) (i.e., as a grammatical subject), and if this means that basho reflects itself in itself, then the abstract concept as a determined basho may, on the contrary, be thought to have a subjective (g) significance; it can be thought of as secondary substance. Depending on one's point of view, the so-called abstract concept can be seen both as subject and predicate; it is a neutral plane between the subjective and predicative directions. The abstract universal does not contain its own mediator within itself; it does not contain a principle of individuation. For this reason, only the relation of "that which is placed within" and basho, i.e., the so-called extensional relationships, remain and by means of this taxonomic conceptual knowledge is constituted from the hierarchy of species and genus.[4]

What does it mean to say that the abstract universal does not include its own principle of individuation? Simply that one cannot start from any abstract universal and, by narrowing the intension, arrive at an individuum rather than a predicate that is true of only one individual. The abstract universal is merely a class of individua; no matter how narrowly it is specified, it is still a class and not an individual. Still we do make judgments about individuals and the individuals that are the subjects of those judgments must also have their place, their basho. To recall Noda's phrase, it must be a universal concept that is "adequate to the individual."

If these predicates are not adequate to the subject, if they do not contain it as color contains red, then there must be some predicate that does. This is what Nishida designates the universal of judgment. The universal of judgment contains the various subjects (g) just as the system of color contains individual colors. And just as a system of color is broken down into the specific colors (subject) and the general character of color (predicate), so, too, the universal of judgment breaks down into subjects (g) (individua) and clusters of predicates (properties).

The basho in which these individuals are located cannot be an abstract universal but must be a universal that has the character of being predicate but never subject:

> The true concept must be concrete; the concrete concept contains within itself its own principle of individuation, its own mediator. For a concept to contain its own mediator within itself is for it to include what is truly subject, i.e., Aristotle's primary substance that is subject but never predicate. I term such a thing the universal of judgment.[5]

The universal of judgment is a concrete universal that is equated with consciousness and frequently referred to as the "transcendental plane of predicates."[6] This transcendental plane of predicates is the general term for the categoreal determination of the type of predicates that can be employed and the types of subjects that can be characterized.

What does Nishida mean by a concrete universal? It is nothing more than a convenient fiction to extricate himself from the difficulties that result from conducting his analysis in terms of "an abstract universal"? At first glance this would seem to be the case, but a more sympathetic reading discloses that there is more involved than a verbal sleight of hand.

Because Nishida takes the basic pattern of thought to be given in the subsumptive judgment where the subject is located in the predicate (the particular in the universal), he wants to extend this relation to judgments concerning concrete individua. Individua cannot be the subject of subsumptive judgments. If knowledge were restricted to the content of abstract universals, it would be impossible to have knowledge of individua. However, we do have such knowledge. To make judgments concerning an individuum the individuum must be located in a universal, but abstract universals are incapable of fulfilling this function.

Nishida executes his general method by formulating a parallel transcendence in the direction of the predicate. In one sense, the pattern of analysis remains the same as before, with the subject (g) located in the universal. In another sense, however, the pattern changes, for now Nishida applies the "over and up" approach in both directions of subject and predicate, rather than merely to the subject as is commonly done. Not only does the subject on this level lie beyond the scope of those in the subsumptive relationship, so, too, does the predicate.

If the individual is beyond specification in terms of abstract universals, what Nishida calls the transcendental plane of predicates occupies an analogous position in the opposite direction. Just as no abstract universal can be something that is subject but never predicate, neither can it be something that is predicate but never subject. The problem with talking about something that is always predicate but never subject is that since it does not become the subject of a proposition, it seems impossible to say anything about it. This is the very position Nishida had hoped to arrive at in his second stage of the analysis, which leads to absolute nothingness. The model for knowledge has not changed; the notion is still one of the subject of the judgment being located in a universal. What has changed is the character of the subject and the predicate. Both the subject and the predicate that subsumes it are beyond the scope of a system of abstract universals.

This parallel transcendence in the direction of the grammatical subject as well as in the direction of the predicate allows for an analysis to be made in the basic form "A is B." Moreover, the relation between the individuum as subject (g) of the judgment and the transcendental predicate plane can be treated as logically analogous to the relation between the subject and predicate of the subsumptive judgment, between species and genus. The subject of the judgment, the individuum, has its place in the transcendental plane of predicates, just as red was said to have its place in a concrete color system. So, too, the transcendental predicate plane is nothingness when viewed from the standpoint of the subject, on the same pattern that color is seen to be nothingness from the perspective of individual colors.

That said, the relationships do not seem strictly parallel. When one speaks of a species as being located in a genus, one thinks of a subject reflected in the predicate, but in the relation of the individuum to its basho, the relation is not merely one of reflection but of determination. The difference is mitigated in Nishida's treatment of the subsumptive relationship. While there is a sense of the predicate determining the subject, the contrast remains, since both the subject and predicate are thought of abstractly in the subsumptive relation. One of the recurring failures of philosophy has been the attempt to explain the relationship between an individual and its properties on the model of the subsumptive relation without recognizing the difference between the two kinds of relationship. Or, if the difference was recognized, then no attempt was made to explore the similarities.

> Thus the true subject (g) in a judgment is not a particular but a universal. What is completely outside the predicate can not become subject (g). Even the irrational can become the subject (g) to the extent that it is possible for it to be universally conceptualized. Taken this way, judgment becomes the self-determination of a universal and all universals must be concrete universals. There is, strictly speaking, no such thing as an abstract universal. Of course what I am here terming judgment is not the so-called act of judgment, but simply the basis for an act of judgment.[7]

Here again Nishida emphasizes the basic point that if there were a complete separation of subject and object, we could never connect the two, and that the same holds true of the relation of the particular and the universal.

While we need to distinguish between abstract and concrete universals in order to clarify the nature of the logical relations that Nishida wants to develop, the distinction is not an absolute one. Indeed, the whole point of his argument is that if abstract universals were simply abstract universals and if they were all we had to work with, it would be impossible to account for how we attain knowledge. We could not even frame the question, let alone answer it.

Abstract and Concrete Universals

While Nishida's predilection for looking at a given structure from various points of view is often confusing, in many ways it is one of the most productive aspects of his thought. The procedure is often confusing because he does not inform the reader that he is shifting perspectives. The casual juxtaposition of seemingly contradictory statements may startle the reader, but the adoption of logically interlocking viewpoints is at the core of Nishida's philosophical method. Only by taking seriously the restrictions inherent in the traditional notion of universals does it become clear that the unity of judgment cannot be established on that basis alone. The same is true when speaking of the universal of judgment. Even though it is necessary to speak of self-determination and ultimately of self-consciousness, these notions take us beyond the universal of judgment. For the universal of judgment to be what it is, it must be based on self-consciousness, but this self-consciousness does not become apparent until one moves to much deeper levels, to the universals of self-consciousness, the intelligible universal and the acting universal.

Here the reference to deeper levels is simply a reference to sets of categories that could not be accommodated within the simpler models but that must be accommodated given the fact that they are actually used. A deeper level, therefore, contains a more adequate concept of self-consciousness than the shallower one. Once again, the effort is always directed toward showing that the restricted categoreal structure of the shallower level will not permit the construction of the more complex categories that are required. If we were in fact bound by the limits of the categories of the shallower level, we would not even be aware that there is problem, since there would be no way to gain access to the more complex categories that need reconciling with the simpler ones. But we *are* aware of these more complex categories. They function to structure our conceptual scheme and we are conscious of the fact that they do so. The level of self-consciousness, Nishida tells us, deepens as the complexity of the categoreal structure that is its object increases.

Nishida's proposal is that the shallower levels, such as the level of the abstract universal, will be productive of knowledge insofar as these levels are derived from the deeper levels that ultimately bring one to the self-conscious determination of absolute nothingness. By the same token, if any of these shallower levels are taken to be complete representations of the ultimate structure in and of themselves, the ensuing explanations will prove to be utterly inadequate.

This subordination or incorporation of levels is seen quite clearly in the discussions of the universal of judgment. Not only does the individual reside there, but so does the abstract universal and in fact the whole system of abstract universals. It is for this reason that Nishida will refer to the universal of judgment as the "universal of universals." The abstract universals are subjective (g) determinations of the universal of judgment; they are partial specifications of this universal that display or mirror its predicative character in an abstract way.

In every case the transition from a shallow to a deeper level is generated by a contradiction that becomes apparent on the shallower level, and this in turn is connected with a deepening in the direction of the grammatical subject and the predicate. The appearance of the contradiction and the recognition of it as a contradiction require a shift to a new set of categories, in other words, to a new basho that can accommodate the type of entity required to resolve the contradiction. This transition marks a deepening of self-consciousness since it depends on the recognition of contradictions that occur when a set of restricted categories is applied universally.

In this way Nishida sees the predicate as important not only at a given level but also in the transition from one level to another. In speaking of a predicate logic he does not, of course, mean to divert attention from the true subject of judgment. In his view only the concrete individual can be the true subject of judgment. He understands the concrete individual here to be in contrast to the abstract individual that is the lower limit of the system of abstract universals. Only concrete individuals exist in the most fundamental sense, which is why Nishida emphasizes that "being" is always related to a field or set of categories, and that the sense of "being" changes with changes in the topos or basho in which the being is located. (The term *existence* is reserved for actual concrete entities.) The field of basho in which a being is located has, unlike a being, a predicative character. It cannot be defined in purely objective terms since it is not a potential subject of judgment, at least not on that level. Nishida therefore speaks of a logic of predicates, a scheme in which the predicate is accorded at least as much attention as the subject of judgment.

To repeat, the option for a logic of predicates is an option against a move toward something like the abstract universal. Traditional interpretations of universals have been intrinsically bound to a logic oriented toward the subject of propositions. Nishida sees the move in the direction of the universal or the predicate as a move toward the concrete. His aim is to track the subject-object distinction down to its birthplace, and this implies an understanding of a self, a knower, and not merely an understanding of the known. To do so he needed to develop a system that would treat the predicate as seriously as it does the grammatical subject. For this reason, the analysis of the self must be carried out in such a way as to not make it into an object.

All of this needs to be read in the context of what we had to say earlier in this chapter on the subsumptive judgment and, in particular, in reference to intuition as being the ultimate subject of judgment, the ground of both the grammatical subject and the predicate. The reason for connecting this intuition with the predicate rather than with the subject is this: when is treated as a subject (g), it no longer functions as a determiner but only as something determined by something else. Language being what it is, we are obliged to speak in active and passive forms of speech, but the point Nishida wants to drive home is that this sort of distinction does not refer to anything fundamentally real but only to our way of partitioning what is fundamentally united.

The key to the argument lies in self-consciousness, but the traditional method of dealing with this elusive concept demands treating the self as an object, which is doomed to failure. The sole course remaining, Nishida thought, was to shift the focus away from being and on to the predicate, to nothingness.

The Elaboration of the Universal of Judgment

In his "General Summary" to *The System of Self-Consciousness of the Universal*, Nishida makes frequent reference to the universal of judgment, but nowhere does he mention the "syllogistic universal,"[8] a concept that plays a significant role in the main body of the work. A detailed study of the universal of judgment and the syllogistic universal is beyond the scope of these pages, but a brief word on their interrelation is needed to understand how the natural world can be said to be determined or defined by the universal of judgment. The transition to the syllogistic universal again represents a change in the categoreal structure from one of substance and attributes, the structure proper to the universal of judgment, to that of an enduring substance that undergoes change.

This move from the notion of a substance that possesses attributes to an enduring substance that undergoes change is crucial and brings into play the idea of activity, causation, and even the "shadow of subjectivity." The key to this complex transition lies in the role that Nishida accords to time in his system. Before looking at the impact of the category of time, I think it best to add a few comments and admonitions.

The two most important features of what Nishida calls the syllogistic universal are that it provides a categoreal structure for the full-blown physical world, complete with objects in interaction, and that it highlights the essential elements for the transition to subjectivity. The introduction of time as a categoreal feature of the syllogistic universal is central to both of these features.

In naming his new universal "syllogistic" and in using terms like "major term," "minor term," and "middle term," Nishida is not interested in offering his own analysis of the classical form of the syllogism. He is only concerned with two general traits of the syllogism, which he will use to take his next critical step. Essentially, the syllogism is a means for relating two terms by means of a third, the middle term. In doing so it also brings to light a dynamic relationship between two judgments, judgments that might otherwise seem unrelated. It is here that Nishida introduces time as a category to connect two statements that cannot be connected on the level of the universal of judgment. Take, for example, the two propositions "x is red" and "x is non-red." Relating the two statements entails the assumption of a subject of predication that endures through time and is capable of undergoing change. Time, as he sees it, plays the role of the "middle term" that links the two. And in the same way the middle term does not explicitly appear in the conclusion of a syllogism, in Nishida's syllogistic universal time is not made an object that needs to be related to anything else. It is rather the medium through which such relations are established. This same pattern is at work in his discussion of the relation of a multiplicity of objects through cause and effect.

Time is also important for the transition to subjectivity. Nishida seems to have been influenced by Kant's treatment of time as the form of inner sense. In any event, the move to subjectivity appears to rest on the notion that the experientially primary example of a thing that endures change is the self or the ego. Time is therefore to be seen as the "middle term" connecting the ego, seen as part of the natural world, to the natural world itself. Nishida uses the expression "minor term" to refer to the ego and "major term" to refer to objects. His references to the "plane of the minor term" and "plane of the major term" refer to the respective fields or spheres in which the ego and objects find themselves, an opposition that amounts to no more than a truncated version of the subject-object opposition. Thus, the physical world with its objects and laws is referred to as the plane of the major term. More than merely an analogical way of speaking, Nishida's use of the syllogism seems to be intended to show the increasing complexity of categoreal structures.

Against the background of these preliminary remarks, let us return to the next stage in Nishida's argument. Central to the notion of the universal of judgment is the type of being said to be defined by that universal, namely, the individual object. The universal defines its categories and the categories, in turn, define the type of object with which one is dealing. For the universal of judgment, the categories permit objects, but there is no subjectivity in these objects. They cannot be construed as selves, even in an objectified sense. Here again it is useful to note that the universals can be seen as "domains of discourse," but more concretely as basic intuitions defining both a set of categories and the entities constituted in accordance with these categories.

The abstract universals are seen as attributes of individuals that are transcendent with respect to the system of universals expressed in the subsumptive relation. An individual is said to have its place in the transcendental plane of predicates; that is, the individual is located in the basho of being. The transcendental place of predicates is a predicate appropriate to the individual. It is the ground of both the subject (g) and the predicates of substance-attribute judgments. For their part, these predicates are essentially objectifiable, capable of serving as the subject of judgments. The conceptual universal (the system of abstract universals) is thus said to be a noematic determination.[9] In other words, it is a determination in the direction of the grammatical subject of the universal of judgment because the abstract universals that comprise it are seen to be attributes of individuals. The abstract universal is a basho, but it is a determined or objectified basho. The universal of judgment is, thus, a universal of universals. In the language of *Intuition and Reflection in Self-Consciousness*, the universal of judgment is an "a priori of a prioris": that it encompasses—or perhaps better, *is*—the basho in which those universals are grounded.

Individuals are located in the transcendental plane of predicates, but this plane is not itself determined or objectified. It remains nothingness with respect to the beings of the universal of judgment, that is to say to the individuals, just as the system of color was nothingness from the standpoint of the specific colors. Individuals can be said to be reflected in the abstract universals that serve as predicates in judgment, but this reflection is only partial. In other words, to assert that an object is red, heavy, solid, spherical, or the like is not to imply that these predicates exhaust the object. On the contrary, it implies that full characterization is essentially impossible. Perfect reflection can be achieved only on the transcendental plane of those predicates in which the individual is located. The universal of judgment has the meaning of being "the actual concrete structure of the relationship of basho and the individuals located in it."[10] The individual unites various predicates, and the transcendental plane of predicates of which the various predicates are abstract determinations guarantees the validity or objectivity of the judgments.

In the sense that it does not include change, the universal of judgment itself has to be considered an abstract universal. This marks the point at which Nishida makes the transition to a deeper level of analysis, though still retaining the same basic analytic framework. The basis of the analysis remains basho, the beings in that basho, and the abstract characterizations of those beings. What changes is the basic character of the categories. There is a shift from categories of substance and attributes to categories of an enduring subject and change, that is, time. Knowledge of individuals, determined by the universal of judgment, is merely knowledge of an individual as the unifier of various predicates. The notion that contradictory predicates could be attributed to the same individual is completely foreign to the realm of the universal of judgment; it does not accord with the intuition that is the ground of the universal of judgment. The categories of the universal of judgment are merely those of substance and attribute.

If the individual were only the unity of a fixed number of attributes, it would follow that as the attributes change, so will the object. But if we are to include change, we can do so only in the context of something that survives change and remains the same. To see change we have first to see unity. Thus, there is no notion of change in "A is B" and "C is D"; there are only two different statements. There is still no change and no conflict in "D" and "not B"; one simply has two individuals with different attributes, "A is B" and "C is not B." However, if "A = C," then we have a contradiction, for now we would be forced to say "A is B" and "A is not B." If "A" is to provide that unity, it cannot be merely an individuum. Even the attempt to bring the notion of time into the picture vis-à-vis the individua will not work. We land ourselves in paradox when we try to speak of the objects and time as somehow being on the same level. This is analoguous to the problem we met earlier of how to deal with relations that emerge on the level of the subsumptive judgment.

In a word, if we take "time" to be something objectified, then we are forced to admit either that the object changes while time does not, or that time changes while the object does not. Both of these alternatives fail to give any adequate account of change.[11] After a lengthy discussion Nishida arrives at the conclusion that time can be construed only as the form of change.[12] It cannot, however, be construed as such simply in terms of the universal of judgment. A mediation between two conflicting and even contradictory judgments is needed, for example, the judgments that "A is red" and "A is green." Since what is required is something that relates judgments in a way that judgments relate subject and predicate, Nishida calls this new universal a syllogistic universal. The universal of judgment and the syllogistic universal are both concrete universals; they are distinguished from one another by their degrees of concreteness:

> However, at the core of the concrete universal there must be a plane of transcendental predicates, a plane of consciousness that includes it. It is only then that it truly can be said to be concrete, or to understand itself. However, saying that the predicate plane is transcendental is to say that it cannot be thought of objectively; it means that there can be no objective knowledge established with respect to it. It is at this point that we must go beyond the world of so-called conceptual knowledge and enter the world of intuition. Taking one direction from this concrete universal one can think of the abstract universal and taking the other direction one can think of the plane of consciousness as the transcendental predicate plane. But even in the concrete universal one can distinguish the universal of judgment from the syllogistic universal. If the universal of judgment is that which includes within it its own subject (g), then the syllogistic universal is that which further envelops the universal. No matter how far one pushes the relation of particular and universal concepts, the individual that is subject but never predicate cannot be contained in the abstract universal. It is only upon reaching the universal of

judgment that it can be said to be contained within the universal. Yet, there is still an objectified individual; it is determined in a universal that is itself determined, and it is not yet something that determines itself. That which contains things that determine themselves must be something that goes beyond this universal. When we reach the syllogistic universal we have a level that can at last be said to include that which is self-consciously determined; we can think of something like the world of objects of reflection.[13]

This passage brings together a number of strands in Nishida's thought. It not only spells out the relationship between the universals that are at the foundation of all discursive knowledge, it also clarifies the relation of these universals with what Nishida calls the transcendental plane of predicates. These various levels of universals, each more concrete than the last, are taken to be none other than levels of the self-determination of the transcendental plane of predicates. As noted earlier, this allows a transition to a set of richer categories that more adequately represent the character of our actual experience and are not reducible to the more abstract categories. The term *self-determination* is important here, since Nishida does not want to set up the transcendental predicate plane as an abstracted set of categories manipulated by something outside of it. It is more like a fundamental intuition that spells itself out in the categories and the objects constituted within these categories. The deeper the level of the self-determination of the transcendental plane of predicates, the closer one approaches self-consciousness. The move from one level to the next is occasioned by the demand for a basho to accommodate some object of knowledge, an object that cannot be dealt with adequately on the basis of the categories of the shallower level.

The system of abstract universals is a hierarchy of concepts and as such cannot incorporate individuals. Even the universal of judgment, which gives knowledge of individuals, only gives knowledge of *abstracted* individuals, individuals that have properties but are not susceptible to change. Only on the level of the syllogistic universal can one speak of changing objects. In fact, the syllogistic universal remains, in an extended sense, a universal of judgment, since it is essentially concerned with objective determinations, that is, with the natural world.[14] In the strict sense, it differs essentially from the universal of judgment in that there is only a glimmer of the notion of self-consciousness at the level of the syllogistic universal.

Kōyama suggests it is fitting to call the syllogistic universal that enfolds the universal of judgment a universal because the syllogism is simply a judgment that relates judgments.[15] What still remains to be explained is how we arrive at the awareness of change. Nishida follows the same pattern as he had in speaking of the universal of judgment: to have knowledge of something objective is for that thing to be in a basho, and therefore to be determined by that basho. Thus, the changing thing will be located in an unchanging basho. In this way, the parallel with the universal of judgment is preserved. The basic logical structure is maintained by taking the minor term to correspond to the subject, the major term to the predicate, and the middle term (time) to the copula in judgment. But just as the copula cannot be thought of as establishing a relation between two things on the same level, so time "is not something that changes nor is it something unchanging, but it is rather the medium that makes the changing thing a changing thing in an unchanging basho."[16] In other words, time is a basic category, just as attribution is in the universal of judgment.

What are we to make of this "glimmer of self-consciousness" that is seen on the level of the syllogistic universal? Kōyama speaks of the syllogistic universal as the level on which individuals are finally spoken of in a full-blooded sense, as individuals that interact with one another. This kind of give-and-take cannot be considered to take place on the level of the universal of judgment, where the only type of judgment that can be made is the delineation of the attributes of an unchanging individual. The interaction among individuals is "rationalized" in terms of the category of cause and effect. Thus while substantial relations (the relation of substance and its attributes) constitute the general form of knowledge in the universal of judgment, in the syllogistic universal this general form of knowledge is to be understood in terms of causal relations, as categories that have now become an enduring substance and change in time. As we now have temporal as well as spatial relations on this level, it is possible to speak of the natural world as the object of knowledge.[17]

Now to speak of individuals mutually interacting, changing, and determining each other implies that these things have lost their self-identity and that this self-identity must revert to something that underlies them, something like energy. This seems to me close to what was said in the previous chapter concerning the energy field, where things that were formerly conceived of as objects are now taken to be simply accumulations of energy. This is not as odd as it might sound, as it is not uncommon for physicists to talk in similar terms, as if energy were a kind of "filmy matter." Here particular objects disappear and the acting things become activity pure and simple. Such activity is not an object; it is constituted when the basho determines itself, when the plane of the major term of the syllogistic universal determines itself. It is a determination in the predicative direction rather than in the subjective (g) direction. Here again we see Nishida emphasizing the point that objectified activity is not activity insofar as the unifying function is lost.

Pure activity may be thought of as a phenomenon of consciousness, thus giving us the transition from the syllogistic universal to the basho in which the phenomena of consciousness are located. At first glance, the transition seems artificial. True enough, Nishida does not present his discussion of the syllogistic universal in the relatively straightforward fashion of Kōyama's summary, which build on the universal of judgment without bringing in the notion of self-consciousness until the very end. Kōyama's explanation does, however, accord with Nishida's own characterization of the syllogistic universal:

> By thinking of the minor term and the major term as being in opposition, with the minor term not being immediately in the plane of the major, the syllogistic universal can be distinguished from the universal of judgment. If this were not so, then, since the subject (g) would be immediately in the predicative universal, there would be no way in which it differed from the universal of judgment. The minor term, which has the sense of being the subject in the syllogistic universal, has not only the sense of being simply an individuum that is subject but never predicate, but it must also have the sense of not being establishable as a mere subjective (g) unity. It must have the sense of being an immediate self-determination on the transcendental plane of predicates, i.e., it must be something that is located in self-conscious awareness. To say the same thing from the opposite point of view, we begin by having self-awareness, upon which the transcendental predicate plane is reflected, and it is by means of this that the syllogistic universal is constituted.[18]

The above passage seems to conflict with what was said a few pages earlier regarding the logical structure of the syllogistic universal as analogous to that of the universal of judgment, but the contradiction is only apparent. The difference between the universal of judgment and the syllogistic universal is that the objects defined by the former do not *do* anything; they can only be said to possess properties. The objects defined by the syllogistic universal, in contrast, act on each other. This notion of acting prompts Nishida to say that the "minor term" is not fully explicable as being a "subjective (g) unity." Thought of strictly as a "subjective (g) unity," it would be nothing other than the individuum defined by the universal of judgment. To say that something is a purely "subjective (g) unity" is to say that it is purely objective, that it is static, that it cannot act. In fact, Nishida takes the minor term to be essentially the cognitive subject (in the sense of subject as opposed to object).

The central point to be kept in mind with respect to the syllogistic universal is that the plane of the minor term is in the plane of the major term. The subject (the self) is seen as an entity in the natural world, but at the same time it is not completely or wholly in this world. The human person is not just a table or a rock or a flower. As humans we are bound by the laws of physics, physiology, and the like since we are part of the natural world, but we are also cognizing subjects that view the world as an object of knowledge. In other words, there are categories that are applicable to the human person that are not applicable to the other objects of the natural world. And these psychological categories are not strictly reducible to those of the physical world.

This would seem to explain the opposition between the major and minor planes and account for why the one is not in the other but must be related to it through some medium. With respect to the syllogistic universal, we come to have a notion of the self as a particular that has as its object the natural world. The opposition between the knower and known only arises on this level. But the relation is not yet truly that of the knower and the known; it is still objectified. At the level of the syllogistic universal one can conceive the natural world either in terms of a relation between a self that views the natural world through the medium of time as an object of knowledge or as a system in itself apart from this relation. On this level we are faced not only with the fact that objects have certain relationships to one another, but also with the fact that these relationships are an object of knowledge. One has not only the fact of the natural world, but also the fact that it is cognized as the natural world.

The natural world, the world of physical objects interacting in accord with the laws of physics, is seen as self-contained and developing or determining itself through time. But this notion of an objective world that incorporates change is not conceivable in terms of a universal of judgment whose categories are restricted to substance and attribute. To view this natural world as a self-developing, changing structure, there must be something that encompasses contradictory predicates. This role cannot be played by the purely objective individuum, by a mere substance having properties. To encompass contradictory properties, it must be something characterized as predicate but never subject; it must have the character of basho.

That which is predicate but never subject is consciousness. In order to conceive of a subject that as something more than the individuum (something that is needed to incorporate the notion of change), it is necessary to think of something like the self or the "I." This would mean that that which is predicate but never subject, the transcendental predicate plane, must be taken as subject (g); it must reflect on itself. This in turn requires that the transcendental predicate plane be capable of objectifying itself or determining itself as an object. Conceptual knowledge cannot be established without to some extent objectifying itself, but at the same time it cannot completely objectify itself and still be that which is predicate but never subject. Thus the claim is made that judgment is the self-determination of the universal, and that for the universal to determine itself is for the universal to "see a subjective (g) unity within itself."[19] In other words, in order to have a judgment, the judgment must be about something; and that something must be of the sort that allows judgments to be made about it. Thus, the object would have to be a result of the objectification of the concrete universal.

With respect to the syllogistic universal, Nishida says that the minor term plane must be thought of as a universal of judgment. He adds:

> However, it is not a simple universal of judgment, but, rather, since it is something located in basho, it must already have the sense of determining itself self-consciously; it must have the sense of an active determination.[20]

What is spoken of here as being in basho is a universal of judgment and not a particular or an individual; this is why Nishida refers to it as the plane of the minor term. Contrary to first impression, this does not conflict with the statements made about the syllogistic universal being a universal of judgment in the broad sense. The difficulty is resolved if one recalls that when Nishida calls this universal "the syllogistic universal," he uses the title descriptively and not as a mere decorative flourish. If the abstract form of the syllogism is taken to be "A is B, B is C, therefore A is C," Nishida's language is altogether suitable.

Nishida sees the opposition that first appears on the level of the syllogistic universal but is not apparent on the level of the universal of judgment to result from the fact that the judgment expressed in the conclusion could not be made without the middle term, B, which links the major and minor terms. Although it is doubtful how far this analogy can be taken, the main point is clear enough. Both the plane of the minor and that of the major terms determine themselves through judgment and are, therefore, universals of judgment. The plane of the minor term is a direct self-determination of the transcendental predicate plane of the universal of judgment.

This is not the place to follow Nishida through the considerable details of his argument about the role of time as the medium that provides the unity in the syllogistic universal and about how the various interpretations of time lead to different experienced worlds. In terms of Nishida's logic, the essential point lies in the nature of the syllogistic universal vis-à-vis the universal of judgment and in the transition from the syllogistic universal to self-consciousness. It is precisely here that he faults Hegel's logic for failing to clarify the relation of objects to self-consciousness. How Nishida himself does so is critical for the development of his thought.

The Syllogistic Universal as a Transition

The hierarchy that Nishida has developed to speak of the structure of discursive knowledge—species-genus relations, the universal of judgment, and the syllogistic universal—is treated as a series of levels of the self-determination of the transcendental predicate plane. On each level, an object of particular character is conceived in accordance with the universal, the determination of a universal being the determination of an object, or more precisely, of a multiplicity of objects of a particular sort. Each stage has both a greater degree of complexity and a greater degree of concreteness than the preceding. This hierarchy of complexity and concreteness becomes obvious if we examine the "entities" encountered at each level. Thus, the abstract universal, taken as the subject (g), is merely subsumed by a universal. It is located in a universal or, considered concretely, is seen as "part of the universal." The individuum, however, not only is located in a universal but can be thought of as having qualities. Finally, on the level of the syllogistic universal we have things that act and are, of course, also located in a universal.

Now the general feature of this hierarchy, as we have been saying all along, is that none of the more complex levels is explicable in terms of the less complex. The transition from a simple level to a more complex level, from a "simpler being" to a more complex one, is never made by a mechanical arrangement of the entities on the simpler levels. At each stage the entity of the more complex stage is "transcendent" with respect to the simpler stage, that is, the more complex entity cannot be encompassed by the categories of the simpler stage. The general form of the transition may be expressed as follows: If one were strictly bound by the categories of level s, entity T would be inconceivable, since entity T would have to be such that it had properties that would be contradictory in terms of level s. Since we do, in fact, conceive of T, it must be done from the framework of some level other than s. In this model, the individuum is not explicable strictly in terms of the species-genus relationship, since it is not capable of becoming a predicate when all of the entities that are conceived strictly in terms of this relationship necessarily have the character of serving as the predicates. Further, the individual can serve as the subject for a multiplicity of predicates, predicates that are not related in terms of species-genus relation. Thus, one can say "This box is blue and six cubic inches in volume" even though "blue" and "six cubic inches" are incommensurable qualities. Such individuals must be conceived in some terms other than the relation of species-genus, although it is possible to give some indication of what they would be in terms of this relationship; that is, they are subjects, but never predicates. The same relation holds between acting things and the universal of judgment in the strict sense.

Although the transition from the universal of judgment in the strict sense—where the categories are simply those of substance and attribute—to the syllogistic universal can be seen as merely a transition from the second to the third level of the universal of judgment in the inclusive sense of the whole structure of the three levels and their interrelationships, the importance of the transition is more wide-reaching. Of themselves the categories of the universal of judgment are so restricted, strictly speaking, they are incapable of yielding the natural world. Not even Newtonian physics could be described in terms of those categories, since time is a necessary feature of physics and yet is not one of the categories of the universal of judgment in the strict sense.

In contrast, Nishida's analysis seems to indicate that once one has a set of categories adequate to the constitution of the natural world, these same categories yield some form of subjectivity that must be included as part of that world. In a word, whenever one is confronted with the natural world of objects, one is also confronted with some form of subjectivity. It could, of course, be argued that even the more abstract categoreal schemes are not completely without relation to subjectivity, since if they were, it would not be possible to speak of a conceptual system at all. Granting the point, it remains the case that only at the level of the syllogistic universal does subjectivity becomes part of the conceptual framework.

The crucial point here is the way in which the active thing transcends the universal of judgment. Nishida characterizes this transcending as something that changes and argues that this change is essentially dependent on a notion of acting that is nothing other than an objectification of self-consciousness. The active individual located on the level of the syllogistic universal is a subjective (g) unity, but not merely a unity (for it is not the individuum); it must possess the character of that which is predicate but never subject. Thus, it has the character of a self, which means that there must be a "determination of the sort 'I am'" at the foundation of all judgments.[21]

In a broad sense, the whole of the universal of judgment is said to be a basho of being[22] precisely because all the entities that are taken to be central are objects, which is to say that in reference to the basic relation of the subsumptive judgment they all have the character of the subject rather than the predicate of judgments.[23] To clarify the relations between the various levels of the universal of judgment and the terminology connected with them, the following scheme may prove useful:

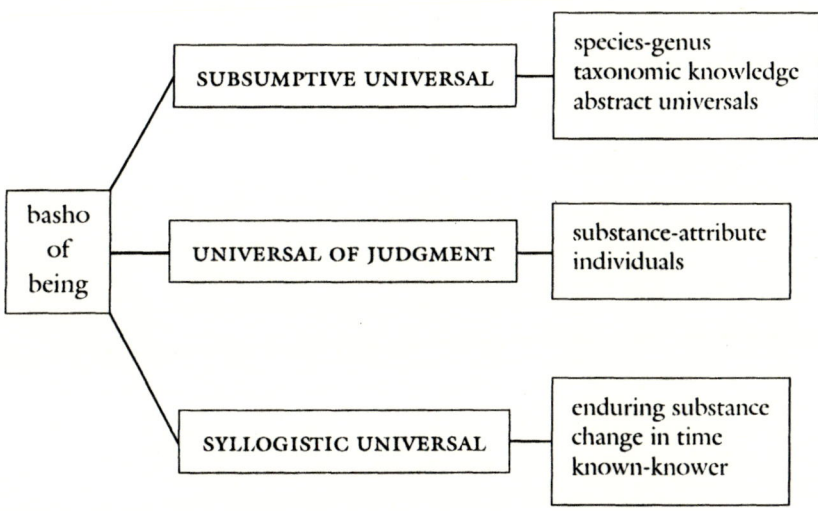

The objects are all objects of knowledge but lacking the character of something that knows. This applies to all levels of the universal of judgment, even though one approaches closer to the basho itself when moving through the hierarchy. Thus, on the level of the syllogistic universal, the entity that is the subject (g) is not completely determinable as subject (g); it is not completely objectified, and this accounts for the transition to the level of self-consciousness.

The cognizing self on the level of the syllogistic universal is considered to be very nearly on a par with the natural world, the knowing self being imagined as an eye that sees and the natural world as something that manifests itself to itself through the medium of time. The cognizing self is an object that is related to other objects. But because the self is not completely determinable as an object, the transition to self-consciousness becomes necessary. The ever deepening levels of the universal of judgment represent a growing demand for self-consciousness. To speak of self-consciousness in terms of logic, it needs to be seen as a kind of determination of a predicate plane embracing an infinitely deep subject (g).[24] One may also consider it as something that acts as a subjective (g) unity, but this is not sufficient to describe self-consciousness. We need to posit a deeper level. This follows a pattern similar to the way in which, when speaking in terms of the relation of species-genus, an individuum could be spoken of only as that which is subject, but never predicate.

The distinction of subject and object is, thus, made on the level of the syllogistic universal, but the distinction is one that treats the relation between these as a relation of objects, which is not sufficient. If it were, there would be no explaining how that relationship can itself become the object of knowledge. Self-consciousness, therefore, becomes the key to unlocking the solution to the problem of completeness. To explain self-consciousness in terms of logic, one can go no further than an explanation in terms of the syllogistic universal, and even here, one has less an explanation of self-consciousness than a demand for it. This is what Nishida means by the remark, "Instead of trying to explain self-consciousness in terms of object-logic, I take the form of self-consciousness to be the basic logical form."[25]

SELF-CONSCIOUSNESS AND THE LOGIC OF BASHO

The concept of self-consciousness was central in all of Nishida's works including *The System of Self-Consciousness of the Universal*, and it stands to reason that a final solution to the problem of completeness would hinge on that concept. Prior to the work, Nishida has thought of self-consciousness, including the relationship of knowing, as an activity. Only in forging his notion of basho was he able to provide an interpretation of self-consciousness free of the entanglements of reflexivity. We have followed him as he proceeded from an analysis of judgment to show that all judgments ultimately have their roots in self-consciousness. The transition from the abstract universal to the concrete universal of judgment and, finally, to the syllogistic universal clearly points to the need for deeper levels of consciousness than can be expressed by these levels on their own. His appeal to the Cartesian *cogito* is not new; we have seen it already in *An Inquiry into the Good* and later in *Intuition*. But the nature of the appeal has changed. Previously his concern was to derive an active principle from the *cogito* that would assist him in constructing a system of self-consciousness capable of solving the completeness problem. Now it is no longer a principle of activity that he seeks, but a logical relationship between the notions of basho and nothingness. This is part of a larger shift of perspective, a transition from viewing the problem as primarily epistemological to viewing it as primarily logical, and, at the same time, to construing the central concepts of that logic in the light of the Zen concept of nothingness.

The crux of the appeal to the Cartesian *cogito* is simply this: whereas judgments are usually analyzed with emphasis on the grammatical subject, this will not do for the "I am" of Descartes. In judgments analyzed in terms of the universal of judgment, the predicates represent no more than a partial explication of the subject (g). The abstract predicates are not suited to explaining the subject. No multiplication of predicates could ever suffice to give an adequate picture of the subject (g). When speaking of "I am," the situation seems to be reversed. Here it is rather the subject (g) that is inadequate. As Nishida puts it:

> The *sum* of Descartes' *cogito, ergo sum* does not mean subject (g) existence, but must have predicative existence. Since "I" is a thinking "I" and not a thought "I," it can never be found in the direction of the subject (g) of judgment; what is more, everything subjective (g) must find a place in it.[26]

To say that the subject (g) is not adequate to the predicate sounds unsettling at first. What Nishida appears to mean is that when one attempts to make the self, or "I," the subject (g) of a judgment, one can never fully succeed. The concept we have of the self, when taken as an object, never seems to capture completely or to describe satisfactorily the whole of our personal experience. The objectivized self can be characterized precisely because it is already an abstracted entity, a conceived self, a construct—that is, because it is no longer the concrete subject of experience. One may attempt to obtain a more complete concept of this self, but no matter how complex the concept becomes, it never approaches the concrete living self. The thinking "I," Nishida tells us, is predicative in nature and because it is not an object or a thing in any sense, it is not to be found in the direction of the subject (g) of judgment.

It is this very impossibility of complete objectification that led Nishida to distinguishing various worlds or levels and the corresponding universals that make them up. Each specific level demands a deeper level to account adequately for our experience. Thus, in the previous section, there was a steady progression from the more to the less abstract, and, in the end, there was a requirement for a type of being that could not be totally objectified. This provided the basis for a transition from the physical world to the world of consciousness. For Nishida the transition is one from the universal of judgment to the universal of self-consciousness.[27] It is a shift from the plane of the major term to the plane of the minor term of the syllogistic universal.

The transition is a change in the form of judgment insofar as what occupies the position of an occupant of the new basho is something essentially predicative in nature, namely, the self. But the self that is posited as the occupant of this new basho is at least partially an objectified self insofar as it is the correlate of the objects in the universal of judgment. That is to say, this self is the being that is proper to this basho, which Nishida terms accordingly the basho of relative nothingness.[28]

This new basho, enveloping the universal of judgment, has the same formal structure as that of the previous basho. It envelops the universal of judgment by virtue of the fact that its categories are richer than the categories of the universal of judgment. Self-consciousness is in no way accommodated within the categories of the universal of judgment, and yet the basic categories of the universal of judgment can be seen as limitations of the categories of this new basho. Each basho that Nishida speaks of is structured such that there is a "being" that is the occupant of that basho and whose nature is determined by the nature of that basho. In addition, there is an abstract plane of determination that functions as a field where the nature of the being that occupies that basho is spelled out. Both the being and the characterizing field are said to be the unfolding or the explication of the basho itself. in much the same way that the specific colors and the abstract concept of color can together be said to be the unfolding or the making explicit of the basic intuition of color.

Each basho except the last is treated as a concrete universal that determines or specifies its particular and general content. Furthermore, there are various levels within the basho itself. Nishida distinguishes three levels in each of the three basho: the formal, the static, and the active. The reason for this is that the universal, or world-determining, category is made explicit in varying degrees. The more the characterizations approximate the character of the universal itself, the more apparent it becomes that the universal is limited or determined by some new basho.

Each of these basho can be interpreted as particular perspectives or standpoints in the sense they they do not merely denote a set of particular categories but represent a more general schema of interpretation. It is also possible for a perspective to include within it a more limited perspective, a viewpoint recognized to be limited. As we have seen, the transition from the limited perspective to a more inclusive one would not be possible from within the more limited sphere alone.

Putting things this way amounts to trying to give a purely objective account of how the how the shift in perspectives can take place. Since the perspectives in question are those of a knowing subject, the problem is to explain how the knowing subject can shift perspectives and realize that first the earlier and then the later perspective was limited. This amounts to trying to explain self-consciousness in purely objective terms, an attempt that Nishida rejects for the simple reason that he takes self-consciousness to be an irreducible fact of experience.

His reasons for alluding to Descartes should now be clear. The "I am" is the starting point of philosophical inquiry, not its rationalized conclusion. No objective explanation of the fact that "I am" is possible. What is possible, and needed, is an elaboration of its nature that will show how it forms the the basis of all our knowledge. To attempt to delineate self-consciousness in terms of the categories of formal logic would be putting the cart before the horse. This is why Nishida argues that logic is merely the most abstract, objectified form of the structure of self-consciousness.

Self-consciousness is an experiential fact, but it cannot be known as merely one more fact or object. It needs to be uncovered through logical form.[29] In other words, the levels of self-consciousness need to be laid out in a structural fashion. The uncovering takes place through a progressive discovery of contradictions at the more abstract levels. Once the deepest level is reached, the structure as a whole discloses the sense in which the Cartesian *cogito* can be considered primary:

To be sure, self-conscious experience is immediate and indubitable, but it can only be thought of as the starting point of an academic discipline if it has already been conceived in various forms.[30]

THE STRUCTURE OF THE THREE WORLDS

As indicated in the preceding chapter, the elaboration of the various forms of self-consciousness will be an elaboration of the structure of the three major basho: the basho of objective existence, of relative nothingness, and of absolute nothingness. These are the grounds of the three worlds: the natural world, the world of consciousness, and the intelligible world. Their interlocking is possible only because ultimately they have the same foundation. We have seen how a detailed analysis of judgments as the self-determinations of the universal of judgment ultimately resulted in the necessary positing of an entity that, by nature, resisted full explanation as the subject of judgments. This demand for an entity of this sort means that, at least implicitly, a transition has already taken place from the confines of the universal of judgment into a new basho. That new basho is the basho of the universal of self-consciousness.

The transcendental predicate plane that had been the topos of the universal of judgment is now, in effect, taken as the abstract plane of determination for the universal of self-consciousness. As indicated earlier, each basho has a structure within which it can be said to determine or display itself in terms of a "being" that is taken to be within basho and an abstract plane that is a partial explication of that being. In the universal of judgment, that being is the individuum that is subject but never predicate, and the abstract plane on which it is explicated is the plane of predicates. Thus, the content of the individuum is spelled in terms of the various predicates that can meaningfully be attributed to it. Finally, the meaningfulness of any attribution is guaranteed by the referral of the individuum and the predicate to the intuition upon which the judgment was founded.

In the new basho the transcendental predicate plane of the universal of judgment now occupies the place that the abstract plane of predicates had occupied in the universal of judgment. The new basho is therefore said to enfold the former. That is to say, in the universal of judgment, judgment had been considered only in terms of content. The logical structure of judgment as self-determination or the immediate analysis of a concrete universal into particular and general aspects had been given in a purely objective fashion. A contradiction showed up on the level of the universal of judgment in that it was necessary to take as the subject of judgment something that could not be regarded as completely determined by the universal of judgment, something that was not merely subject but never predicate. Recognition of the contradiction for what it was signaled that one had already stepped on to a new basho capable of accommodating such a being.

On this new basho the transcendental predicate plane is taken to be a plane of consciousness. What were previously taken to be objects are seen as no more than the content of that field of consciousness. A transition of this sort, from an enfolded basho to an enfolding basho, first shows up in a purely formal way. The knowing self, the first occupant of the universal of self-consciousness, is a purely formal self, the minimum self that is required to speak of a self. Its content, spelled out on the plane of consciousness, is not the content of the knowing self but only a given noematic content. It is the self regarded as a plane of consciousness, a plane whose content has both the sense of being an element of consciousness and the function of mirroring things beyond the field of consciousness. The character of consciousness at this level is, therefore, purely intentional.

The content of the plane of consciousness has an essential reference to the objects of the universal of judgment. This referential character dominates the nature of consciousness at this level. Considered from the point of view of the syllogistic universal, the appropriateness of this intentional character is clear, since the universal of self-consciousness corresponds to the plane of the minor term that stands in opposition to the plane of the major term in the syllogistic universal. This relationship can be likened to an eye viewing the natural world (with the self taken as an object in the natural world), but the metaphor cannot describe the relationship of the universal of self-consciousness to the universal of judgment. At this point in his analysis Nishida speaks of the universal of self-consciousness as enfolding or encompassing the universal of judgment, so that the contents of the universal of judgment appear to become the contents of the field of consciousness. This is not to say that chairs and tables actually occupy the field of consciousness, but only that impressions of chairs and tables do so. One has a congeries of ideas, but these ideas are always *of* something or other.

The structure of the universal of self-consciousness parallels precisely that of the universal of judgment. In fact, as Nishida delineates the structure of the three universals one finds an identical structure in all three basho. Previously we presented sketch of the structure of the basho of being or the universal of judgment, but the general features of that basho are applicable to the other two as well. As touched on above, each basho contains three levels that might be considered various degrees of abstraction. The gradation of the levels is determined by their degree of abstractness, with the most abstract said to be the shallowest level and the least abstract the deepest. The three levels of all three basho are (from the most abstract to the least): (1) the formal, (2) the static, and (3) the active. On each level, there is a set of categories appropriate to that level and defining the character of the being or entity that finds its place at that level. The categories are such that at the formal level, there is no concrete entity at all, only formal relationships. The subsumptive relation in the universal of judgment is a purely formal relationship, and individual objects are not included within the categories of that level. The individual is not constituted by the limitation of abstract universals, but rather represents the formal limit of such specification. The only individual on this level is one of pure form; there are no actual individuals. This same general feature holds for the shallowest, or formal, level of all the basho. Thus, the shallowest level of the universal of self-consciousness is the level of the formal, intellectual self, where there is only a "congeries of ideas." These are not properties of the self; if anything, the self can be seen only as a limiting concept, as a completed whole of the congeries.

The second level, the static, has as its basic categoreal structure things and their attributes. I use the term *static* here because the judgments all have to do with given entities and their characteristics. These entities are not seen as creating or causing these characteristics, only as possessing them. Thus, the individuum is described as red, heavy, round, and the like; and, as we will see, the emotive self will have its own specific characteristics, such as the ability to recognize the elements of the field of consciousness as its own.

The third and deepest level, the level of activity, has categories that refer to change and agents of change. In the universal of judgment, it is at this level that one speaks of physical causes and the interaction of individuals. In the universal of self-consciousness, the causal nexus appears as willful self-action that brings about change in its own character.

Structural Parallels among Basho

These three levels can be seen as independent categoreal structures that specify entities, but is it more appropriate to see them as articulations of basho. One can speak of an entity proper to the universal of judgment, an entity proper to the universal of self-consciousness, and an entity proper to the intelligible universal, but the nature of each such entity can be articulated only in terms of categoreal structures, and these differences in degree of articulation depend in turn on the level of abstraction of the structures. The character of the entities will differ according to the basho in which they are located, but the mode of articulartion of their character will have the same logical structure, regardless of the basho. Thus, the entities of the universal of judgment are purely objective in character, while the self of the universal of self-consciousness is largely subjective in nature.

The three worlds delineated in terms of these basho interpenetrate one another and depend on one another. Theirs is not a temporal or physical interdependence but rather one of determination, abstraction, or specification. As such, one would expect the structure of the three worlds to be isometric, at least with respect to their major features. It is as if one were viewing a scene through a lens fitted out with a series of filters. The view one has with all three filters in place would be structurally similar to that had through two filters or only one filter, even to the view obtained without using any filters at all. The analogy is not precise, but it does illustrate the interdependency of the three basho and the progressive uncovering of the essential richness of experience. What the analogy lacks is any reference to the subject-object dichotomy.

The structure of the three worlds described in Nishida's essay "The Intelligible World"[31] is one of a dependency functioning in a variety of ways. Thus, the universal of self-consciousness is said to envelop the universal of judgment, with the transcendental predicate plane of the universal of judgment taken to be the field of consciousness. At the same time, the universal of judgment directly determines the intelligible universal. Still, Nishida posits a comparable structure at work in each of the three universals determining the three worlds. Thus, in the universal of judgment, the most abstract level of determination is represented by the subsumptive relationship. The being that is said to be present in the basho is something that is subject and never predicate, which means only that it reaches the boundaries of the subsumptive relationship. The formal relationships are not capable of yielding the individuum, but the abstract universals are. And yet not even the individuum, considered as the subject of predication, is capable of accounting for the structure of the natural world. For that a transition is required to the notion of activity.

The true occupant of the natural world must be something that is active, that is, it must include properties that look to be contradictory when viewed within the universal of judgment. That which is most properly the occupant of the universal that determines the natural world will thus contradict the categories of universal of judgment. Only the transition to a more enveloping universal can accommodate the contradiction.

As we have seen, activity is a necessary feature of the syllogistic universal, but the full concept of activity cannot be unfolded without reference to self-consciousness. Although the leap to this higher level resolves the contradiction that prompted it, another contradiction quickly makes itself apparent, since the structure of the universal of self-consciousness is precisely the same as that of the universal of judgment. On the most abstract level lies the plane of consciousness. Here the self is a formal self and the content is not a self but a "given" content of the self. The elements of the plane of consciousness intend something beyond the plane. They are not self-determining, just as the abstract universals in the universal of judgment were not.

The abstract universals, we recall from our earlier discussion, functioned as a network in which the content of the individuum was determined or specified. In this sense it served as a "plane of mediation" between the basho and that which was located in the basho. In the same way, the field of consciousness becomes the plane of determination of the universal of self-consciousness once it is seen as the plane of consciousness of the emotive self. The transition to the emotive self from the purely intellectual self in the universal of self-consciousness coincides with the shift from a purely subsumptive relationship to a relationship of possession in the universal of judgment. Only on the level of the feeling self can the content of the plane of consciousness be said to be the content of a self. Emotions are the attributes of the self.

The transition in question is from a level where one can only say that a thing occupies the field of consciousness to one where the thing is an actual attribute of the self. The example of the field of force given in the previous chapter may be of help. The transition from the formal to the emotive self is analogous to the transition from entities interacting on a field of force to a conceptual framework in which the entities are seen as patterns of the field. In both cases we see a parallel progression from the abstract to the concrete, from purely formal being to being that has determined itself, the individuum as a substance with attributes corresponding to the self with feelings. Noetic qualities of the self are seen as attributes of the self they are said to describe, just as the individuum was characterized by the predicates.

The emotive content is not merely something given from the outside; it is what characterizes and "gives substance to the self." The feeling self is determined in the plane of consciousness, in much the same way as as the individuum in the universal of judgment is determined in the plane of abstract universals.

However, just as the notion of an individuum is not the deepest or most concrete explication of the "being" appropriate to the universal of judgment, neither is the notion of the emotive self the most concrete articulation of the "being" appropriate to the universal of self-consciousness. The feeling self simply *has* properties; it does not *give* them to itself. But because these properties can and, in fact do, change, a willing self is implied, a self that not only recognizes the content of consciousness as characterizing itself, but also sees that content as its own products and, therefore, as subject to alteration.

The noetic aspects of the content of the plane of consciousness are a direct result of the activity of the willing self, so that in changing the noetic quality of the content of the plane of consciousness, the self can be said to be determining itself in that plane. In this sense, the willing self is not merely confronted with content given to it from some outside source, as is the case with the formal self; nor is it simply presented with content that it recognizes as its own, as was the case with the emotive self. The willing self acts to change its own nature, the content of the field of consciousness, on the basis of desires and goals. The willing self is not bound to the present, fluctuating field of consciousness, since it needs to act on the basis of goals that are not part of the present field of consciousness (as, for example, sensations are) in order to recognize some content as the result of its own activity. Goals direct activity and determine change. A change in the field of consciousness represents a change in the willing self, and, since this change is due to the activity of the willing self, the willing self is said to determine itself.

The intellectual or formal self, in contrast, does not determine itself. It is simply determined or characterized in the plane of consciousness, a plane that reflects objects outside itself. The fact that its content is merely given is is what makes it a formal self. It represents only the formal structure that accounts for the order and arrangement of its given content, and as such corresponds to the abstract individuum considered as the lower limit of the abstract universals. Further, just as the individuum taken as an object possessing qualities was a static notion, so, too, is the emotive self. But while the individual in the universal of judgment is thought of as self-determining, in the case of universal of self-consciousness it is the willing self that determines itself.

The above comparison shows the analogous structure of the universal of judgment and the universal of self-consciousness, but there is one more parallel to be drawn. The characteristic that makes each of the occupants of that basho its true occupants is also responsible for the transition to a deeper basho. This point is essential, and merits closer attention. As described previously, all the basho have a tri-level structure in terms of which the nature of each basho can be formulated. The nature of an occupant of a particular basho is determined by the nature of that basho and by the nature of the entity in question, since the various levels of a basho represent levels of concreteness of the entity. The deepest level represents the most concrete (and accurate) description and specification of the nature of the entity proper to that basho. Although one can speak of numerous entities in a particular basho—for example, the formal, emotive, and willing selves in the universal of self-consciousness—these should not be conceived of as independent entities—in this case, as three independent selves—but as different degrees of specification of the entity proper to that basho. Even when one finally arrives at the most concrete characterization of an entity proper to a particular basho, and thus to a characterization of that basho itself, one sees that the precise nature of that entity could not possibly be understood only with reference to the categories specified of that basho. Each basho represents a partial viewpoint and the recognition of this is what makes necessary the transition to some fuller and more adequate view.

Take, for instance, the deepest level of the basho of being, the syllogistic universal. This universal specifies the nature of the objects in the natural world. The true occupants of the natural world are objects that determine themselves, objects that not only are capable of change themselves but can effect change in other objects. But when viewed in terms of the categories specified by the universal of judgment, these objects appear contradictory. In that framework they cannot initiate action, and yet the initiation of action is required to account for the network of physical objects interacting in accordance with the laws of physics in the natural world. Realization that there is a contradiction obliges forces one to conceive of a basho in which this contradiction is resolved. If there were none, if we were restricted to the categories of the basho in which the contradiction occurs, Nishida argues, we would not have been able to see the contradiction in the first place.

The same holds true of the universal of self-consciousness that belongs to the basho of relative nothingness and the world determined by that basho, namely the world of consciousness. In this world, the content of the natural world is transmuted into the content of consciousness. But this does not suffice to resolve the contradiction, although it does fulfill a necessary condition of the resolution The formal, or intellectual, self is not yet a self in any concrete sense, even though in order to conceive of a formal self, one must use categories that allow for conscious activity.

Conscious activity is not enough to constitute a self; there has to be deliberate variation within that activity where activity itself, the noesis, becomes an object of the self's activity. The willing self is seen as the self in the fullest sense because it is only then that one can speak of self-consciousness. One has a self-conscious self only when the different noetic aspects of the content of the plane of consciousness are incorporated within the willing self as stages of its development.

Accordingly, a self that merely observes, such as the formal self, is not able to explain the richness of our experience. What is demanded is a self that can act and recognize the results as being the consequence of its own actions. But a self that acts in terms of goals is inherently contradictory when viewed in terms of the categories of the universal of self-consciousness. Goals give direction to activity, but they are not given to the self in the way impressions or sensations are given. Desires, for example, are not just sensations; they serve to direct activity, the goal of which is the satisfaction of that desire.

This means that the concept of conscious activity is not sufficiently rich to describe the fullness of the willing self. We need more than activity; we need what Nishida calls an "activity of activities." We cannot get around the idea of goals in speaking about the actions of a willing self, but no mechanism in the universal of self-consciousness can supply us with an explicit recognition of goals, except insofar as goals can be reduced to sensations or feelings, which completely ignores the critical fact that goals direct activity. In short, the willing self is contradictory because contradictory states are seen to belong to same subject, but this subject cannot be described in terms of the plane of consciousness because that plane is an abstraction of the universal of self-consciousness and as such merely displays a set of representations. That the content of the plane of consciousness changes, and that these various dissimilar fields are taken as the determinations of one and the same self, demands something that will support the transition from one field to another.

The Intelligible Universal

The contradicion we have just described provokes the move to what Nishida calls the "intelligible universal."[32] This is a level of immediate intuition wherein the self is immediately aware of its own content as "ideas." These ideas, taken in a broad Platonic sense, are the standards and ideals that guide behavior and, as such, serve as the ground of goal-directed activity. In the universal of self-consciousness, the goals that direct activity are not explicitly part of the categoreal structure, and yet they are seen to be necessary to an understanding of characteristics of the entities proper to that basho. In the intelligible universal these ideals become an explicit part of the content of the basho.

What Nishida means can best be seen by looking at the most abstract determination of this universal, namely the intellectual intelligible self, which is the equivalent of Kant's "consciousness in general." This self is analogous to the intellectual self in the universal of self-consciousness in the sense that it is purely a formal self. The plane of consciousness for this intellectual-intelligible self is none other than the universal of self-consciousness. As such it is conceived of in terms that would fulfill the formal requirements for having the universal of self-consciousness as its abstract plane of determination. Nishida remarks:

> The simply intellectual (knowing), intelligible self is a formal self such as intellectual self-consciousness, it does not yet truly see the content of the intelligible self, i.e., it does not directly see its own content. Truth is merely a formal "idea."[33]

His point is that the intellectual-intelligible self does not recognize the content as its own content. The content is given and the self is nothing more than the formal structure of the given.

The content of the intelligible self first becomes apparent on the level of what Nishida calls the feeling-intelligible self, or the level of artistic intuition. It is only on this level that the content is recognized as the self's own and not simply as something given it from the outside. The "idea" corresponding to this level is the idea of beauty, which is seen as an expression and explication of the feeling self. The pattern Nishida adopts here is that of an entity and its attributes, the same basic pattern we saw in the case of the emotive self in the universal of self-consciousness. Its aim is to arrive at a better understanding of the nature of this self through the ideal of beauty.

The richer the expression of this ideal in works of art, the more fully the nature and content of this self is made explicit.

But this is, and remains, a static level. Not that works of art are not creative or that there no activity involved in their creation. The focus is rather on the sense in which artistic creation expresses the nature of the self. The creation of a work of art may result in a character change for the self, but a work of art is not created with that intention. Thus, in terms of the categories of the intelligible universal, this feeling-intelligible self does not act; it simply reveals the character of the intelligible self. It is on this level that the full content of the intelligible self is revealed. Fittingly, Nishida names this universal "the universal of intellectual intuition." The acting of the feeling self is a seeing, as is the acting of the feeling intelligible self. The transition from the feeling self to the feeling-intelligible self is effected "by forgetting the conscious self, by loving the object as oneself by becoming directly one with it."[34] Artistic intuition will then be manifested as the content of our emotions.

The deepest layer of the intelligible universal is not to be found in the idea of beauty that expresses the content of the feeling self, but rather at the level of the willing intelligible self, or the self of practical reason. As we have seen, the feeling-intelligible self belongs to the static level of the intelligible universal in the sense that the point of artistic creation is the expression of the content of the self and not the changing of the self's nature. In fact, however, we do act at times with the express purpose of changing and developing the self, and this has to be taken into account. Hence the need for a transition to a self that is active in terms of the categories of the intelligible universal, namely, a transition to the willing-intelligible self. The parallel to transition from the feeling self to the willing self in the universal of self-consciousness is patent. The willing-intelligible self does not merely *express* its own content but deliberately acts to *change* it. On this level, the development of the self is not something that merely happens but something that is actively sought. Here the modification and indeed the creation of the self is an explicit goal.

Full self-determination is achieved only on the level of the willing-intelligible self. The "idea" appropriate to this level is the idea of the good, the idea of a style of life that the self ought to follow, of a standard with which the self should be in harmony. As an ideal, the good does not have any specific content. The good can be specified in any number of ways, and acting in conformity with these specifications will no doubt modify the character of the person who so acts, but none of this can provide a complete explication of the "idea" of the good. This is the very reason why we find ourselves reviewing, evaluating, accepting, and rejecting various concrete formulations of the good. The "idea" as such has no specific content; it is the form of an idea, the bare notion that there *is* a standard and not a specific formulation of *what* that standard is. This is reflected, Nishida says, in the fact that it is on this level that conscience[35] makes its appearance. It is in the immediate apprehension of conscience at the depths of the self that the moral world, including the various conceptions of standards of goodness and moral rules, is constituted.

But here a contradiction arises in the character of the willing-intelligible self. The idea of good guides and directs our behavior, but it is not formulated in a specific manner at the level of the willing-intelligible self. In a sense the role of conscience is essentially negative in that it stimulates dissatisfaction with the present state of one's character but does not provide a final goal. Its function is only to make us aware of the limitations of our nature and our ideals. Hence the contradiction: the willing-intelligible self acts to determine itself, but it does so on the basis of an idea that cannot be fully explicated. The nature and activity of the willing-intelligible self cannot be comprehended without reference to conscience, but the precise functioning of conscience cannot be accounted for on the level of the willing-intelligible self. All we can say is that we act in accord with ideals in order to modify our character; we cannot explain how or why these ideals change.

The recognition of this contradiction at the deepest level of the intelligible universal calls for a shift away from the intelligible universal, but there is no higher universal to which we can turn. There is no new set of categories to be specified, and any attempt to do so would result in nothing more than a reintroduction of existing categories with new names. The shift away from the intelligible universal is a shift to the immediacy of absolute nothingness. The shift is made because of a contradiction embodied in the feelings of guilt that show up as the conscience becomes more acute:

> As long as the seer and the seen confront each other in that which sees itself, it is not something that truly sees itself. It is for this reason that moral free will is contradictory as a "being."[36]

Here we arrive at the crux of the matter. Even at the very deepest level of the intelligible universal a contradiction arises because of our attachment to the distinction between subject and object. The journey from one basho to the next has been moving steadily in the direction of debilitating that distinction, but even at the end of the road, at the level of the intelligible universal, enough of the distinction remains to generate a contradiction similar to what we saw on more superficial levels of analysis. The resolve to see the morally free will, the moral self, as a "being" or a thing gives rise to this final contradiction, which only a transition to absolute nothingness can overcome. The only possible solution is to reject the subject-object dichotomy, but to do so is to forsake the possibility of saying anything at all about the place or basho in which the contradiction has been resolved. This is why Nishida names this final basho the basho of absolute nothingness. All that can be said about it has already been said in the presentation of the entire structure and the logical interrelations of the structure's elements. Absolute nothingness cannot be presented or described, and the structure of the theory shows why this is so. We have arrived at the core of the solution of the problem of completeness.

We have seen the precise parallel that Nishida sets up in describing the logical structures of the three basho. Our rather abbreviated summary of the three worlds determined by the three concrete universals has also helped to explain why Nishida insists that the basho, especially the basho of absolute nothingness, are not to be interpreted merely as concrete universals. The intelligible universal may have been the deepest of the three universals in the sense that it enfolded or contained the other two, but the distinction between noesis and noema, between the knowing subject and the known object, remains even if only on a transcendental plane. Unless it is disabled, Nishida will not have resolved the problem of completeness.

A number of other points concerning the outline of the system given above are needed to clarify the nature of the three universals and their relationship. To begin with, there is an important parallel that has been overlooked up to this point. In the discussion of the universal of judgment, it was noted that the transition to self-consciousness was effected through what Nishida termed the syllogistic universal. We also remarked that Nishida did not refer to this universal in his "General Summary." The introduction of this "extra universal" seems to set up a marked imbalance in the symmetry of the system. In fact, not only is this universal necessary in the transition to self-consciousness, it is representative of a general feature of the system as a whole. Nishida puts it this way:

> As the self-determination of any universal deepens, that determination is transferred to "that which is within," which can then be thought to be self-determining. At the same time the universal itself can no longer be

determined and it merely confronts "that which is within" simply as law.[37]

In the syllogistic universal, the world of physical law confronts the active individual. Through the medium of time a universal is constituted—the natural world. Although not as convincing, an analogous sort of opposition can be found in the universal of self-consciousness. In the intelligible universal, the last "being," the moral self, is confronted by moral law. Good is not an object or even an idea, but a pattern or mode of being. Hence Nishida speaks of a moral world, although in this case he understands it as a creation of the moral self and not merely as something confronting it from without.

A second point concerns the transition from the universal of self-consciousness to the intelligible universal. Nishida is most emphatic that this is not to be construed as a transition to a world of transcendent objects lying outside our experience. The transition is made on the basis of a deepening of self-consciousness. Nishida refers to this self-consciousness as a transition from the willing self to the acting self.[38] The acting self is a self that cannot in any sense be viewed as an object. The objectifiable self (or selves, if we consider the three levels as distinct) is the empirical self or the self on the level of the universal of self-consciousness. There the noetic aspect of the acting self does not figure in the picture at all; only the noematic content of this self is visible at the various levels. For this reason the universal in which the various levels of the acting self are determined is named for the ideas that are expressions of the acting self.

Throughout Nishida's system, the dynamic of development is always linked to a basho. The systematic structure of the three universals should not be construed as a linear progression commencing with the subsumptive judgment and ending with absolute nothingness. The move from the self-conscious universal is a move to the level of the behavioral self in its entirety. Thus, all the levels of the intelligible world are levels of one world. There are not three different selves in the intelligible universal or in the universal of self-consciousness. The self is not merely an intellectual self, an emotive self, or even a willing self. These are distinguishable features of a self, but the fact that they are distinguishable does not imply that they are independent. The distinctions merely indicate various degrees of specification in the nature of the self.

Third, there is no direct link between the level of the cognitive-empirical self and the level of the transcendental self, since this would imply the possibility of moving to the highest level without passing through the level of the willing-empirical self. Nishida describes the difference between the worlds as a deepening of self-consciousness marked by a progressive weakening of the distinction between subject and object. It is only by virtue of this deepening that it is possible to return to one's original state; there are no shortcuts. It is worth noting this because the presentation of Nishida's system as a hierarchy of three levels, each containing three distinguishable sublevels, might lead the reader to imagine it as a kind of stepladder that takes one further and further away from one's starting point the higher one climbs. Nothing could be further from Nishida's mind. Nothing is left behind; it is opened up, deepened, enriched. The deepening of self-consciousness, for example, does not entail an abandonment of the natural world but its enhancement. As Nishida makes clear, the end is the beginning:

> In the depths of noetic determination there must be something that has gone beyond so-called intuition. There is behavior that cannot intuit its own content—indeed, this is everyday behavior.[39]

THE VIEW FROM THE TOP

Now that we have completed our investigation of the manner in which Nishida constructed his system, we are in a position to understand the answer that the system provides to the problem of completeness. The investigations thus far have concentrated on displaying a rigorous and structural account of the reasons why any theory that pretends to give an adequate account of our experience must reject the subject-object dichotomy as ultimate. This is Nishida's answer to the first half of the problem of completeness: to disable the ultimacy of the subject-object dichotomy and, at the same time, to offer an alternative.

What we have yet to see clearly is how Nishida introduces the "looping" feature into the system. How is the possibility of conceiving the structure accounted for in the theory itself? To appreciate what Nishida has done, we need to take view of his system "from the top." This will require a slight change in emphasis and the addition of a few more technical terms, but nothing to compromise the structure as we have presented it. In particular, we will shift our focus from the logical and ontological features of the theory to an emphasis on what we might call its psychological or creative features.

This is not unlike the shift in language that Hisamatsu makes from spatial descriptions of Nothingness to its identification with No-Mind. It is a transition from the "objective" to the "subjective" features—not merely to *objectified* subjective features but to radically pure subjective features. In taking this step we are better able to see just how drastic a step the rejection of the ultimacy of the subject-object dichotomy is. In stepping away from the objectified logical structure to the creative and dynamic aspect of experience, the structure remains the same. As was the case with Hisamatsu, for Nishida only the perspective changes. Only such a shift will allow him to show how the structure he has developed marks the transition from an interpretation of self-consciousness as activity to an analysis in terms of basho or fields.

Since the structure of the system remains the same, we can draw on what has been said earlier to explain what this means. The basic feature of "the view from the top" is that it enables us to see the relationships of the various universals as they emphasize or deemphasize the noetic or noematic aspects. The actual structure becomes rather complex because this concentration on a particular aspect requires keeping more than one level in mind at the same time, so that the noetic or subjective aspect of which we will speak will be an objectified noesis without ceasing to be noesis. At the same time, it is possible to envisage a nearly pure noema, lacking all subjective attributes. Thus, in terms of the structure already presented, the universal of judgment eliminates nearly all reference to self-consciousness or subjectivity. As Nishida says:

> A determination of the universal of judgment is nothing more than what remains when one excludes from such a self-conscious determination the sense of being a noetic determination.[40]

The universal of judgment is what remains after all references to subjectivity have been removed. The categories of the universal of judgment contain no reference to psychological characteristics, only to substances, their properties, and their objective relationships. Now, as we have seen previously, this universal itself cannot stand alone because the categories proper to it are not sufficient to describe completely the being that is proper to it. It should now be much clearer why this is the case for the universal itself and why the type of entity proper to it is now seen to be the end result of a process of abstraction.

But to say this does little more than whet the appetite. To see clearly what this means, one must supply a context, which in this instance is a brief view of the entire system from the top. In the development of the system, we spoke of three basho: the basho of being, the basho of relative nothing-ness, and the basho of absolute nothingness. The entities that were said to be the proper occupants of these basho were, respectively, individual sub-stances, the empirical or perceived self, and the intelligible self. The beings characteristic of each level were determined by three universals: the univer-sal of judgment, the universal of self-consciousness, and the intelligible universal. These universals then determined three worlds or spheres in which these beings were said to reside: the natural world, the world of con-sciousness, and the intelligible world. At each level there appeared a con-tradiction to the effect that in order fully to understand the entity on a given level required reference to a category or set of categories not found among the categories of that level. The final contradiction on the deepest level of the intelligible universal was attributed to the lingering presence of the subject-object dichotomy. Disabling that dichotomy resulted in the transition to absolute nothingness itself, which entailed the complete and utter dissolution of the subject-object dichotomy. The outcome of this process is that no structure can be assigned to absolute nothingness other than the structure that characterizes the system as a whole. In a sense, the entire system is a description of absolute nothingness, indeed the only pos-sible description.

The point is that absolute nothingness expresses itself in terms of the subject-object distinction on various levels, but this distinction is not a characterization of the nature of absolute nothingness except in the sense that the models or explications of it are couched in those terms. This way of stating the point may be obscure, but I think what he means can be clarified in the light of the structure already given.

One of the major difficulties is the way Nishida uses the terms *basho, uni-versal,* and *self* in such a way as to suggest that they are interchangeable, even though at other times he seems to want to maintain a strong distinc-tion among them. Roughly stated, the differences come to the following.

Basho is a neutral term that Nishida employs when he is concerned with the logical relationships among the various elements that make up the structure he has developed.

Universal is used when he is concerned with the structure taken primarily in an ontological and epistemological sense but to some extent objectified. This is why he speaks of a final universal or a universal whose categories are ultimate in the sense that there are no more categories beyond them, since that would require their objectification. This final or ultimate universal would find its place in the basho of absolute nothingness, but that basho cannot be characterizable as a universal except by objectifying it, which would amount to reinstating the subject-object dichotomy he had been at pains to dispose of. The point is crucial for Nishida's resolution of the completeness problem. To speak in terms of universals is to speak of basho in a noematic or objective sense, but this must not entail that the basho exclude any and all reference to subjectivity. As we shall see, there are various gradations of objectifying basho or diminishing its noetic, subjective aspects.

As we would expect, Nishida uses the term *self* when he wishes to emphasize the noetic, or subjective, aspects of basho. Here, too, the use of the term does not refer to an exclusively subjective or noetic aspect at all levels of the system. There are various levels of selves, some of which are marked by strong objectivity, such as the self of the universal of self-consciousness or the empirical self. This is not to say that such selves are regarded as objects that can be perceived internally by a knowing subject. The more nearly a self can be characterized in terms of subjectiveity alone, the less it is possible to view the self as an object. The limit of characterization of the self is the self that can in no way be taken as an object. This can be referred to only as a no-self, or as Nishida says, "a self that sees without being a seer." In short, any attempt at characterization will involve distinctions between the subjective and the objective.

There has long been a tendency in philosophy to make sense of the purely objective and even to make the purely objective the basic ontological category, a tendency that Nishida find pernicious, and all the more so because it is so pervasive. At the same time, since everything that counts as knowledge seems to demand an object of knowledge, there seems to be no other choice. Indeed, the very phrase "knowledge without an object" sounds self-contradictory. What bothers Nishida most is that the goal of objective knowledge, however common, is impossible to attain because the very conceptual apparatus we use to generate talk of "pure objectivity" already entails a reference to subjectivity. Failure to see this is at the heart of the problem of completeness.

Nishida's response is to stress the search for pure subjectivity. Although his way of expressing himself is at times somewhat excessive, he has no mind to reduce noema to noesis, or objectivity to subjectivity. This would land him in some form of idealism, which he finds unsuited to the reality of what we experience as subjectivity. Instead, he tries to show that the entire distinction between the subjective and the objective is misconceived. However necessary the distinction may be, in the end it fails to describe the structure of reality. Insofar as the limitations of language oblige us to think in these terms, all description of the structure of reality is foredoomed. This is especially true if one uses the distinction other than to show how the distinction operates, why it is unsuited to describe reality, or how it is constructed out of the fabric of experience.

As we have seen in the development of Nishida's system, the level of absolute nothingness is one in which no distinction between subject and object is conceivable. Even so, and granted that any attempt to structure it is an abstraction, it can still be experienced. Indeed, it *must* be experienced if it is to serve as the ground of all conceptualization. The self-conscious experience of nothingness, according to Nishida, is the deepest religious experience. It is the state "that recognizes form as void and void as form, i.e., the state in which there is neither a seer nor that which is seen."[41] This is the very thing he had earlier tried to express with the concept of pure experience and failed.

Nishida insists, as indeed he must, that there is no specific content to religious experience. If there were, the experience would be capable of being described, but because this is a state in which there is no distinction of subject and object, such description is impossible. Nevertheless, the experience as well as our reflections and thoughts about it are crucial to determining the various levels of Nishida's system. Each level represents a partitioning of the total fabric of experience into noetic and noematic aspects, culminating in a point at which the system "goes beyond itself" by including in the structure the recognition that such partitioning is just that—a partitioning.

Both the partitioning and the ability to see that the partitioning is not an ultimate characterization of the nature of reality rest on the irreducible fact of self-consciousness. The structure and interrelationships of these partitionings make up the logic of basho, and it is critical for self-consciousness that they be objective in some degree. This seems to be the thrust of his remark that "all self-conscious determinations are necessarily reflected in the noematic plane of the self-consciousness of absolute nothingness."[42] The phrasing is dense but the point is essential to the solution of the problem of completeness since it expresses the character of the "looping" that makes Nishida's system work.

If we must say something about what Nishida calls the self-consciousness of absolute nothingness, the state in which there is no distinction of subject and object, we must tread carefully and avoid being misled by his terminology. Whatever descriptive account we give of the self-consciousness of absolute nothing, it is not something done from outside of self-consciousness. Self-consciousness of absolute nothingness is the basic pattern by which self-consciousness determines itself and discloses its nature.

The deepest or most adequate level of characterization, as we have seen, is what Nishida refers to alternatively as the acting universal in the broad sense or the universal of expression in the broad sense. This latter is what he has in mind with the phrase "the noematic plane of self-consciousness of absolute nothingness." This is the broadest possible way of describing in objective terms a state in which there is no distinction of subject and object. Insofar as it is an objective model, of course, there must be some distinction of subject and object, of noesis and noema, at this level. And because it is the broadest model possible, its descriptions incorporate the system of universals developed earlier with its distinctions between self and objects, the noetic and the noematic.

What is more, since the noesis-noema distinction is a coordinate one, any talk of a noematic aspect of the state in which there is no distinction of subject and object will necessarily involve talk of the noetic aspect. This noetic aspect is what Nishida calls "the flow of internal life." But note: Nishida will not refer to it as a determination, since nothing we say could possibly characterize it. The various selves that have been introduced in the various levels of universals are, to the extent that they are characterized, objectifications and abstractions. The logic of self-consciousness requires a noetic aspect, even on this level, but that aspect itself is not susceptible to description or objectification. If one describes it, it would have to be as an element in the ultimate universal.

The question may arise why Nishida uses two terms when speaking of this final universal. The answer is that this final universal contains all the specifications, determinations, and characterizations of self-consciousness, which means that it will include within it all selves, objective structures, objects, worlds—indeed, every noetic and noematic structure that can be employed. In labeling this universal, one can focus on the noetic features or on the noematic ones. One can accent the ground of behavior, the active process of self-determination, or, taking "universal of expression" in its wide sense, one can stress the result of such self-determination, the structures, objects, and worlds created by such self-determination. The choice of terms for Nishida is dependent on whether he wishes to emphasize the active, creative aspects of the universal or the objective structure. But even when the objective aspects are being emphasized, they are always understood as a reflection of self-consciousness.

The main point in all of this is that, even taken objectively, the final universal expresses a state in which there is no distinction between subject and object. One may object that an expression can be only the expression of a self, and indeed Nishida does at times talk in this way. But he is careful to note that the self he has in mind is a "self that sees while making itself nothing" or a "self that sees without being a seer." The self expressed in the final universal is a no-self, a self that can no longer characterized as a self. In the state of absolute nothingness, there is no differentiation of subject and object, even though reference to that fact requires a language of subjects and objects. The distinction may be linguistically ultimate in the sense that it is ineluctable when it comes to expressing one's thoughts and reflections, but it is not ultimate in the sense that it can adequately describe what that experience is apart from our reflection about it. This is what Nishida's system shows by its very structure. It is the quintessence of his solution to the problem of completeness.

We need also to consider the universal of expression and how it relates to the structure developed for the universal of judgment, the universal of self-consciousness, and the intelligible universal. Briefly put, the structure of the universal of expression in the wide sense is the structure of the three universals described earlier, but now seen as expressions of self-conscious reflection. This is why Nishida describes this universal noetically as the acting universal in the narrow sense and identifies it with the intelligible universal.

In examining the development of Nishida's system, the intelligible universal was characterized as the level of the acting self. While both subjective and objective aspects were discernible within this universal, the ideas of truth, beauty, and the good were seen as based on the self proper to each level, indeed as expressions of these selves. The focus was on describing the nature of the self appropriate to this intelligible universal, the acting, truly self-conscious, self-determining self.

Here the self is viewed in terms of its activity and the results thereof. The emphasis is on the ground of activity, and attempts to objectify the self by and large fail on this level because of the degree to which "full-blown" subjectivity is present. Not even the ideas, the noematic aspect of the intelligible universal, are objects in the sense that physical objects are. Moreover, to say that they are ideas does not mean that they are arbitrary or that they do not each make an essential contribution to the structure of existence. The three worlds are not separate worlds. Nishida is not saying that one has to make choice among various interpretations of experience, only one of which is correct. Rather his structure aims to account for the way these various interpretations take shape. The intelligible universal does not supplant the universal of self-consciousness nor the universal of judgment. Without these two universals, the intelligible universal would be a phantasm, a dream world.

The way in which Nishida analyzes experience in terms of the three basho may be likened to the construction of a woodblock print through a series of overlays. The final product is not possible without all the layers being in place. None of the overlays, by itself, is a perfect representation of the painting, although some of them may in some sense be more crucial to the final outcome than others. One can even rearrange the overlays to create a different impression. Strictly speaking, there is no print apart from the overlays; they are its matter as well as its form. This is a good image of what Nishida tries to do in the "General Summary" when he presents various combinations of the elements as objects and the self as the field in which those objects are observed. There is no need to line up all the possibile permutations to appreciate the overall structure of his analysis as a series of "overlays."

The intelligible universal is said to enfold both the universal of self-consciousness and the universal of judgment. How does this relate to the notion of a universal of expression? Since the relation of enfolding to enfolded in the development of the system was expressed in terms of the utterly subjective or noetic enfolding of the objective or noematic structures that were projections of it, one would expect a noematic or objective description of the universal of expression to include reference to both the universal of self-consciousness and the universal of judgment. In fact, Nishida labels the noematic or objective characterization of the final universal "the universal of expression" in the strict sense. He further states that the acting universal in the strict sense is the basho of the universal of expression in the strict sense, although even it is essentially determined by the universal of expression in the wide sense. Consequently, the universal of expression has the universal of self-consciousness as its noetic characterization and the universal of judgment as its noematic characterization. Both of these are extreme forms of the objectification of the basic self-conscious intuition. In the universal of judgment, there is no self at all and in the universal of self-consciousness the self is an abstract, objectified self.

Viewed in this way, the system is an enfolding of the basic intuition of

self-consciousness. Its structure depicts the fact that, while self-consciousness is intuited, it is not fully conceptualized. It also shows that all characterizations of this basic self-consciousness will be reflected on the level of
the ultimate universal, the universal of expression in the wide sense. This
feature of the system represents the final part of the solution to the problem of completeness.

A diagram may help one visualize the relationships:

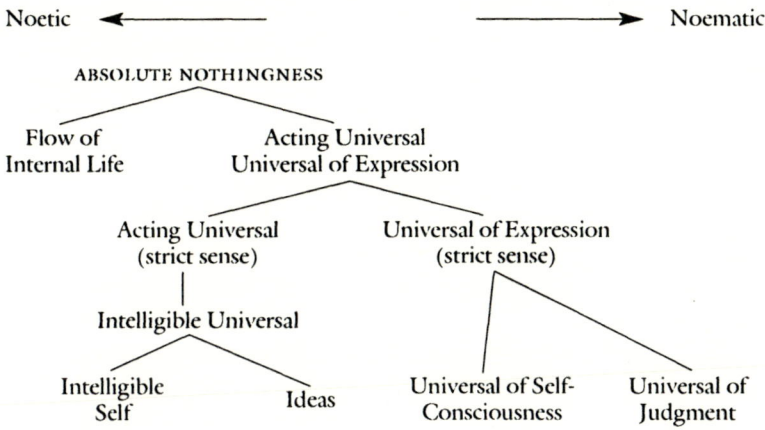

Seen from the top, the diagram depicts a process of greater degrees of
objectification, culminating in the objects of the universal of judgment.
Seen from the bottom, it is a process of deobjectification of the noetic
aspects, culminating in the "flow of internal life and absolute nothingness."
In Nishida's term, it is a process of returning to the concrete origin of conceptualization, pure experience.

The diagram fails to show each of the partitionings as a self-conscious
determination, but it does depict a crucial feature: that the universal of
judgment is directly grounded in absolute nothingness. The world of physical objects is not simply reduced to mental activity of some sort. For this
reason, Nishida's structure is not an idealism but a realism.

Objectivity, in a sense, disappears in absolute nothingness, but so, too,
does subjectivity. Acts, conceived of as acts, fall properly within the scope
of the ultimate universal, the universal of expression in the wide sense. The
self-consciousness of absolute nothingness is not an act, therefore, but an
irreducible fact, a fact that is the ground and goal of all reflection.

CONCLUSION

The main outlines of Nishida's solution to the problem of completeness are now laid out before us. The scheme presented in this chapter distinguished three basho or fields of experience, nested one within the other in such a way that a description of their relationship displays the nature of all experience and knowledge.

In Chapter 4 we saw that the basho have logical, epistemological, and ontological significance. Epistemologically, the basho can be considered schemata, of varying degrees of adequacy, for interpreting experience. The more basic the scheme of interpretation, the more aspects of experience it will interrelate and rationalize. Ontologically, the basho are fields whose occupants are concrete individuals that owe their existence to the field in which they are located. Logically, the basho exhibit and prescribe the forms of the interrelationships between the individual beings as well as the modes of awareness of these interrelated beings.

The three basho are characterized as concrete universals that determine the natural world, the world of consciousness, and the world of ideal value. These three worlds are not seen as independent or unrelated; nor is the relationship among them something imposed from the outside. Indeed, from the point of view of the system, there is no outside. The relationship between one basho and another is always one of enfolding and being enfolded. Thus, the universal of judgment is, at least in part, enfolded by the universal of self-consciousness, which is, in turn, enfolded by the intelligible universal. The diagram on the facing page may help to clarify these relationships.

Because it does not completely determine the content of the universal of judgment, the universal of self-consciousness is said to partially enfold the universal of judgment. The empirical self knows the world of nature, but it is also confronted by it. Viewed in terms of the enfolding, the relationship is one of determination, specification, or abstraction; viewed as enfolded, the relationship is one of "support" or "a transcendence in the depths" of the enfolded. Each enfolding basho is, therefore, already implicitly recognized in the enfolded, and this can be so if one is not bound to the standpoint of the enfolded basho. In recognizing the fact of being enfolded, one is at the level of the enfolding basho. That is, the transition from one basho to another begins with the awareness that the basho that one is in is restricted or limited. This progressive deepening of self-consciousness is carried on until the point is reached at which there is no longer any distinc-

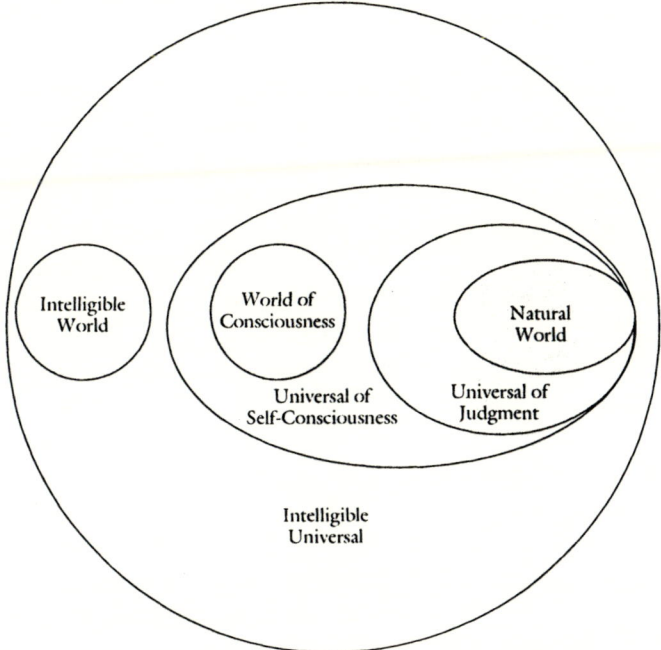

tion between the conscious self and the contents of consciousness. This is the basho of absolute nothingness.

It is worth noting here that the levels of the basho characterize not only types of knowledge but also types of objects known. For Nishida, to be known is to be in a basho; similarly, to exist is to be a thing of a certain sort, and this means to be in a basho. In the final analysis, the distinction between epistemology and ontology is erased.

In the introduction I remarked that the structure of Nishida's logic of basho is best grasped when seen both as a structure showing various stages of completion and as a completed whole. Although the bulk of this chapter has been directed to an examination of the process of construction, a brief description of the view of the whole structure "from the top" is necessary to see how the structure itself has solved the completeness problem. That view centers on the self-consciousness of the universals, the most concrete or conceptualized level of which is the universal of expression in the wide sense.

The introduction of the universal of expression allowed Nishida to present in explicit form the "looping" that is required to answer to the problem of completeness. As the final universal that enfolds all other universals and reflects the content of the various selves, it contains within itself the contrast of noesis and noema. In fact, all constructions out of experience are contained in or reflected in this universal of expression — including Nishida's theory itself. Thus, the expressive universal in the wide sense represents the noematic aspect of what Nishida referred to in *An Inquiry into the Good* as pure experience. The noetic aspect is what he calls the "deep flow of internal life," although he is careful to note that the reference to the qualification *internal* is not to introduce any opposition between internal and external. Indeed at this level the distinction between noesis and noema itself becomes something of an absurdity. At this level there can be no real distinction since that there is no distinct noetic aspect to point to. It is in this context that Nishida claims the self can no longer intuit its own content, that there is only "the flow of infinite life." Reference to a noetic direction is required for formal analysis of self-consciousness, but here we have arrived at the end of the analysis. The visible, distinguishable self has completely disappeared and all that is left is the expressive universal in the wide sense, a universal that contains all content and grounds all knowledge.

The Zen masters speak of this disappearance of the self as a stage at which things are just as they are. The difficulty Nishida has in speaking of this stage, the fact that he will use a phrase like "internal life" in one breath and repudiate it in the next, argues in his behalf. Any attempt to characterize the noetic aspect at this stage would be to dislocate it and make it an object in the universal of expression:

> ...one can say no more than that basho determines itself. All that remains is something like the determination of the noematic plane of self-consciousness of absolute nothingness. Its noetic determination cannot even be seen since it is simply our profound inner life. It is for this reason that basho-determining-itself is construed as the self-determination of our deep inner life, which is to say that the basho of the universal is a mirror wherein life reflects itself.[43]

6

Conclusion

THE EPISTEMOLOGICAL and metaphysical structure presented in the previous chapter constitutes the "philosophical foundation for the demand to see the form of the formless" that Nishida had sought.[1] I have argued that the concept of basho was conceived by Nishida as a means of solving a philosophical problem—the problem of completeness—in philosophical terms, and that the elaboration of the logical structure based on that concept contains Nishida's answer to that problem. Since the structure ascribes a place within the theory for the possibility of the construction of the theory itself, it seems fitting to consider Nishida's view of the nature of the philosophical enterprise as an integral part of assessing the system as a whole.

In this regard I would like to pick up a statement on the nature of philosophy from an essay entitled "Conscious Activity as the Self-Determination of Basho":

> It seems to me that philosophy is a kind of true anthropology. But it must be an anthropology of the self-conscious person; it must be the study of *homo interior*, not *homo exterior*. As Augustine says, "The *homo interior* is the direct image of God."[2]

I cite the passage with a certain misgiving. While it can be illuminating, it can also be misleading. The reference to philosophy as the study of human beings seems to stand in direct conflict with what was said in the introduction concerning Nishida's aversion to anthropocentrism, but the contradiction is only apparent. Nishida is no more interested in doing anthropology or psychology than Kant was when he elaborated the categories—even less, since he did not share Kant's assumption regarding a thing-in-itself lying beyond experience, not even as a limiting concept. I do not mean to deny the similarity of Nishida's project to Kant's description of the role the forms of intuition and the categories play in the constitution of objects as a form of anthropology.[3] Nishida emphasizes at many points that he sees his work as a metaphysics of experience, which is in the tradition of Kant.

That said, there are any number of critical differences between the two thinkers. Most notably, perhaps, Nishida emphasizes the dilemma of Kant's critical philosophy with respect to the problem of completeness. As we remarked in Chapter 4, Nishida felt that the failure of the critical philosophy to solve this problem stemmed from an inadequate treatment of self-consciousness and its reliance on a logic oriented to the subject (g). The Kantian scheme is an attempt to get at *homo interior,* but it fails to make explicit the character of self-consciousness and to that extent fails to display the nature of consciousness as well.

The reference to *homo interior* reflects another central feature of Nishida's thought: his emphasis on will and feeling as integral aspects of experience. For Nishida a reconstruction of the categories presupposed in scientific judgment does not of itself constitute an adequate metaphysical view. The purely cognitive subject is only an abstraction, a truncated projection of the true self. This does not mean that the true self is to be equated with an emotional or volitional self, since these, too, are mere objectifications or projections of the true self. The true self, for Nishida, is the no-self of which Hisamatsu speaks. It is discovered by transcending the categories that we use to describe particular, objectified selves. It is not a transcendence aimed at a self that lies somewhere beyond the boundaries of the particular self, but a "transcending in the depths of the self" to a more profound and adequate level that both grounds the particular self and expresses itself in the particular self. Even to refer to Nishida's project as a discovery of the true self is mistaken insofar as it implies that he intends to describe a self apart from the particular selves we know through experience. If a true self were describable, it would by that very fact be only one more projection of the true self, not the ground of all descriptions of the self.

The process of uncovering the plurality of selves or levels of the self is intimately bound up with the notion of self-consciousness. Only by formally acknowledging the limitations of the categories in terms of which we describe the self at various levels of self-consciousness can we hope to arrive at what is presupposed by the recognition that these categories are limited and imperfect.

This talk of levels of the self culminating in the true self should not be understood as an attempt at a distinction between the real or essential self and the mere phenomenal selves that are in principle unnecessary, or even unwanted, distortions of that essential self. To reach the ultimate depths of the self is not to be cut off from the "shallower" levels; it is only to see the manifold of levels, each in its proper perspective.

Nishida's scheme stresses the notion of the self as an explanatory device, a fact, as we noted in the introduction, that typifies the deep religious motivation behind his thought. At the same time, the way the self functions in his thought implies reference to a structure apart from any immediate reference to the self. The scheme that Nishida presents is not intended merely as a description of the categories by which experience is structured and rationalized. It is also an attempt to display the mechanism whereby these categories themselves become the object of knowledge, a feature, as we were at pains to show, that is essential for the "looping" required to solve the problem of completeness. As we have also seen, insofar as philosophy uses language and uses it intelligibly, the categories of thought need to be objectified to serve as explanatory devices; at the same time, insofar as they are objective they no longer structure experience, which is beyond the distinction of subject and object.

Since Nishida is primarily concerned with displaying the structure of all knowledge and the nature of reality at their ground, which lies beyond all objectification, the attempt would seem doomed to failure. One reply is that there is a difference between using language to speak of things that are already the objects of knowledge and using language to suggest that these things are essentially not objectifiable.[4] Indeed, this is why Nishida is concerned with the development of a logic. Given a suitable logic and demonstrating it at work on levels that admit of objectification, he hopes to show that at least in principle it is possible to speak analogously of the ultimate ground of reality without objectifying it.[5] Yet throughout the course of the "General Survey" included in the appendix we see Nishida treating the various sorts of universals as objects for thought, as abstractions, thereby eliminating them from serving as the ground of reality.

The question remains: Does the appeal to analogy succeed in the end? Does Nishida solve the problem of completeness or is the whole structure an elaborate disguise for what amounts to no more than a wave of the mystical hand? How does Nishida's move from the various delimited structures to the ground of these structures, absolute nothingness, differ from the analogical arguments concerning the nature of God made by the medieval Christian mystics or the analogical representations of Oriental Nothingness presented by Hisamatsu?

I have neither the intention nor the knowledge to survey the history of analogical thought, but a few general observations may prove helpful in assessing Nishida's views. One of the paradigmatic methods used by the mystics to characterize the nature of the ultimate ground is to attribute contradictory properties to it with the aim of showing it to lie beyond all our distinctions. Nishida not only specifically cites these mystical descriptions with approval, he adopts a similar idiom in characterizing the level of absolute nothingness as a seeing in which there is neither a seen nor a seer.

There is no doubt that Nishida saw the deepest level of self-consciousness and, thus, the ground of all knowledge as essentially religious in character. This is why he can speak of the self-consciousness of absolute nothingness as "the religious experience in which form is seen as void and void as form."[6] It comes as no surprise, therefore, to find him sympathetic with mystical experience and mystical modes of expression, though none of this argues one way or the other for the philosophical integrity of Nishida's system.

Or again, the analogies adopted by Hisamatsu in his descriptions of Nothingness are often strikingly similar to Nishida's own characterizations of basho. Hisamatsu cites Takuan, the seventeenth-century priest of the Jōdo sect, to the effect that the mind is an actor that plans every role; and when the mind is left with no role to play, it is called Emptiness. This is entirely reminiscent of Nishida's characterization of the self that sees while making itself nothing. There is also ample evidence in Nishida's work of the analogies of space and the reflecting mirror that Hisamatsu cites. The similarities between the various Zen characterizations of nothingness and Nishida's basho were touched on in Chapter 3 to corroborate the great influence that Zen had on the development of his notion of basho.

The primary difference between Nishida's thought and attempts to characterize the ultimate ground of all knowledge by means of analogy lies in the complex logical structure of Nishida's system. Nishida leaves no doubt that the ultimate ground of all knowledge could not possibly be displayed or characterized in a way that it would allow us to treat it as just one more object of knowledge. It may be possible to lead a person to this ultimate ground through the disciplined practice of meditation. This is one way of reaching religious insight, of eliciting knowledge by acquaintance. But the experience of conversion is not the same thing as philosophizing. The philosopher has also to demonstrate how such knowledge by acquaintance is possible and why.

Nishida's philosophical scheme does in fact argue that such knowledge by direct acquaintance is possible. Already in *Intuition and Reflection in Self-Consciousness* he had attempted such an argument, only to reject the results as a capitulation to mysticism. What of the present structure based on the logic of basho? Surely the phrase "the self-consciousness of absolute nothingness" is every bit as mystical as "absolutely free will." The difference lies not in the choice of terminology but in the logical rigor of the structure as a whole. In *Intuition*, the appeal to an "absolutely free will" seems to have been made in despair. The system he had been trying to erect lacked the foundations to hold it up, and only a leap into "dazzling obscurity" could save it. In the system based on the notion of basho, however, the final move to absolute nothingness is not a leap away from the rest of the structure; it is the last in a steady progression of logical moves. It is the logical culmination of the system, not its rejection. In particular, we see in hindsight that Nishida always introduced activity as the last or deepest mode of being in each universal, and that this activity or, rather awareness of it, was what propelled one to a deeper level. In the course of remarks on Heidegger, Nishida writes apropos of this:

> That which determines itself does not emerge simply from the questioning self. The questioning self must be an active self, a behaving self. The ontic is uncovered as the noematic determination of the behaving self. The answer must be anticipated in the question.[7]

The fact that he was able to integrate the transition to absolute nothingness within his system argues in favor of Nishida's claim to having developed a logic of mysticism. If mysticism is an immediate appeal to ineffability—to the private nature of experience—then Nishida is no mystic. He is too committed to uncovering the necessary structure of the whole of experience. If, on the other hand, mysticism is the claim that the ultimate ground of knowledge cannot itself be an object of knowledge, then Nishida may be numbered in the ranks of the mystics, albeit as one who seeks to demonstrate the reasons for his position with logical rigor.

In sum, I am persuaded that Nishida provided a plausible solution to the problem of completeness he set out to solve. He showed that the acceptance of the ultimacy of the subject-object distinction necessarily leads to contradictions, and that this distinction cannot simply be accepted as ultimate. What is more, he suggests a viable alternative to the assumption of the dichotomy, namely his theory of basho. The looping in the theory, provided by the universal of expression, overcomes the primary difficulties that confront such traditional theories as idealism and materialism. The central paradox of the problem, it will be recalled, was that any system that attempted to give a complete account of experience was doomed because it could not explain its own status. Nishida's logic of basho is able to incorporate the construction of the system itself as part of the system's own structure, without appealing to anything outside the system, because his main focus is on self-consciousness. His final basho is not a particular standpoint that could become the object of another inquiry. Any attempt to objectify the basho of absolute nothingness is viewed as talk about something in the universal of expression. Having analyzed the nature of basho on levels where it is possible to leave the basho and view it from the outside, he closes the circle with the final basho by naming it an absolute nothingness.

The account Nishida gives of self-consciousness in the course of developing the system seems generally solid. From the start he saw it as a fundamental feature of experience, but the fact that any attempt to analyze it as a hypostatized ego leads to the paradoxes that we have called "the problem of completeness." Accordingly, he sets out to interpret Descartes' *cogito* without falling into the trap of reifying the self, on the one hand, or inviting a Humean reductionism, on the other. The logic of basho needs to be seen as a gradual but inevitable progression away from conceptualization. The core of the problem of completeness is self-reference, and by taking self-consciousness as the most basic form of thought, Nishida not only neutralizes the threat that self-reference poses to his analysis but turns it into an explanatory device. To say that the world and our relation to it can be viewed from any number of different perspectives is obvious; to give a coherent explanation of how this is possible requires genius. Nishida's analysis of self-consciousness in terms of basho shows such genius. In the final analysis, the plausibility of the logic of basho and Nishida's analysis of self-consciousness are not separable. The key to both lies in the concept of nothingness.

As plausible as Nishida's solution to the problem of completeness appears to be, it is not without serious difficulties. I would like to conclude by singling out three of them, none of which is insuperable but all of which are bothersome in the extreme.

First, the opposition Nishida sets up at one level between the material world and the self is not as convincing as he would like. True, he does stress the body as a necessary component of experience—even going so far as to say that there can be no activity of the self without a body—but the point is not sufficiently developed. Let it be noted, however, that Nishida does go on to treat the body in later works.

Second, the emphasis throughout his system on the self leans in the direction of idealism, despite his best efforts to argue that he is oriented toward a radical subjectivity that goes beyond the idealist categories. Even when elaborating what he means by radical subjectivity, Nishida tends to stress the noetic features of basho to such a degree that the reader is naturally led to see it as merely another form of idealism. I have argued that the impression is a false one by pointing out how Nishida's direct grounding of the physical world in absolute nothingness avoids the criticism of being a simple mental construct. Nishida himself says as much on several occasions, but never at any length until his later works. In any case, his argument that the deepest level of experience is the level of ordinary behavior and not some exotic and mysterious realm seems inherently consistent.

Third, Nishida fails to clarify the social character of experience. Scattered allusions to the point references exist, but he was not able to find it a place of importance in his overall scheme. Nishida himself seems to have been aware of the fact, witnessed by the continued attempts he made, right up to his final essay, to rework and refine his system in such a way as to better highlight the historical dimensions of experience.

Whatever the ultimate fate of Nishida's formulation of the logic of basho, it stands as a radically new, and viable, approach to the problem of completeness. In the ongoing search for understanding who we are as self-conscious beings and what place the human self—if indeed, there be such a thing as the self—has in the world, Nishida's thought marks an important milestone in the history of philosophy.

7

Appendix

A Translation of Nishida's "General Summary"
from *The System of Self-Consciousness of the Universal*

I

IN ORDER TO help the reader understand what I have tried to say
in this work, I think it advisable to clarify two crucial points where my
position differs considerably from the mainstream of traditional philosophy. The first concerns my view of the universal that is the foundation of
discursive knowledge (knowledge through judgments), and the other concerns my views on the way self-conscious experience is to be understood.

When we think that we predicate something with respect to an objectively existing thing by means of a judgment, the entity that becomes the
grammatical subject is taken to be the foundation of discursive knowledge.
Aristotle established the individual as that which could be a subject but
never a predicate. Universals, since they are secondary substances, can
become grammatical subjects, but a universal can also become a predicate
that applies to something other than itself. Thus the truly real, that which

* 『一般者の自覚的体系』「総説」, NKZ V, 419–64. The translation is my own.

186

can be subject and never predicate, must be the individual. However, as long as it is possible to predicate something of the grammatical subject as the grammatical subject, this grammatical subject must be determined by a universal. The same is true of the individual when it is thought of as being a grammatical subject, for it is possible to predicate something of it only insofar as it is determined by a universal. In this sense then, judgment is established by the self-determination of a universal. Even Aristotle thought that *to ti en einai* (the being-what-it-is of a thing) had a definition, but that which has a definition must be determined by a universal. The same point can be made with respect to present-day object-logic.

If one makes a sharp distinction between problems of value and problems of existence, and seeks the foundation of truth in that which is objective (pure object), then one cannot avoid arriving at something like Lask's "unopposed object." However, in order for such an object, as the foundation of truth, to have a normative sense for our judging consciousness, it must come into being through something like Kant's synthetic unity of consciousness-in-general (apperception), i.e., it must be founded on the self-conscious determination of pure self. If such an object were completely transcendent with respect to our consciousness it could not have normative meaning for our judging consciousness. Just as there must be a universal that envelops and determines the individual insofar as something is predicable of it, so too must there be a self-conscious determination behind even a transcendent object insofar as it has a normative meaning. Yet it must be noted that this universal is not the so-called universal concept and that this self-conscious determination is not to be confused with so-called self-conscious determination.

If one takes the universal concept as one's point of departure, one can never, no matter how far one particularizes, reach the individual; the *infima species* is not yet an individual. One can reach the individual only by transcending these determinations. Thus, what determines the individual must be something that transcends the determinations of the so-called universal. But then how can one think of such a thing as being a universal? Mere transcendence of the determinations of the so-called universal (abstract universals) does not in itself yield an individual: an individual is determined with respect to an individual. As in Leibniz' monadology, what is unique is determined by universals. In order for one to be able to think of an individual there must be a universal that envelops and determines all individuals. My "transcendental predicate plane" or "topos" is just such a thing. Further, if our self transcends, in the direction of the grammatical subject, the individual that is subject but never predicate, then the universal that determines the individual can be thought of as our plane of self-consciousness, and the transcendental predicate plane, or topos, is the plane of consciousness of Kant's transcendental self (consciousness-in-general). Combining Aristotle's logic and Kant's philosophy in this fashion makes clear, I think, the true foundation of discursive knowledge.

It was Hegel who thought of judgment as the self-determination of a universal, and it must be admitted that this logic is a systematic and exceedingly fruitful working out of that idea. However, even Hegel's logic does not explicate the meaning of what I have referred to as the universal that envelops and determines the individual. It does not clarify the relation between self-consciousness and the universal that forms the basis of discursive knowledge. Thus, no satisfactory foundation can be given to the transition from the object to that which is conscious; nor is it made clear why the Idea itself must be self-conscious. In this sense, Hegel's logic is still characterizable as a logic of the grammatical subject, an object logic. Of course, there is a sense in which as a logic it is quite natural for it to be objective and oriented to the grammatical subject. Even so, experiential content, that based on self-consciousness, cannot be merely objective. Further, the very fact that we can think of such content makes it imperative that we clarify the structure of this thought. Instead of trying to explain self-consciousness in terms of object logic, I take the form of self-consciousness to be the basic logical form, i.e., I argue that it is precisely because we are self-conscious that we are able to think logically.

What, then, is self-consciousness? Self-consciousness is the knower knowing the knower himself; in self-consciousness the knower and the known are one. But then what is knowing? The knower must always be of a higher dimension than the known; the knower and the known must be such that they can never be thought of as being on the same plane. The knower must in no way be objectifiable, for to the extent that it is objectified it is no longer the knower. In this sense, the knower is nothingness, i.e., non-being with respect to the known. This is, however, not to say that the non-being that is simply opposed to being is the knower, for knowing does not arise from the simple relation of being and non-being. Just as we are said to intend an object when it is in our consciousness, so too must the knower envelop the known and determine it within itself: the known must be that which makes itself nothing and determines being. In such a situation that which has form is the shadow of the formless.

When we think of the self as the unity of conscious phenomena, what we have is the known self, not the knowing self. Even if one goes further and sees conscious phenomena as forming an infinite process and the self as a (substanceless) pure act, one is still left with something that is objectified and thus not the true knower. The true knower can never be determined categoreally, but rather it is that which does the categoreal determining. If one follows out this line of thought, then that which truly knows must be what I called earlier the transcendental plane of predicates, or topos. Knowing is usually thought to be an activity, but that which truly knows must envelop activity: it must be that which actively determines its content within itself. Since we usually take something objectified as activity to be the self, we cannot see that which envelops this, i.e., what I call topos, which is thought to be transcendent. However, speaking from the viewpoint of true knowing, topos is the true self and that which is active becomes immanent only as it approaches the topos: to be evident means to be immediately in topos. From this viewpoint it is that which acts that must be transcendent. That we conceive of conscious activity in terms of (substanceless) pure acts is due to the fact that, since acts are immediate to topos, they are immanent and thus substanceless; it is non-being that determines their being. The more clearly the acts are recognized as having their initial points in non-being, the more they are seen to take on the character of consciousness.

If we think of knowing in this fashion, then self-consciousness means that topos determines itself in itself; thus topos and that which is in topos are identical. To say that the knower and the known are the same is not just to say that a certain thing is identical with itself, nor is it the unity of a continuous activity as when what acts and what is acted on are one. All these senses of identity refer to the unity of objects and, as such, do not make clear the sense of identity that is meant when the knower is said to be identical to itself.

How is it that we are able to think of self-identical things? The self-identical is thought to be characterized by the fact that it becomes its own predicate, but how is this possible? It may be thought that when the universal is radically particularized and the individual is reached by transcending the *infima species*, then we have self predication, for the individual is identical to itself. However, as I have indicated above, the individual is the self-determination of the transcendental predicate plane of the universal, i.e., of topos. The individual is situated in the topos of the universal and can be thought of as the self-determination of topos itself. When one takes the individual as a self-identical thing that becomes its own predicate, there are two ways of looking at the matter. The first is that the predicate unites with the subject, and the second is that the subject unites with the predicate. The former self-identity is obtained by thinking of the predicate as being absorbed into the subject and it thus has the sense of an objective self-identity. However, if one takes the position that judgment is formed by the self-determination of a universal, then, from this point of view, self-identity is obtained by thinking of the subject as approaching the predicate ever more closely and finally uniting with it. So-called individual self-identity is found in the confines of the determination of the universal of judgment that determines itself discursively. However, knowing is the universal determining the universal itself, and in the determination of a universal that transcends the determinations of the universal of judgment it is possible to see a self-identity that transcends individual self-identity. This is self-conscious self-identity. The knower, i.e., the universal that determines itself, cannot, of course, be logically determined, but if we conceptualize this universal while extrapolating on the notion of logical form, then we can say that self-consciousness is the identity of the enveloping and the enveloped, the identity of topos and "that which is placed within." Moreover, from this identity of whole and part we obtain the infinite process of self-consciousness.

I think that the relation between self-consciousness and the self-determination of the universal has been made sufficiently clear from what has been said. If one thoroughly and consistently exploits the position of predicate logic, where judgment is established by the self-determination of a universal, one can think of the self-determination of a universal that transcends the determination of the individual. It is our awareness of self-consciousness that reveals this determination. This is not to say that one can go beyond the transcendental predicate plane and still think of the determination of the universal in logical terms alone. Purely logical determination is completely exhausted within the determinations of the transcendental predicate plane. Our self-conscious experience, which determines being while it itself is nothingness, proves the existence of a universal that goes beyond the universal of judgment. Self-consciousness is not something simply known as fact but rather, as has been shown, it is thought through logical form. If we reflect on this, then what was previously termed the determination of the universal is essentially nothing more than objectified self-conscious determination. That discursive knowledge is thought to be the determination of the universal is due to its being a self-conscious determination in the sense of the self-conscious determination of consciousness-in-general. If we think of the form of self-consciousness from the stand-point of logical form, then in predicate logic there is already the sense of self-conscious determination present in that determination of the universal. Further, if we can think of this form of self-conscious determination as the basic form of the determination of the universal, then, since the form of our self-conscious determinations becomes ever richer and deeper, we can go beyond the determinations of the universal of judgment and think of the self-determination of a universal that is immeasurably deep and rich.

The shallowest level of self-conscious awareness is representational or ideational consciousness. Self-conscious determination is not yet apparent in ideational consciousness since that which is situated is merely inten-tional. It is only upon reaching intellectual self-consciousness that self-con-scious determination can be clearly seen. The determinations of the univer-sal of judgment are simply the objectifications of intellectual self-conscious determination. But the meaning of self-conscious determination, wherein nothingness determines being, is not exhausted in mere intellectual self-consciousness. In intellectual self-consciousness the self is still determined as an objective being. In volitional self-consciousness, however, not only is the meaning of self-conscious determination much deeper, but also we are conscious of our self in a much deeper sense. Even volitional self-con-sciousness is, however, not the ultimate level of self-consciousness. We reach the consummation of self-consciousness when we reach the level of seeing without anything that does the seeing.

On the other hand, if we move in the opposite direction and minimize the sense of noetic determination in self-conscious determination, which is to say objectify self-conscious determination, then it approximates discur-sive determination. Intellectual self-conscious determination becomes dis-cursive determination when it loses the sense of noetic determination. It is for this reason that the transcendental predicate plane of the universal of judgment corresponds to the noematic plane of intellectual self-conscious-ness, to the objective plane of determination. The plane of predicates is the plane of consciousness that no longer has the sense of self-conscious deter-mination. But how is it possible to think of self-conscious determination losing its sense of noetic determination and becoming objectified? As self-conscious determination becomes deeper, determining being while remaining non-being is, when seen from the rear so to speak, like the fol-lowing. The content of the noetic determination of the shallow self is, when seen from the standpoint of the noetic determination of the deeper self, noematically determined.

Having made the universal of judgment the point of departure for this exposition, I was able to say that what goes beyond its transcendental predicate plane and determines itself, i.e., that which determines being while being itself nothingness, is self-consciousness. Speaking from the point of view of self-consciousness itself, however, self-consciousness is the self seeing the self in the self. Seeing without a seer is the "self (as subject)" becoming "in the self," i.e., it becomes topos itself. Now, once one transcends this topos where the "self (as subject) unites with "in the self" (for example, seeing the volitional self behind intellectual self-consciousness) the "self (as subject)" is seen, and as self-consciousness accordingly becomes deeper, one is inevitably led to see once again a topos where this "self (as subject)" unites with "in the self." When we reach that which truly sees and which can no longer be seen by a deeper self, then "in the self" is all that remains. In such a topos, the entire content of the noetic determination of the self is reflected and objectified.

Since I wanted to clarify the nature of the internal relations obtaining between logical determinations and self-conscious determinations as well as elucidate the logical structure of the latter, I began my investigations with the study of the self-determination of the universal of judgment. And I said that by transcending in the subject and predicate directions one will come upon a universal that encompasses this. This will no doubt engender certain apprehensions and questions such as "Does this not lead to an infinite number of universals each of which is enveloped by another?" or "Precisely what is it that determines the universal?" At this point, however, one must keep in mind that my "self-determination of the universal" essentially has the meaning of self-conscious determination. As I have indicated, when one thinks of judgment as being established through the self-determination of the universal of judgment this sense of self-conscious determination must already be present. These doubts and apprehensions are perceived from the viewpoint of a logic that is oriented to the grammatical subject. Thus, if one thinks of a transcendence of a transcendence purely in terms of objects, it is possible to continue this series abstractly as far as one wishes. From this viewpoint it is also reasonable to claim that when there is a determination there must be something that affects the determination. However, my "self-determination of the universal" has the meaning of self-conscious determination, and so to speak of a determination of nothingness over and above the determination of nothingness is like speaking of a zero over and above zero. Moreover, one can ask what determines it only if it somehow has the sense of objective being.

What I call the self-determination of the universal is a form of cognition in the broad sense, and further, I think it is the deepest and most comprehensive form of cognition. What were heretofore taken to be the forms of cognition were such that their relation to self-consciousness was not at all clear; something active survived in the depths of subjectivity. I, however, see logical form as the form of self-consciousness and, conversely, the form of self-consciousness as logical form. Just as the individual is thought of as the self-determination of the universal of judgment, so too the self is nothing more than an object (a being that is a grammatical subject) that is determined in a universal that transcends the universal of judgment. When the "in the self" unites with the "self as grammatical subject," there appears something like Kant's consciousness-in-general. Here, I am not saying that first one has a universal and that it is then either determined by something or determines itself. Nor am I saying that the content of the universal is determined and that from this the particular is deduced. That which is most concrete and immediately given is given to the self. To be immediately given means to be given to the self. That which is in the deepest level of our self-consciousness is that which is most concrete and immediate. However, if self-conscious determination has a logical meaning, then that which is most concrete and immediate must be given in the topos of nothingness. What many people refer to casually as the immediately given must necessarily be given in some form or other. Even those who start with immediate experience think of immediate experience as some form of givenness, e.g., Bergson's pure continuity. But since the logical form is not immediately apparent, these thinkers are led to speak of it as a reality that transcends thought, i.e., they fall into metaphysics. My "determination of the universal," whose fundamental form is found in self-conscious determination, is a form that also determines immediate experience, but more than that, it is a form that determines all "being." All being is located in what I call the topos of the universal.

Descartes can be considered the first to take self-conscious determination as a form of cognition in opposition to those who espoused a more metaphysical view that saw the self-conscious self as a metaphysical reality. Descartes' *cogito ergo sum* is my transcendental predicate plane determining itself. But when Descartes took this as the fundamental cognitive form of certain knowledge, it immediately acquired a metaphysical meaning for him. It was Kant who made self-conscious determination the cognitive form of the objective world, but in Kant's "I think" there still remains the sense of self-consciousness as activity. Present-day phenomenology can also be said to take some sort of conscious self to be the basic form of cognition. However, this cognitive self is nothing more than a purified internally perceived self and, as such, it has not yet attained the form of the true self-conscious self. Even if one speaks of intention as being grounded in given objects, it is nonetheless the case that because the form of that intending is imperfect, it is not possible to intend the content of full-blooded concrete experience. To be sure, self-conscious experience is immediate and indubitable, but it can be thought of only as the starting point of an academic discipline if it has already been conceived of under various forms.

II

Since what I call the self-determination of the universal has the meaning of self-conscious determination, if one wants to clarify the structure and levels of the universals, one must start by giving an accurate account of the structure and levels of self-consciousness. To say that the knower and the known are one while at the same time taking knowing to be a type of activity is no more than taking the viewpoint of objectified self-consciousness. For objects to be known by me they must be immanent in me; I must be the topos in which these things are situated. In this sense then I am utter nothingness with respect to things and merely reflect them. Yet, insofar as I know things, these things must be determined by me; what is in the self must be what is determined by the self. The self knows by determining and reflecting its content within itself. One can say that by making itself nothing it determines being. This is the sense in which self-consciousness can be said to be the self seeing its own content in itself. Further, this self-conscious determination must form the foundation for all knowing.

The "in the self" is that ideational consciousness we take to be the ordinary plane of consciousness, and that which is placed in it reflects — that is to say intends — something. But just what is it to intend something? It seems clear that one cannot intend anything that is completely external to the self. In the sense that the self determines its own content in itself, what is intended must also be the content of a self that is reflected in the self. It is just that at the level of intention we have not yet arrived at an intuition in which the content of the self is directly apprehended within the self. If one takes the viewpoint of "in the self," then consciousness must be radically intentional. Further, since being "in the self" cannot be separated from self-consciousness, intentionality is seen to constitute one of the most basic characteristics of consciousness.

Nonetheless, the self must be what determines the self in the self. But how is it possible to conceive of the self seeing the self in the self? It cannot be that we reflect the self in the self's ideational plane of consciousness, for the reflected self is the seen self and not the seeing self. At this point we may begin to think of the self as the unity of consciousness, but this unity is not at all something that can be reflected in the plane of consciousness. Even supposing that what is reflected is the content of consciousness, it is still not that which unifies. The self must always be thought of as being in the depths of the plane of consciousness, and when we think of it reflecting itself in itself, then this self is necessarily seen as an infinite process. It is in this way that the notion of conscious acts comes into being. (If this unreachable something that underlies the process is thought to be external, then this process is merely a causal activity. It is only when the goal of the process itself is enveloped by a plane of consciousness that there can be conscious acts.) But in the depths of a conscious act there must be something that sees the act itself; there must be something that envelops the conscious act within it. This something is the self-conscious self.

Now in order for us to be aware of this self-conscious self, it must be in some plane of consciousness, but this plane of consciousness cannot be the ideational plane of consciousness that we have discussed. No matter how one deepens the ideational plane of consciousness, it is impossible to reach a plane of self-consciousness where one is aware of the self itself. Normally the self-conscious self is taken merely to be an infinite process that simply reflects the self in itself, but awareness of the self does not emerge in this way. Seen from the ideational plane of consciousness, the self-conscious self is taken to be an infinite process, but this expression "from the ideational plane" means that the self-conscious self is always thought of as being behind the ideational plane, i.e., it is always thought of as transcendent. Nevertheless, the fact that I am self-conscious means that something transcendent in this sense is immanent in the self: it amounts to returning to the origin of the infinite process. The more intuitive our consciousness becomes the more this process fades from view; the active process approaches the plane of consciousness itself and ultimately submerges into it.

The plane of self-consciousness must be a plane of consciousness that differs from the ideational plane; in fact, it is only the former that is a plane of consciousness in the strictest sense. Consciousness without a self is inconceivable; self-consciousness is the fundamental form of consciousness. Self-consciousness is the self seeing the self in the self, and when the "self (as subject)" is obscured, and further the "in the self," i.e., the plane of consciousness, is taken to be the "self (as object)," we have the ideational plane of consciousness. When the plane of consciousness that reflects the content of the self loses the character of self-determination and is thought of simply as the plane of the "self (as object)," we have nothing more than the reflection of external content. Of course, without the "self (as subject)" there is no "self (as object)" but even so it is possible to think simply of the "in the self" as the ideational plane of consciousness. Properly speaking, however, there is no "in the self" without the "self (as subject)." When the "in the self" is thought to be the "self (as subject)" or when, conversely, the "self (as subject)" is thought to be united with the "in the self," we have ideational activity, and all the elements in this plane of consciousness (i.e., the ideational acts) are conceived of as intentional.

In contrast, when the "in the self" unites with the "self (as object)," i.e., when it becomes a plane of the "self (as object)" it becomes a plane of self-consciousness that directly reflects its own content. What is in this plane does not reflect external content but is conscious of itself, i.e., it is self-conscious. The self-conscious self that is commonly spoken of is nothing other than the content of this plane of consciousness; it is the content of the self-determination of the plane of self-consciousness.

The so-called self-conscious self is a self conceived of as an infinite process that comes into being by thinking of the self reflecting the self in the ideational plane of consciousness. The plane of consciousness that is aware of this self must be something that envelops the process within it and that, further, sees this process-self as a determination of itself in itself. When I talk of self-consciousness as being the self seeing the self in the self, the notion of activity has already crept in. It is basic to the "self (as subject)" and the "self (as object)" that they are not thought of as "beings" in the ordinary sense. There is no plane of consciousness apart from the self, but by the same token there is no self apart from a plane of consciousness. It is not the case that there is first a self that then proceeds to determine itself. Rather, the plane of the "self (as subject)" determines the plane of the "self (as object)." Topos determines itself. In this sense, self-conscious determination can be thought of as a type of categoreal determination. Just as the natural world is determined by judgments, the world of consciousness is determined by self-conscious determinations. From the point of view of the ideational plane of consciousness, that which is in the plane of self-consciousness is always taken to be noetic while its content is taken to be noematic. Thus, instead of saying that the self sees the self in the self, it is possible to say that what is in the ideational plane of consciousness, i.e., what is located "in the self," has contrasting noetic and noematic vectors, assuming that one takes the plane of the "in the self" to be the central axis.

How does one proceed from this self-conscious determination to the self-determination of the universal? Normally, the self-conscious self means the intellectually self-conscious self. This self-conscious self is thought to be the limit of an infinite process that is engendered by thinking of the self reflecting itself in the ideational plane of consciousness. The topos that accommodates this sort of self-conscious self is what I have called "the plane of self-consciousness." However, our self-consciousness does not terminate here, for we are aware of a much deeper self in the form of our volitional self, and even more so in the form of our acting self. The plane of self-consciousness is endlessly deepened. Yet, even the volitional self and the acting self are still, like the intellectual self, objects of consciousness. They are in a plane of consciousness. They are perceived selves. They are basically thought of as things that transcend the processive intellectual self and they cannot escape being a form of active self. Properly speaking, what is really in our plane of self-consciousness must be the volitional self, for the intellectual self is at the boundary of this plane of self-consciousness and the ideational plane of consciousness.

Once we are at the level of the acting self, however, our self can be considered external to the so-called plane of consciousness, which is the noetic plane supposedly submerged in the depths of the ideational plane of consciousness. We get to the acting self when what is in the plane of self-consciousness transcends this plane in the noetic direction. It is only in the acting self that we reach a self that sees without a seer. One might be inclined to think that in such a case the self simply disappears, but actually it is only the objectively viewed self, the self as seen in the plane of self-consciousness, that disappears. The self as such becomes the truly seeing self. The so-called self-conscious self is a noetic self that determines its own content in the ideational plane of consciousness, but it has not yet freed itself of the sense of merely being an internally perceiving self. Further, from the viewpoint of the true self, which sees in the most profound and proper sense, this internally perceiving self is nothing more than a determined self and can thus, on the contrary, be called external.

When we reach the position of the acting self, just what is this plane of self-determination wherein the self determines its own content? It is possible to think of it as the expressive plane of consciousness in the wide sense, so that everything in this plane expresses its own content. What is in its noetic plane can no longer be seen; only that which is in the noematic plane is visible. At the level of the acting self, the self has the sense of an intuition that objectively sees its own content. The content of expression may be thought of as the content of intuition in the wide sense, and given this position, that which has its noetic determinative aspect reduced to a minimum, i.e., the content of the most objective expression, is the object-world for consciousness-in-general. That which further excludes all sense of noetic determination from this transcendental self is what I call the self-determination of the universal of judgment.

How is it possible to remove noetic determination from the transcendental self? I have said that in the acting self we arrive for the first time at the self that truly sees (sees while making itself nothing), but even the acting self cannot be said to completely avoid being a sort of internally perceiving self. But when one reaches the level of the self-consciousness of absolute nothingness, there is no longer even the acting self. At the conclusion of "The Self-Determination of the Universal" I referred to the content of such a self as the content of internal life. At the level of the self-consciousness of absolute nothingness even the noetic determination of the acting self is rejected. Thus what I have been calling the self-determination of the universal is more properly termed the determination of the noematic plane of the self-consciousness of absolute nothingness. Insofar as one can see the noetic determination of the acting self in this determination of the noematic plane, the content of this (noematic) determination must be construed as expressive. Further, insofar as that determination of the acting self is taken to be a determination of the transcendental self, that expressive content, the content of the universal of judgment, is truth.

Seen from the standpoint of the universal of judgment, the self-conscious self becomes the individual substance, and the self-determination of the self-conscious self becomes the act of judgment. Universal concepts refer to the various planes of determination. As the sense of a noetic determination of the acting self is added to the determination of the universal of judgment, this latter gradually acquires the sense of being a determination of the self-conscious universal. The internally perceiving self is, however, nothing more than the self-as-process based on expressive content. This expressive content, as the content of the acting self itself, is ideal content (in Plato's sense of Idea), and the self that actively intuits its own content is the intelligible self.

In this way, the determination of the universal that envelops all other universals must be a noematic planal determination of the self that truly sees. That is to say, the ultimate universal has the sense of being the noematic plane of the self-consciousness of absolute nothingness. Our entire life is reflected here. In fact, all that is objectively reflected or seen is reflected or seen here. In this way, objective determination receives its deepest, most profound foundation. Since the ultimate self cannot at all be seen noetically, the noematic plane of this self must have the meaning of an objective determination with respect to the noetic determinations of all seen selves. Thus, even if one speaks of a noetic determination of the self, if one supposes that it can be seen as a noetic determination, then precisely to that extent it must be determined in the noematic plane mentioned above. By virtue of the fact that this plane of determination reflects life in its entirety, the noetic determination of the seen self can also be said to be reflected in it. Because of this, the universal has a plane of self-determination in itself and one can say that self-consciousness determines itself in itself. As long as self-conscious determination is reflected in this plane and insofar as it itself is a self-conscious determination, it must have its own plane of determination. This plane of determination is the plane of self-determination of the universal. To the extent that the universal determines self-conscious content, that is, to the extent that it is a concrete universal, it has a plane of self-determination within itself. From one viewpoint, the very fact that what is self-conscious has a plane of self-determination means that we have not yet reached that which truly sees itself, i.e., it is not yet true self-consciousness. Having this plane of self-determination implies that it is reflected in the noematic plane of that which truly sees.

By being reflected in the ultimate noematic plane, what is self-conscious has its own plane of determination; and by having its own plane of determination, what is self-conscious can be said to be the object of consciousness, to be what is thought of. Seen from this plane of determination, what is self-conscious is transcendent; it is what determines its content in this same plane of determination. However, the self-determination of the universal is essentially grounded in the noematic plane of the self that truly sees (sees while being nothing). Since it reflects what is self-conscious, the self-conscious is seen; and to the extent that this is so it is determined by a universal, it has its place in a universal. What envelops the noetic self is what I have called the topos of the universal, namely, the universal itself. If one looks at what is in the topos from the vantage point of what is in the plane of determination of the universal, it will be seen to be something that determines itself in the plane of determination, but that can in no way be determined solely in this plane. This is the sort of thing the individual is. From the plane of determination, innumerable determinative processes can be seen in all directions, which is to say that an infinite number of individuals can be conceived. Thus topos envelops these individuals and can be thought of as the extensional determination of individuals.

This is not to say that what I here call topos is at all like a topos that merely has individuals in it. I mean only that it can be viewed in this fashion from the plane of determination. Since the self-determination of the universal is a determination of the noematic plane of the self that truly sees, its topos necessarily determines the noetic. In other words, it necessarily determines acts, and that which is in this topos must be actively self-conscious. Thus, to say that topos determines itself comes to mean that the elements of topos determine themselves, that they must be self-conscious. It is just this determination that one has in mind when one speaks of intuitive determination. To paraphrase, the "in the self" becomes the "self (as subject)."

The self's determining itself in this sense is the self seeing the nothingness of its self, the disappearance of the seen self, the inability any longer to see noetic determination. When this determination is carried out to the extreme, one can say no more than that topos determines itself. All that remains is something like the determination of the noematic plane of the self-consciousness of absolute nothingness. Its noetic determination cannot even be seen since it is simply our profound inner life. It is for this reason that topos determining itself is construed to be the self-determination of our deep inner life: the topos of the universal is a mirror wherein life reflects itself.

When we think of the self intuiting its own content, i.e., when the "in the self" becomes the "self (as subject)," this self still has the sense of a seen self, a noematic determination. When it becomes the true "self (as subject)," it is nothing other than the unfolding of our life. That is to say, the "self (as subject)" necessarily determines the "in the self" and sees the "self (as object)" in itself. From this standpoint then, to say that self-consciousness has a plane of self-determination within itself means that life determines itself, that it is conscious of itself. Therein is included the meaning of the universal determining itself, of topos determining itself.

Accordingly, this plane of determination also has the sense of being a self-conscious determination that in turn determines its own plane of determination. When this sort of self-conscious determination is brought about, the occupants of topos, when viewed from the plane of determination, are conceived of as innumerable recursively formed individual selves. The occupants of topos determine their content in the plane of self-determination, in other words, they are self-conscious. Further, the self-determination of topos itself can be seen in their depths as the deep flow of internal life.

A determination of the universal of judgment is nothing more than what remains when one excludes from such a self-conscious determination the sense of being a noetic determination. Its noematic plane of determination is the plane of abstract predicates, and what is in its noetic topos, i.e., the plane of transcendental predicates, is the individual that becomes subject but never predicate. Furthermore, depending upon how one thinks of topos determining itself, the predicate straightaway becomes subject and then finally something that cannot be determined as subject. In other words, together with becoming active, it leaves the domain of the universal of judgment. Conversely, even the plane of abstract predicates, which is the plane of determination of the universal of judgment, can itself be construed as a topos—the abstract universal—since it is an immediate self-determination of the topos referred to above. What is usually called a general concept refers to the content of a plane of determination of this universal.

Thus, the universal has its own plane of self-determination, and the occupants of topos (individuals) determine their own content in the plane of determination. As the universal determines itself, i.e., as topos determines topos, its occupants become things that determine themselves, and having finally become active, leave the domain of that universal. To say that the universal determines itself or that topos determines itself is to say that life determines itself. Thinking of a higher universal that envelops this universal is just to think of a hierarchy of noetic determinations of that which truly sees (sees while being nothing).

When, at the extreme limit of self-conscious determination, we reach the self-consciousness that is a seeing without a seer, the content of the noetic determination of this self is the content of our internal life. We should note, of course, that at the level of this self-consciousness of absolute nothingness there is neither anything that sees nor anything that is seen, since object is immediately mind and mind is immediately object. But such a state is beyond the realm of logical disputation, and in terms of rational thought one can say no more than what is stated above.

When the "in the self" merges with the "self (as object)" we have ideational consciousness, and when it merges with the "self (as subject)" we have self-consciousness. However, when it truly arrives at the plane of the "self (as subject)" it can be conceived of only as the content of deep, rich life. In the depths of the self-conscious (intuitive) self a still deeper life flow is visible. That which determines the topos of all beings ("that which is placed within") must be the noesis of this life, since it determines the universal of universals. When this noesis determines itself, thereby making the determination of a noetic self visible for the first time, we have before us the acting self in the broad sense. The noematic determination of the acting self in this broad sense is also expression in the broad sense. The determinations of the acting universal are established here. However, since what I call the acting universal in the wide sense has the meaning of a self whose content cannot be seen noematically, from the point of view of its noematic determination it might be better to speak of the expressive universal. Since the occupants of this universal, i.e., the noematically seen content of the acting self, are Ideas (in a sense similar to Plato's), I have referred to the acting universal in the strict sense (characterized by the fact that its occupants see their own content) as the intelligible universal when speaking from the standpoint of its noematic determination.

The topological determination of this universal is such that the true and acting free ego is determined in it as the noetic determination of deep life. Its plane of determination can be regarded as the world of expression that houses all of that which has the character of an expression. Its plane of the "self (as object)" is best construed as the simple world of expressions. Yet, when the plane of the "self (as object)" becomes the plane of the "self (as subject)" it is the plane of intuition of the intelligible self, and its occupants are things that see ideal content. The world of Ideas is now just the plane of intuition of the intelligible self. The true "self (as subject)" that transcends this intelligible self can no longer be seen as a noetic determination in any sense, and the most that can be done is to think of it as an infinitely deep noetic determination in the depths of the acting self. In this sense, the content of the acting self as the content of the acting self is ideal, but it cannot be seen in the way Ideas are seen. I call this self the historical self.

Where topos is thought to determine itself, even the intuitive self disappears. When topos determines itself in the universal of judgment, the occupants of that topos can no longer be construed as grammatical subjects. Indeed, it is almost as if they were active things that had left the domain of the universal. Thus, even the intelligible self disappears in the plane of the true "self (as subject)." This state is what we ordinarily term religious experience, for in religious experience the seen self completely and utterly disappears: we become truly selfless even as we are are immersed in a profound and rich internal life.

As noted previously, when our profound internal life determines itself noetically, the acting self makes its appearance, and expression, in the broad sense, emerges as its noematic determination. Now the acting self is founded on that noetic determination while expression is founded on that noematic determination, but true life itself is something that fundamentally and essentially determines the universal, not something founded on the universal. Thus, we do not have here the self-determination of the acting self in the sense of seeing all expressive content as its own determination. We cannot be self-conscious of the noetic determination that determines all expressive content. Such a self-consciousness could only be said to be the self-consciousness of absolute nothingness, but this is no longer something that could possibly be determined as a universal. Properly speaking, the acting self is the seeing of oneself while being nothing. But the self as seen cannot be the self that sees, for the latter, being nothing, could not possibly be seen. This is the contradiction inherent in the acting self. It is here that the distinction is drawn between the determination of the acting universal in the narrow sense that emphasizes the noetic determination of the acting self on one hand, and something like the expressive universal that emphasizes the noematic determination of the acting self on the other.

The acting universal in the narrow sense is established in the direction of the noetic determination of the self that truly sees (sees while being nothing) while the expressive universal is established in the direction of its noematic determination. The former can be construed as the self-conscious plane of the acting self where the "in the self" merges into the "self (as subject)." And insofar as the acting self sees its own content in this self-conscious plane, it can then be said to be the intelligible self. In contrast, the expressive universal, since it is the result of the merging of the "in the self" into the "self (as object)," can be regarded as the plane of self-determination of the acting universal in the wide sense. Further, if one excludes the "self (as object)" from this plane of determination and considers only the "in the self," then the result is precisely the simple world of meaning. Conversely, when it is regarded as simply the plane of the "self (as object)," it becomes the universal of judgment.

The acting self itself can never, properly speaking, be construed as the "self (as object)." The universal of judgment is established precisely as this plane of the "self (as object)." Accordingly, as this "self (as object)" takes on the meaning of the "self (as subject)," as it acquires the sense of a noetic determination, the content of the expressive universal shifts from the universal of judgment to the universal of self-consciousness. This is the reason that in "The Self Determination of the Universal" I insisted that these universals are founded on expression.

The intellectual intelligible self, where noetic determination is minimized, i.e., the plane of determination of the transcendental self, lies on the border between the simple expressive universal and the acting self in the narrow sense, i.e., the intelligible universal. If the acting universal in the wide sense is thought of as the self-determination of the self that truly sees (sees while being nothing), in its noematic direction we have the expressive universal that encompasses both the universal of judgment and the universal of self-consciousness, while in its noetic direction we have the acting universal in the narrow sense, or the intelligible universal. This latter can be said to be the plane of self-consciousness of the expressive self. The plane of consciousness of the transcendental self can be regarded as the first of these planes of self-consciousness. Since it is a plane of consciousness of the intelligible self that is in the intelligible universal it can be considered as the plane of consciousness of the intellectual intelligible self that has minimized the sense of noetic determination. Further, regarded from the point of view of the expressive universal it is topos. This plane of consciousness of the transcendental self is characterizable as a plane of self-determination of the intellectual intelligible self, the sense of intelligible noetic determination having been minimized. For this reason it is regarded as lying directly behind the universal of judgment. Further, if its sense of noetic determination is completely excluded, we have the topos of the universal of judgment, that is to say, the transcendental predicate plane in which the natural world is determined. Thus, the natural world can be said to be expressive content seen through the noetic determination of the intellectual intelligible self. It is the noematic content of the intellectual intelligible self.

We must, however, take care at this point. Even though one asserts that the intellectual intelligible self is that which has minimized the sense of noetic determination, it still is an intelligible self and thus, to some extent at least, it intuits its own content. By deepening this sense of noetic determination, it can be regarded as determining the noetic content contained in expressions, i.e., it can see the content of the "self (as object)." It is here that the universal of self-consciousness is established as its noetic determination. In this way, the determination of the self-conscious universal the "self (as object)" must be seen to correspond to expression. There must be a self that is seen as the unity of expressive content. Of course, deepening the sense of the noetic determination of the intellectual intelligible self means that a transition has already been made from the intellectual intelligible self to the emotive-volitional self. Further, the self-determination of this emotive-volitional intelligible self must always underlie the determination of the self-conscious universal. That is, behind the self-conscious universal there must be something that always sees itself. This is the reason that we must think of the transcending of conscious acts and the arriving at the intelligible self as the transcending of the self-conscious universal in the direction of its noetic determination.

In short, the expressive universal is the plane of the "self (as object)" of the acting self in the wide sense and thus carries with it the sense of the acting "self (as object)." As we go deeper in the noetic direction, i.e., as the acting self becomes self-conscious, we reach the acting universal in the narrow sense or the intelligible universal. Thus the so-called world of conscious phenomena determined by the self-conscious universal is nothing other than the content of the acting self seen as (viewed on the analogy of) expression. The world of conscious phenomena can be construed only by placing the acting self behind the natural world. Transcending the conscious self and attaining the transcendental self is not simply a matter of transcending the intellectual self, but rather must be a transcendence in the noetic direction of the acting self. Once the determination of the intelligible universal is reached, the acting self intuits its own content; that is, it sees Ideas. Moreover, since the self-determination of the acting self is founded on the noetic determination of our profound inner life, this ideal content can be said to be the direct effusion of this inner life, and it is here that we possess an eternal life that transcends time. In this sense, I fully appreciate the meaning and value of Plato's philosophy, provided we keep in mind that the acting self, as was said above, is nothing other than the noetic determination of the self that sees while being nothing itself.

As long as the noetic self can be seen, it remains the seen self and not the self that truly sees. As one continues to go deeper in the noetic direction of the self that truly sees (sees while being nothing), as one reaches the level of the historical self, both the noetic self and ideal determination can no longer be seen. Objectively speaking, a historical "idea" cannot be observed. All that can be seen are the forms, such as a historical period, on the analogy of expressions. These forms—"types" or "wholes"—are, in a word, nothing other than abstract "ideas." Thus, this historical form is something that cannot but be idealized and yet is material that cannot be ideally determined. However, to attempt to determine the meaning or value of the ideal content from the historical form is as great a mistake as attempting to determine concrete individuality by abstract universals. The historical "idea" that has to be idealized even though it can never be seen as an "ideal," may be thought to change in an irrational manner, but that is only so because being abstract it cannot be seen as an "ideal." Yet this does not negate the eternality of the concrete "idea" that the abstract One suggests. After all, the history of art is not art and the history of philosophy is not philosophy. On the contrary, there can be a history of art only after there is art. The same applies to philosophy. History is the acting self trying to see "ideas" as noetic determinations of the profound life. The real matter of history is not sensation (sensual matter) but the deep flow of our life.

I began my analysis with the self-determination of the universal of judgment, but if we reason along the lines indicated above, this self-determination of the universal of judgment can be said to be the noematic plane of determination of the expressive universal. It is what remains after the sense of the "self (as object)" is eliminated from the noematic plane of determination of the acting self in the broad sense, i.e., the plane of the "self (as object)." Thus, viewed from behind as it were, it can be said to be founded on the noematic determination of the self that truly sees. Seen in this way, transcending in the depths of the transcendental plane of predicates—the topos of the universal of judgment—already has the sense of a noetic determination of the self that sees nothingness, of the self-consciousness of the acting universal in the broad sense. When the meaning of noetic determination of the expressive universal is added, the transition is made from the universal of judgment to the universal of self-consciousness; and when the acting self sees its own content, when it becomes self-conscious, the intelligible universal is established. This intelligible self can be construed as the noetic plane of determination of the acting self, in the depths of which one finds the content of a deep profound life. However, since this content can no longer be viewed as a noetic determination, it will be determined by the expressive universal, at least to the extent that it is viewed noematically. In fact, the expressive universal, which has the meaning of the noematic plane of the self that truly sees, comprehends all the self-determination of all the various universals. This is so even with regard to the self-determination of the acting universal, for insofar as this self-conscious determination is seen, it has its place in the intelligible universal as something that determines itself noematically. Thus it is that we are able to construe such things as self-determinations of a universal.

Of course, the noetic determinations of the acting self, being founded on the noetic determination of the self that truly sees, must transcend the determinations of the expressive universal. The acting self in the deep sense must be something that cannot be determined, not even expressively. Intellectual determination and practical determination are always in opposition, and neither can contain or comprehend the other. However, that which is an intellectual determination must always be a determination of the expressive universal. Moreover, since the expressive universal is essentially and properly something founded on the noematic determination of the self that truly sees (sees while being nothing), the determinations of the universal of judgment that are determinations of the noematic plane of this expressive universal can then be considered the basic pattern of our intellectual determinations. However, since a determination of the expressive universal is a noematic determination of the self that truly sees, it must have its own life content. Intellectual determinations themselves are nothing other than a current of life. From the vantage point of the noetic determination of the self that truly sees, all currents converge to form a single flow of life.

The self-consciousness of absolute nothingness

This is the religious experience in which form is seen as void and void as form, i.e., the state in which there is neither a seer nor that which is seen.

Internal life

When the self-consciousness of absolute nothingness determines itself, its noematic plane is the topos of the final universal that determines all that exists, and in its noetic direction we find the flow of infinite life. At this point one might question how absolute nothingness can possibly determine itself. In reply it must be stated that absolute nothingness is not simply not-being-anything but is rather the ultimate noetic determination; it is the essence of spirit. It is both absolute nothingness and absolute being, and as such it transcends the limits of our understanding. This is the very origin of the question.

The acting universal in the broad sense or the expressive universal in the broad sense

The most basic universal established through the noematic determination of the self-consciousness of absolute nothingness is the acting or expressive universal in the broad sense. In its noetic direction there is seen the acting self, and in its noematic direction there is seen expression. However, since the acting self has the sense of being the noetic determination of the self that sees while making itself nothing, its content cannot be noematically determined. For this reason the acting universal is divided into two universals — one based on the noematic aspect and one based on the noetic aspect.

The acting universal in the narrow sense or the intelligible universal

In the sense that the acting self sees its own content, the plane of noetic determination of the acting universal is the intelligible universal. The historical self transcends in the direction of noesis that which is in this intelligible universal, and thus it already has the sense of being in the universal in the broad sense.

The expressive universal

The expressive universal, while being the noematic plane of the acting self, also colligates in its noetic aspect those things that cannot be seen in the noetic determination of the acting self. Within this universal, the universal of judgment and the universal of self-consciousness can be distinguished. Although an objective self such as the intelligible self cannot be discerned in the expressive universal, one can see the determination of the abstract self, the subjective self, as a noematic determination of the acting self in conformity with expressions. Thus, the noetic and noematic planes confront each other in the expressive universal, the former being the universal of self-consciousness, and the latter, the universal of judgment. Moreover, since, properly speaking, the determinations of the expressive universal have the sense of self-determinations of the acting self, one can think of a profound flow of life lying hidden in the depths of what are taken to be simply determinations of the universal of judgment.

III

As I have stated repeatedly, in contrast to previous philosophies that considered the structure of consciousness in terms of acts or processes, I conceive of it topologically, in terms of planes. Thus, I take the structure of self-consciousness to be the fundamental structure of all consciousness and conceive of its center of gravity as being in the plane of consciousness. The plane of the "self (as object)" is usually taken to be the ideational conscious plane, and the occupants of this plane to be things that in some sense intend objects. Objects, however, are occupants of the plane of the "self (as subject)," which is to say that they are the content of the self-conscious. When the plane of the "self (as subject)" is regarded as being the result of the plane of the "self (as object)" being absorbed into the "self (as subject)" it is a plane of self-consciousness in which objects are intuited. Given this, even the things that are in the plane of the "self (as object)" must be regarded as self-conscious entities that should be, but are not yet, self-conscious. The act of intention itself is nothing but a self-conscious act that should be, but is not, self-conscious. Instead of starting from the intentional character of consciousness, I would rather begin from its self-conscious character. Consequently, I think of representational or ideational consciousness as being the result of minimizing the self-conscious character of full-blooded consciousness. When the self tries to reflect itself in the plane of ideational consciousness, an infinite process is invariably set in motion, in the depths of which this self-conscious self must lie.

Conscious acts are thought of in just this way, for construing consciousness as acts always involves taking such a process as the nucleus. Even so-called self-consciousness is nothing more than a process-self of this sort. It is merely something seen in the plane of self-consciousness. However, this process-self must be submerged in that which truly sees itself. The more intuitive our consciousness becomes, the more activity is transcended. The true plane of self-consciousness must be a plane of intuition. It is for this reason that to consider the self seeing the self in the self as the basic structure of consciousness implies that what is in the plane of intuition casts its shadow on the ideational plane. Determination as an infinite process comes about by intuition reflecting itself in the ideational plane, the so-called self-conscious self being that which one is conscious of at the extreme limit of such a process, i.e., in the plane of intuition. The so-called self-conscious self is conceptually grounded in the self-determination of the plane of intuition. Thinking emerges when the occupants of the ideational plane are regarded as self-determinations of that which is in the plane of intuition, and the act of thinking appears when the objects of the intentional acts are thought to determine themselves. Thus, speculative consciousness is the recognition that there is a plane of intuition immediately behind ideational consciousness and that what is in the plane of intuition determines what is in the ideational plane. Seen from the ideational plane, speculative consciousness is always a process linked to the self-conscious self. This is why thought is considered to be spontaneous and active.

However, this self-conscious self is not merely found in combination with speculative consciousness, for as long as one can think of non-being determining being, the self-conscious self will necessarily be found to underlie that infinite process. This process is merely something that can be characterized as lying in the plane of the "self (as subject)" and is thus necessarily submerged in that which truly sees. Fundamentally, the plane of ideation or the plane of consciousness is nothing more than the plane of the "self (as object)." The plane of the "self (as subject)," i.e., the plane of intuition, cannot be conceived of without at the same time conceiving of the plane of the "self (as object)." It must have the meaning of the plane of self-determination of the self that sees while being nothing, the noematic plane.

Ideational consciousness, in contrast, arises from viewing the "self (as object)" in the abstract. This is equivalent to thinking of an abstract universal. But just as there is no abstract universal that is not a plane of determination of the concrete universal, so, too, there is no plane of ideational consciousness that is not a plane of determination of that which is self-conscious. This being the case, why is there always a plane of the "self (as object)" found in opposition to the plane of the "self (as subject)," and why must ideation be thought to be the most fundamental characteristic of consciousness?

The noetic determination of the self that truly sees cannot itself be seen, and even self-conscious determination is something determined by the noematic determination of the self-consciousness of absolute nothingness. In other words, it is determined by the expressive universal in the broad sense. All self-conscious determinations are necessarily reflected in the noematic plane of the self-consciousness of absolute nothingness. In this sense, then, the plane of the "self (as object)" must always be in opposition to the plane of the "self (as subject)." The representational plane and the planes of consciousness, for example, must fundamentally be seen to have this sort of meaning. Thus, in the same sense that one can think of a plane of consciousness of internal perception, one can also think of a plane of consciousness of the transcendental self because the ideational or representational conscious plane itself has transcendental meaning.

It is true, of course, that we intend things in the plane of consciousness, but it must be remembered that the word "things" has various meanings and that there are various modes of intending. Representations lie in different planes of consciousness, depending on whether they are perceptual representations, imaginative representations, or merely signs. Just as the abstract universal has discursive significance by virtue of its being a plane of determination, and a contraction of a concrete universal, so too the intentional conscious plane can be thought of as intentional by being the plane of determination of that which is self-conscious.

The problem is that we inadvertently think of things like the noematic determination of the acting self in the broad sense, even when speaking ostensibly of the representational conscious plane, and as a result we think it possible to go in the opposite direction as well, from the ideational conscious plane to the plane of intuition. In other words, insofar as the acting self sees its own content, it is thought of as the plane of intuition. For this reason, the ideational plane of consciousness that includes various modes of intending must in reality be the expressive plane of consciousness, and the plane of internal perception must, conversely, be determined by this expressive plane. The expressive plane, where everything in it expresses itself, must be said to be the most concrete plane of consciousness. Thus things in the plane of consciousness are thought to intend something, and as long as the acting self sees the content of its self-determination, its self-conscious content, these things are thought to intend objects. But when self-conscious content is seen merely as the self-determination of the expressive universal, it is thought simply to intend meaning. The former is a meaning-fulfilling act, and the latter, a meaning-bestowing act.

Taken this way, consciousness essentially has the sense of being a plane of expression, and as a plane of self-conscious determination of the acting self, it has both a noematic and a noetic direction. At the outer limits of its noematic direction speculative intuition is established by intellectual self-consciousness, while in its noetic direction there is established feeling-willing intuition. In short, various planes of intuition are established as the self-consciousness of the acting self that sees while being nothing. Accordingly, various conscious acts can be conceived of in relation to the expressive plane of consciousness. To think of the plane of ideation as simply intentional is to take this to be an intellectual plane of determination, and the intuitive plane that is behind this can then be thought of as the plane of intellectual intuition referred to above.

Even from the plane of ideation in the sense of the noematic plane of the acting self there is a plane of intuition to be seen in the noetic direction. It is precisely because of this that what is felt and what is desired can be thought to be reflected ideationally. Moreover, the true ideational plane is the expressive plane. By deepening this position we ultimately come into contact noematically with the self-consciousness of absolute nothingness, and thus we can conceive of something like the neutralizing act of consciousness. In contrast, the more our self becomes something that truly sees, the more consciousness becomes intuitive. Acts are enveloped and necessarily become reflected (that is, they become objects). It is in this sense that noesis has to be seen in self-conscious determination. Furthermore, it is in this sense that the noetic plane needs to be seen as a plane of intuition. If one thinks of going deeper in this direction and ultimately coming in contact noetically with the self-consciousness of absolute nothingness, one can conceive of a level of intuition of the pure self to which all active positions can be reduced. Such a position is the foundation for an intuition of essences established on an intuition that includes activity.

The notion of self-consciousness as a process arises from the noematic determination of self-consciousness where the self sees the self in the self. Since the result of this noematic determination is an expressive determination, objects must be recognized as expressive determinations in which noetic determination can no longer be seen. Insofar as noetic determination can be seen, objective cognition of objects is established as a self-conscious determination. This is why one thinks one is truly seeing the objective world of facts in the self-consciousness of Kant's transcendental self, a self that lies on the boundary between the determination of the expressive universal and the determination of the intelligible self.

Moreover, when that which is in the depths of this process-self-consciousness sees its own content, i.e., when what is located in the noetic plane of the expressive universal sees noetic content, it has "experience" (*Erlebnis*) in the sense that it sees its own world. But intuition of essences (*Wessenschau*) is not experience in this sense. Intuition of essences is not merely something that lies in the plane of intuition seeing its own content; it must rather be an intuition of the plane of intuition itself. It must be an intuition of that very self that determines itself actively; it must be a state of being conscious of so-called self-consciousness. Thus true intuition of the pure self must be similar to the noetic determination of the self-consciousness of absolute nothingness.

Of course, there is neither noesis nor noema in the self-consciousness of absolute nothingness, but when it is said to see itself, we must think of it as the confrontation of noesis and noema. The ultimate universal is thus determined as its noematic plane and our world of cognition is established through the determinations of such a universal. In contrast, our internal life can be seen as its noetic determination. The content of this internal life can no longer be seen cognitively. Seen from the position of internal life, however, cognitive determination is nothing more than the flow of internal life in which noetic determination has been reduced to a minimum. This noetic self-consciousness of our internal life is the position of true intuition of the pure self; it can be called the self-consciousness of internal life itself. From one point of view we can say that the acting universal in the broad sense is the topos of the expressive universal, which in turn is the self-consciousness of the plane of intuition itself, all three of which can be said to be equivalent. I have said that the deep content of the acting self cannot be determined cognitively and that even the historical self cannot be brought to consciousness noetically. However, from the position of a still deeper noetic determination, the topos of the universal of judgment can be thought to be a plane of self-determination of the intellectual intelligible self. Even though its noetic determination is minimal, it is still a self and as such it must be capable of self-consciousness. Thus it is possible to establish the self-consciousness of self-consciousness, just as it is possible to speak of "reason reflecting on itself."

The self-consciousness of self-consciousness is the seeing of self-consciousness-as-process in the plane of intuition of the "self (as subject)." It is seeing in the plane of the selfless self. From the position of the noetic determination of still deeper life, the acting universal in the broad sense, or the topos of the expressive universal, can be thought of as the determination plane of intellectual life that has minimized the sense of noetic determination. Even if the noetic content of life itself cannot be reflected intellectually, we can think of the intellectual self-consciousness of life in the same way that we can think of the self-consciousness of Kant's transcendental self on analogy with the topos of the universal of judgment. True self-consciousness of the pure self must be something like this. Intellectual life is a topological determination of the acting universal and a noematic determination of the noetic content of life. As such, this noematic plane of determination is reflected in life's noetic plane of intuition, which implies that the self-consciousness of intellectual life is established.

Still, there is no intellectual self-consciousness without a willing self-consciousness, and just as we think of intellectual self-consciousness as the noematic determination of willing self-consciousness, so too we can think of the intellectual self-consciousness of life as the noematic plane of determination of the self-consciousness of internal life. Willing self-consciousness can further be considered to be the noematic determination of the acting universal, but there is no further noematic plane that can determine life itself. The self that sees while being nothing cannot be seen, and therein lies the limit of knowledge. Only things like the self-consciousness of intellectual life remain and retain an intellectual or cognitive sense.

To say that we are thinking of something refers to a fact about an individual self. Something thought is always considered to have its origin in the individual self. But then this active self that is thought to be the point of origin for all things in this sense must, in fact, be the individual self that is in the final noetic plane of determination; it must be the acting self. Thus, the plane of consciousness that is its plane of determination cannot be the ideational plane of consciousness but must rather be the expressive plane of consciousness. Conscious space is not two-dimensional but multi-dimensional. The tendency to think otherwise is due to the fact that we consider thinking a temporal fact, and when the self is thought to be based on temporal facts, then that self, namely, the plane of consciousness of the perceiving self, is regarded as the so-called ideational plane of consciousness. However, the direction and significance of the various intentions cannot be ascertained in the ideational plane of consciousness.

In contrast, since the plane of self-determination of the active self is a plane of expression, intention is to be found in various directions and in various senses in this plane. A plane of expression has both a noematic and a noetic direction. In its noematic direction objective cognition is constituted self-consciously; experience (*Erlebnis*) is constituted in its noetic direction. I feel that this is the proper method of distinguishing objective cognition and "experience."

I cannot help doubting the phenomenologists' claim that what has the character of an object is intuited in perception. What is seen "corporeally" (*leibhaftig*) must be the content of experience seen in the noetic direction. The first objects we make contact with in this direction must be something like artistic "ideas." From this direction it is impossible corporeally to come into contact with objects that determine themselves noematically. The objects of objective cognition must be seen as determinations of the expressive universal where noetic self-consciousness cannot be seen. Perceptions are fundamentally noematic determinations of acting self-consciousness, while impulses are its noetic determinations. Although the acting self is thought of as a noetic determination, it also has in its noematic direction a sense of having transcended noetic determination. Consequently, that noematic content must have a meaning that cannot be grasped corporeally. These are the sorts of unchanging relations we find in self-consciousness.

It is clear, then, that experience must be distinguished not only from objective cognition but also from the intuition of essences (*Wesensschau*). This can be done only from the level of the plane of intuition that reflects the relation of noesis and noema.

What I call the standpoint of internal life is the standpoint of the noetic determination of the self that sees without a seer; it refers to the noesis of the self-consciousness of absolute nothingness. Thus, its noematic plane of determination is supported by the noematic determination of the self-consciousness of absolute nothingness, and the last thing I referred to as a universal, namely, the acting universal in the broad sense, must be the topos of the expressive universal. This universal of the noematic plane of internal life is determined, and it is in this plane that various worlds and individual selves can be thought. But, of course, there still must be a plane of intuition in the direction of the noetic determination of internal life, and there that the determination of the universal itself is reflected. I said previously that the universal itself is determined by internal life, but it is in this plane of intuition that the intellectual self-consciousness of internal life is established.

This, I believe, represents the true philosophic position. Kant sought the foundation of knowledge in the synthetic unity of consciousness, but his critical philosophy as such cannot be erected securely on this synthetic unity of the self. As the self-consciousness of reason itself, it can refer only to the intellectual self-consciousness of internal life. The phenomenological pure self that rejects all standpoints must also be something like this intellectual self-consciousness of internal life. Husserl's pure self, however, does not avoid reduction to a purified, internally perceiving self. From such a position there is nothing more to be seen than Husserl's so-called essences, and this is not sufficient to provide a foundation of the objective cognition of objects that determine themselves.

Since the phenomenological position was, from the start, the standpoint of the intellectual self-consciousness of internal life, the transition from Husserl's phenomenology to Heidigger's interpretive, hermeneutical phenomenology or fundamental ontology was an understandable one. Even so, we still have nothing more than the purification of the self-consciousness of the acting self in the noetic direction; the basis for the objective determination of expressive content is not yet made clear. In other words, the notion of what I call the self-determination of the expressive universal is not yet apparent.

When I speak of internal life, I do not intend a contrast with external life. Internal life refers merely to the intuitive plane of determination where the self that is in any way seen noematically has disappeared. Since we usually take the self to be the process-self, we can think of the self only as either disappearing or uniting with objects. The true self as such does not disappear. Rather, everything that *is* becomes something located in the self. The self that truly sees must be a plane of intuition that includes this process-self-consciousness. Thus we can say that we feel our own life in the shining moon and in the insects crying in the fields.

Even Hegel's dialectical development must have the sense of what I call the self-consciousness of internal life. Everything that is in a topos is, when seen from the standpoint of the plane of self-determination of the universal, self-contradictory. Insofar as the universal is determined, contradictions are seen everywhere, and that which envelops the development of the dialectic must be something like the plane of intuition of internal life.

When I say that intellectual self-consciousness of internal life is the true standpoint for philosophy, I am not saying that I agree with so-called "life philosophy"; the content of experience (*Erlebnis*) is no more than the content of the acting self noematically determined, and since the depths of the acting self can never be made visible, the content of experience can thus never be more than historical knowledge. Philosophy as the self-reflection of reason itself must have validity in and of itself. History may determine what sort of philosophy will appear in what age, but philosophical development must be the self-conscious development of reason itself. As such, it is grounded in the plane of intuition that includes historical development, not the other way around.

Notes

1. Nishida's predecessors

[1] Miyakawa 1961.

[2] Nishimura 1887, cited in Funayama 1959.

[3] The possible exception is the term *soku* 即, which means "at once, immediately, identical," but this term is generally used in Buddhist works and thus cannot be ascribed to the direct influence of the Inoues. Still, there are other factors to consider in assessing their influence on Nishida.

[4] Until rather recently, it was common practice in Japanese academic circles to omit reference to other Japanese scholars in one's field unless one was directly criticizing their views. This was especially true if the scholar in question were still alive, no matter how deeply indebted one might be to that person for one's ideas or basic orientation. Watsuji Tetsurō, for example, makes almost no reference to Nishida in his works, although the influence is strong and unmistakable. Tanabe Hajime makes no reference to Nishida in his published works, except for an article that is a direct criticism of Nishida's thought. Mutai Risaku was a student of Nishida and even wrote an exposition of Nishida's philosophy after Nishida's death, but he does not mention Nishida in his major work,『場所の論理学』[The Logic of Place].

[5] Inoue Enryō, 1886–1887.

[6] Takeuchi 1966, 54, citing Kimura 1932. Takeuchi builds a strong case for the influence of this volume on Nishida, citing passages from his letters that closely resemble closely Inoue's statements. Kōsaka Masaaki also refers to Nishida's appreciation of *An Evening of Philosophical Conversation* (Kōsaka 1947, 19).

[7] Funayama 1959; see also Funayama 1956, 81–4. Piovesanna 1968 contains material on the role of the two Inoues in Meiji philosophical thought.

[8] A rather interesting and amusing feature of this work is that the Master who

provides the synthesis is referred to as Enryō (Inoue's first name), which means something like "perfection and completion." Additionally, each of the students has a name containing one character of the name Enryō 円了, and the two disputants in the cosmological issue have each one character from the Japanese word for *universe*, 宇宙. That the response to the puns was not well received in some quarters is attested to in the preface to Part II where Inoue replies to a critic that he is not attempting to extol his own virtues, but that he could not have used the name of any of the great figures of the past for the simple reason that none of them had given this precise formulation of the problem and its solution. Moreover, he did not want his theory to be misinterpreted as being merely a variation on Buddhism, Confucianism, or Taoism.

⁹ Inoue uses the term 唯理論, literally "principal-only theory." Since "principlism" sounds barbaric and "logicism" would be misleading, I have chosen "archism," basing the term on the Greek word for *principle*.

¹⁰ The term 理即物心 virtually defies translation into English. The key glyph is *soku* 即, whose Japanese reading, *sunawachi*, is used in colloquial language much as English speakers use the expression "in other words." In this technical expression, and others like it, it is meant to convey the idea of essential identity among elements that may be radically different. It is particularly common in Buddhist writings and is the term used in the often-cited phrase from the *Heart Sutra*: 色即是空, 空即是色 (form, precisely as it is, is emptiness; emptiness, precisely as it is, is form).

¹¹ FUNAYAMA (1959, 84) comments on this passage, stating that Enryō is in effect diluting the idealist stance. No doubt Funayama's criticism stems from his own Marxist leanings.

¹² INOUE E. 1886–1887, 20.

¹³ INOUE E. 1886–1887, 26.

¹⁴ INOUE E. 1886–1887, 32.

¹⁵ INOUE E. 1886–1887, 73–104.

¹⁶ Here it seems that Inoue is driving toward the notion of a concrete universal, which is central to Nishida's view, though he does not elaborate, rather than demonstrating a faulty reading of Hegel's writings. See FUNAYAMA 1956.

¹⁷ INOUE E. 1886–1887, 101.

¹⁸ Examples expressing the same sort of relation between the phenomenal and the permanent are common and very much in keeping with Inoue's background. He was a devout follower of Buddhism and defended that faith against numerous criticisms circulating in the Meiji period. He was also very much concerned with showing that Buddhism was not in conflict with the discoveries of modern science and, what is more, that it could be shown to provide the solutions to some of the most perplexing philosophical problems as yet unsolved in the West. The analogy is also used prominently by a major contemporary Chinese philosopher, HSIUNG Shih-li (1885–1968); see CHAN 1963, 769–72. Hsiung also uses the Buddhist notion

of immediate identity to resolve the conflict between principle (理) and material force (気). His *New Doctrine of Consciousness-Only* has interesting parallels with Nishida's *An Inquiry into the Good*, and will be dealt with later.

[19] INOUE E. 1886–1887, 103.

[20] He had just returned from a journey to Europe sponsored by the government and in the same year published his commentary on the Imperial Rescript, which was destined to become the foundation of official moral teaching for many years to come. It might also be noted, as a further indication of his prominence, that Inoue became president of Tokyo University in 1897.

[21] SONKENKAI 1931.

[22] Cf., TAKEUCHI 1966, Chapter 2, passim; KŌSAKA 1947, Chapter 1, passim.

[23] It was primarily because of political difficulties that Nishida left high school without graduating. He rebelled against the authoritarian, even militaristic, restructuring of the school.

[24] 「我世界観の一塵」, (1894);「現象即実在論の要領」(1897).

[25] INOUE T. 1894, 495.

[26] The irreducibility is not easily seen in this example. The claim that cells cannot exist apart from some organic body or another might be met by the response: "If by organic body you mean something composed of cells, then of course there will be an organic body whenever there is a cell, but what does that show other than our particular use of language?" Inoue might reply that what he wants to show is precisely that our concepts are interrelated in such a fashion; distinctions such as objective-subjective are made within the context of some unity and are interdependent and for that reason any attempt to reduce one to the other is foredoomed to failure.

[27] The only difficulty is the example of an extra-experiential world as "an infinitely distant star world" seems to indicate some obscurity in distinctions two and three.

[28] WALSH 1963, Chapter 3, passim.

[29] INOUE T. 1897, 389–90.

[30] Nishida also makes use of this notion of reducing material objects to energy distributions. See NKV IV, 20, and Chapter 3 of this essay.

[31] INOUE T. 1897, 392.

[32] That there must be a ground for the distinction not on a par with the elements of the distinction is central to Nishida's concept of basho as discussed in Chapter 3. His treatment of this intuition, however, is far more penetrating.

[33] INOUE T. 1897, 394.

[34] In this connection, one thinks of the statement by QUINE in his essay "On What There Is" (1963, 1–20): "To be is to be the value of a variable." This point will also be discussed when Nishida's predicate logic is considered.

[35] The influence of T. H. Greene on Nishida, especially with reference to the primacy of the will, should be noted. For further details, see TAKEUCHI 1966, Chapter 1, passim.

2. THE FIRST ATTEMPTS:
RADICAL EMPIRICISM AND VOLUNTARISM

[1] Nishida himself states that his position most closely paralleled Berkeley's and Fichte's in many respects, and this juxtaposition is in itself quite revealing.

[2] NKZ I, 9; *Inquiry*, 3. All the translations of Nishida's works in this volume, including those from 『善の研究』, are my own, but cross-references to the Masao Abe and Christopher Ives translation, *An Inquiry into the Good*, are included for the reader's convenience.

[3] NKZ I, 28; *Inquiry*, 19.

[4] NKZ V, passim.

[5] NKZ I, 9 and 22; *Inquiry*, 3 and 15.

[6] NKZ I, 11; *Inquiry*, 5.

[7] We shall see that the word *encompass* is not a mere coincidence here.

[8] This is, of course, strictly speaking, impossible, for a viewed experience is not pure experience, but an object of thought; that is, it is no longer active or dynamic.

[9] NKZ I, 25; *Inquiry*, 16.

[10] NKZ I, 25; *Inquiry*, 17.

[11] The Japanese 運動表象 literally means "movement representation." The compound 表象 is commonly used to translate the German *Vorstellung*.

[12] NKZ I, 37; *Inquiry*, 26.

[13] The idea that objective unity is always an imposed unity and, thus, is incapable of being the final solution is almost axiomatic in Nishida's thought. It runs throughout his works.

[14] NKZ I, 39; *Inquiry*, 28.

[15] This emphasis on the idea that "given" means "given in a particular context" appears frequently throughout Nishida's work.

[16] The internal necessity to which Nishida refers when speaking of the developing of a pure experience is not to be confused with either constraint or logical necessity in the usual sense. It is more in the nature of a natural development. There is a direction to the development, but not in terms of an ideal that would imply a bifurcation of the pure experience. The ideal and the actual development are one; they have not yet been separated.

[17] It was previously noted that HSIUNG Shih-li attempted to achieve an identity of principle and material force in his *New Theory of Consciousness-Only*. It seems significant that this attempt to analyze the "problem of standpoints" by moving in the direction of utter subjectivity occured in Japan and China at the same time. At any rate, a detailed comparison of the development of the positions of Nishida and Hsiung Shih-li would be a worthwhile project. The fact that both men were influenced by, and yet ultimately rejected, Bergson is of particular interest. See Chapter 1 above and note 18.)

[18] NKZ I, 49; *Inquiry*, 40.

[19] Cf., NKZ V, 430; Appendix, 193-4.

[20] NKZ I, 55; *Inquiry*, 44.

[21] NKZ I, 67; *Inquiry*, 54.

[22] NKZ XI, 60.

[23] NKZ I, 69; *Inquiry*, 57.

[24] NKZ I, 85-6; *Inquiry*, 71.

[25] NKZ I, 87; *Inquiry*, 72.

[26] He uses Berkeleyan arguments against the notion that matter is something independent of conscious phenomena.

[27] NKZ I, 93-4; *Inquiry*, 77.

[28] NKZ I, 94; *Inquiry*, 77.

[29] KOMATSU 1948, 24-37.

[30] NKZ I, 52; *Inquiry*, 42.

[31] SHIMOMURA 1965.

[32] Cf., NKZ XVII, 24-48; cf., TAKEUCHI 1966, Chapter 3, *passim*.

[33] NKZ I, 16; *Inquiry*, 9.

[34] NKZ XII, 64-85.

[35] It might be noted at this point that Nishida expressly rejects the correspondence theory of truth. For him, as for Kant, the act of knowing is a constitutive act that unifies experience for a given category, but he would reject the Kantian notion that there is a fundamental dichotomy between form and content. This contrasts strongly with the view expressed by Inoue Tetsujirō, who expounded a correspondence theory of truth. It is worth noting that Nishida's rejection of a correspondence theory also leads him to deny the possibility of absolute truth in favor of the view that truth can be spoken of only in terms of some point of view. In pure experience it makes no sense to talk of true or false for this would imply a specific, conscious standard or perspective that, in turn, would imply that the unity of the pure experience had been shattered.

[36] There will be a major shift in this emphasis later, reflected in the title of his work *From the Acting to the Seeing*.

[37] Cf., NKZ I, 86; *Inquiry*, 71.

[38] NKZ III, 11.

[39] NKZ II, 12–13; *Inquiry*, XXV–XXVI.

[40] NKZ II, 3–4; *Intuition*, XIX. All translations from 『自覚に於ける直感と反省』 in this volume are the author's. Cross-references to the abbreviated translation of Valdo Viglielmo, Takeuchi Yoshinori, and Joseph O'Leary, *Intuition and Reflection in Self-Consciousness*, will be provided where available.

[41] The notion explicated by ROYCE is that of a self-representative system, which he inherited from a study of the work of Dedekind on the foundations of mathematics. Royce uses the example of a perfect map of England drawn within the boundaries of the country to explain what he means. The idea, of course, is that the map would have to contain a representation of itself in the map in order to qualify as a perfect map. But that would mean that the representation of the original would have to contain a representation of itself; there would have to be a never-ending chain of representations of the original within the original. He then gives a generalized definition of the notion of a self-representative system and discusses its applicability to various philosophical issues, notably the relation of the one and the many to the concept of the self. His idea is that an infinite system can be given a positive definition rather than the purely negative technique of saying that a particular series can never be completed. More than this, the principle is a generative one, for each element of the system is itself reflected, thereby constituting the infinite series. Royce goes on to specify the self as a self-representative system with self-conscious reflection as the generative principle. It is the generative and dynamic aspect of this notion that seemed to appeal particularly to Nishida.

[42] NKZ II, 58; *Intuition*, 31.

[43] NKZ II, 63; *Intuition*, 33.

[44] NKZ II, 164; *Intuition*, 84.

[45] NKZ II, 185; *Intuition*, 92.

[46] See NKZ II, 217; *Intuition*, 109.

[47] NKZ II, 268; *Intuition*, 133.

[48] NKZ II, 275–6.

[49] NKZ II, 279; *Intuition*, 140.

[50] NKZ II, 285; *Intuition*, 142 (incomplete).

[51] NKZ II, 345; *Intuition*, 167.

[52] He quite often uses the metaphor of projection to indicate the relationships in this hierarchy. Thus, for example, the material world is the projection of the spiritual world just as a two-dimensional figure is a projection of a three-dimen-

sional one. The analogy of lines of projection is used to explain the sense of the idea that the lower position is goal-oriented toward the higher.

[53] NKZ II, 11; *Intuition,* XXIII.

3. CONSCIOUSNESS AND THE MYSTICAL FOUNDATIONS OF REALISM

[1] NKZ III, passim.

[2] He later came to consider the position ludicrous since it would involve claiming that we have no knowledge at all, and thus to agree with Kant that the question is not "Do we have knowledge?" but rather, "How do we come to have knowledge?"

[3] NKZ IV, 208–89.

[4] NKZ IV, 5.

[5] NKZ IV, 5

[6] NKZ III, 56.

[7] NKZ III, 64.

[8] NKZ III, 69.

[9] NKZ III, 61.

[10] NKZ III, 70.

[11] NKZ III, 74.

[12] NODA 1955, 351.

[13] SUZUKI 1950, 107.

[14] SUZUKI 1950, 110.

[15] WITTGENSTEIN 1961, 151.

[16] SUZUKI 1949, 23.

[17] SUZUKI 1949, 14ff; see also NISHITANI 1967, III, 36ff.

[18] It is the position of most Japanese scholars that the Southern School of Hui-neng represents the true line of transmission from India through Bodhidharma, explicitly developing the essential teachings of Bodhidharma, which in turn are a direct continuation of Mahāyāna Buddhism and a surpassing of the Hīnayāna approach. Be this as it may, we shall concern ourselves only with the different interpretations put forward by these scholars and not with their orthodoxy.

[19] SUZUKI 1949, 17.

[20] SUZUKI 1949, 22.

[21] This is basically the nature of criticism made by the Mahāyāna scholars against the Hīnayāna schools. Despite the commonalities, it is best not to become

involved at this point with the history and nature of that problem and rather restrict our consideration to this particular criticism.

[22] I have used this phrase throughout since it is the one used in the essay. Incidentally, the essay was not translated as part of Hisamatsu's 1939 volume of the same title, but seems to have been written and translated especially for vol. II of *Philosophical Studies*. Accoringly, I base my remarks solely on the English version as it appears in that volume.

[23] HISAMATSU 1960, 65–97.

[24] The terms *nothingness, non-being, not,* and *negation* have all been used as variations of the single Japanese charater 無. The term *nothingness* has been the most frequent English translation of *mu*, and while it at first sounded somewhat clumsy, it has since lost much of its unfamiliarity in philosophical circles. In any case, it seems preferable to any of the other options. It should also be noted that difficulties with this concept are not made any easier by that fact that a single term has to cover such a wide range of connotations.

[25] HISAMATSU 1960, 71. Here the terms "Buddha-nature" and "non-being" are both used as synonyms for Nothingness. Trying to work Hisamatusu's deliberate choice of capitalized terms into fluent English prose has caused headaches for more than one translator. Here I have used the uppercase to set off Hisamatsu's use of terms from a more general usage or reference to Nishida's thought.

[26] HISAMATSU 1960, 71.

[27] *Sūnyatā* is the Sanskrit original of the terms 無 and *nothingness* (or *emptiness*).

[28] HISAMATSU 1960, 76. The capitalization of Self is intended by Hisamatsu to distinguish the self that is nothingness from the empirical or psychological self.

[29] HISAMATSU 1960, 78.

[30] HISAMATSU 1960, 80.

[31] SUZUKI 1949, 137.

[32] HISAMATSU 1960, 84.

[33] HISAMATSU 1960, 85.

[34] HISAMATSU 1960, 81.

[35] HISAMATSU 1960, 87.

[36] HISAMATSU 1960, 88. In his later works Nishida frequently uses a similar phrase, "the self that sees, not this self that is seen," to much the same purpose.

[37] Notice how this parallels Inoue Enryō's rejection of archism as well as Nishida's stress on utter subjectivity in *Intuition*.

[38] The term "True Nature" is used by Hisamatsu to indicate the same thing that has been designated as "Mind" or "egoless ego" and that is to be contrasted with the self understood in the sense of the empirical ego.

[39] We have already noted Hsuing Shih-li's use of this metaphor to provide a metaphysical grounding for Neo-Confucianism.

[40] HISAMATSU 1960, 92. Hisamatsu does not make the distinction between the subject as a grammatical subject and the subject as the conscious subject, a distinction that will play a crucial role in Nishida's analysis.

[41] HISAMATSU 1960, 96.

[42] TAKEUCHI 1966, Chapter 3, passim; also see SHIMOMURA 1965, Chapter 1, sec. 4, passim.

4. THE CONCEPT OF BASHO

[1] The Japanese term *basho* is one used in ordinary conversation, roughly similar in meaning and connotations to the English *place*. It covers physical place, temporal position, rank or order, situation, and spatial position. As Nishida uses it, basho also has the sense of a field in the expression "force field" (力の場). For the most part I have left *basho* untranslated in this book, except in the translation of Nishida's "General Summary" included in the appendix. In general I prefer the translation *topos* as an English equivalent for reasons of its flexibility of usage as noun, adjective, and adverb, and also to avoid the typical linguistic barbarisms that Nishida's texts drive many translators to. HEISIG (2001) has elected to use *locus* for similar reasons, but I prefer to hold to *topos*.

[2] Examples of Western philosophical concepts serving as occasions for making explicit religious insights are common in Nishida's writings. He did not adapt foreign terms haphazardly, but was selective in integrating such terms into his thought.

[3] KŌSAKA 1947, 128.

[4] KŌSAKA 1947, 130.

[5] NKZ IV, 220.

[6] Some scholars have questioned whether Aristotle was in fact intertwining metaphysics and logic by defining primary substance in this way. See OWEN 1960–1961, 65–90; and SACK 1948, 221–5.

[7] NODA 1955, 345–9.

[8] The term "formal logic" refers either to the traditional Aristotelian logic or to the logic of *Principia Mathematica*. This is not to say that Nishida was not aware of the differences between the two, but only that those differences did not affect the main point he was trying to make.

[9] One might also use the analogy of a two-dimensional projection of a three-dimensional structure, as Nishida himself does in another context to indicate the relationship of formal logic to the logic of basho.

[10] How this relates to Quine's "to be is to be the value of a variable" will be briefly indicated at a later point. See the following note.

[11] This is reminiscent of Quine's often cited statement: "To be assumed as an entity is, purely and simply, to be reckoned as the value of a variable" (1963, 13). A domain of discourse indicates a frame for a range of variables, and something is said to be a member of the domain if it is a possible value of a variable. Quine goes on to speak of the similarity of the acceptance of an ontology with the acceptance of a scientific theory, and comments that our acceptance of an ontology "is determined once we have fixed upon the overall conceptual scheme that is to accommodate science in the broadest sense...." He then suggests that the two competing conceptual schemes for the ordering our experience, the phenomenalistic and the physicalistic, are related in such a way that "from a phenomenalistic point of view, the conceptual scheme of physical objects is a convenient myth, simpler than the literal truth and yet containing that literal truth as a scattered part." He further suggests that this is analogous to the relation of the conceptual scheme of the arithmetic of rational numbers to the convenient myth of the broader arithmetic of rational and irrational numbers.

[12] It might be worth noting here that Quine's problem of selecting among these conceptual schemes differs from the problem that concerned Nishida, namely, to show the necessary relationsship between these schemes and their ground. Further, Quine does not discuss a principle of determination for these domains of discourse, but only presents them as alternative modes of speaking about our experience. His question, therefore, is not precisely the same as Nishida's. Quine is concerned with deciding on the most workable, most useful scheme to interpret experience, whereas Nishida is trying to explain how it is that the nature of experience necessitates the development of these schemes in the first place.

[13] In his youth Nishida had seriously considered a career in mathematics, and the choice between mathematics and philosophy was a difficult one (TAKEUCHI 1966, Chapter 1). His sophisticated understanding of mathematics is shown by the numerous citations he makes of the work of mathematicians such as Dedekind, Cantor, Zermelo, Russell, Poincare, and La Place. The mathematical examples in *Intuition* attest to the depth of his appreciation, as do the essays he authored on "The Foundation of Mathematics" (NKZ XI, 237–85) and "Logic and Mathematics" (NKZ XI, 60–114).

[14] *An Inquiry into the Good*, NKZ I, 3–200.

[15] NKZ IV, 225. The term *oite aru* をいてある can be rendered as either "placed in" or "located in" or even simply "is in." It has both a concrete and abstract sense.

[16] NKZ IV, 225.

[17] This notion of projection is also used in *Intuition* where he speaks of a "world" as being a projection of a "higher point of view" onto a lower.

[18] NKZ IV, 113.

[19] Note how this example of an energy field compares with the analogy used by Inoue Enryō of the waves and the water. Nishida does not mean to be merely giving an analogy.

[20] NKZ IV, 210.

[21] NKZ IV, 293.

[22] Nishida characterized his solution in terms of "pure experience" as excessively psychological and lacking in structure.

[23] COPLESTON 1964, VI/2, 224.

[24] STENIUS 1967, 214.

[25] WITTGENSTEIN 1961, 6–54, 151.

[26] CARNAP 1956, 205–22, passim.

[27] See FITCH 1946.

[28] This refers strictly to the simple theory of types, but little clarity would be gained by digressing into the ramified theory of types in all its detail.

[29] There are, however, a number of difficulties with this theory as well as with several other paradoxes that it is inadequate to handle. See RAMSEY 1931, Chapter 2, passim; QUINE 1963, Chapter 2, passim.

[30] Corresponding processes of the brain would be involved, but not in this context.

[31] NKZ IV, 5.

[32] NKZ IV, 233.

[33] NKZ IV, 313. The final phrase reads 意識されたもの.

[34] Nishida uses the example of geometry's foundation on the universal or a priori of space, his point being that in order to speak of knowledge derived from thought alone, as opposed to the union of thought and perception, there must be a fundamental intuition at the ground of that discipline. He then goes on to argue that the same holds true for knowledge of the empirical world when speaking of it as discursive knowledge.

[35] NKZ IV, 321–2. The word *reflective* in this passage is a translation of the Japanese 反省的, which refers to a self-conscious reflection, and not 反射的, which refers to reflection in a mirror or the like. Nishida does, however, adopt both terms.

5. THE LOGIC OF BASHO

[1] Nishida continued the development of his philosophical speculation many years after the publication of this work. In fact, many commentators, among them Noda and Kōsaka, see the publication of the *Philosophical Essays* as marking a new stage in this thought. Be that as it may, the book does not represent a reversal of

his position or a disenchantment with the notion of basho, which continues a crucial role in any number of later works, such as "The Philosophical Foundations of Mathematics" and "The Logic of Basho and the Religious Worldview." He is inclined to treat his logic of basho in a more dynamic sense in his later writings, equating it with a logic of historical constitution (NKZ XII, 265); but this represents a development of the concept, not its rejection. For this reason, the present essay restricts itself to the structure developed by Nishida in *The System of Self-Consciousness of the Universal*.

[2] 判断的一般者.

[3] 有るもの.

[4] NKZ V, 60; cf. KŌYAMA 1935, 48.

[5] NKZ V, 61.

[6] Nishida uses only one term 超越的 to mean both transcendental and transcendent. Normally *transcendental* is the more appropriate sense, but in phrases such as "x is seen to be 超越的 from y," *transcendent* seems the better choice.

[7] NKZ IV, 274.

[8] 推論的一般者.

[9] NKZ V, 427; Appendix, 191.

[10] KŌYAMA 1935, 55.

[11] This treatment of time as object yields the various temporal paradoxes.

[12] See his essay「知るもの」NKZ IV, 324–88.

[13] NKZ V, 22–3.

[14] NKZ V, 53.

[15] KŌYAMA 1935, 60–77.

[16] NKZ V, 24.

[17] Spatial character can be said to belong to the level of the universal of judgment in the sense that the determination of an individual as an individual necessarily implies the determination of a multiplicity of individuals.

[18] NKZ V, 37.

[19] NKZ V, 28.

[20] NKZ V, 52.

[21] NKZ V, 35.

[22] 有の場所.

[23] Cf. NODA 1955, 345–59; NKZ V, 124.

[24] NKZ V, 41.

[25] NKZ V, 422; Appendix, 188.

[26] NKZ V, 18.

[27] 自覚的一般者.

[28] Cf. NODA 1955.

[29] NKZ V, 425-6; Appendix, 190.

[30] NKZ V, 430; (See also Appendix, 194).

[31] NKZ V, 123ff.

[32] 叡知的一般者.

[33] NKZ V, 167.

[34] NKZ V, 161.

[35] 良心.

[36] NKZ V, 172.

[37] NKZ V, 163.

[38] 行為的自己.

[39] NKZ V, 478.

[40] NKZ V, 444; Appendix, 201.

[41] NKZ V, 451; Appendix, 207.

[42] NKZ V, 456; Appendix, 201.

[43] NKZ V, 440; Appendix, 200.

6. CONCLUSION

[1] Cf. NKZ IV, 6.

[2] NKZ VI, 112.

[3] The word here translated as *anthropology* is 人間学, literally the study of human beings. The discipline of anthropology is 人類学 in Japanese.

[4] Cf. KŌYAMA 1935, Chapter 2, passim. See also Chapter 5 on the point that all theoretical constructions, including this one, are in the universal of expression.

[5] Note the frequency with which the phrase "on the analogy of..." appears in the translation in the appendix. The original Japanese is に即して, which can also mean "based on...". As noted in Chapter 1, note 10, the term 即 is used frequently by the two Inoues, and by Buddhist writers in general, to signify something like "dynamically identical."

[6] NKZ V, 451; Appendix, 207.

[7] NKZ V, 477.

Bibliography

Works by Nishida Kitarō

NISHIDA Kitarō 西田幾多郎

1965–66 『西田幾多郎全集』 [Complete works of Nishida Kitarō]. Tokyo: Iwanami Shoten. 19 vols. [abbreviated as NKZ]

1987 *Intuition and Reflection in Self-Consciousness.* Trans. by Valdo H. Viglielmo with Takeuchi Yoshinori and Joseph S. O'Leary. New York, SUNY Press.

1980 *An Inquiry into the Good.* Trans. by Masao Abe and Christopher Ives. Princeton: Princeton University Press.

Works by other authors

CARNAP, Rudolph

1956 *Meaning and Necessity.* Chicago: University of Chicago Press.

CHAN, Wing-sit

1963 *A Source Book in Chinese Philosophy.* Princeton: Princeton University Press.

COPLESTON, Frederick J.

1964 *A History of Western Philosophy,* vol. VI. New York: Image Books.

FITCH, Frederic B.

1946 "Self Reference in Philosophy." *Mind* LV. Expanded and reprinted in Copi and Gould ed. 1967, *Contemporary Readings in Logical Theory.* New York: Macmillan.

FUNAYAMA Shin'ichi 船山信一

1956 『日本の観念論者』 [Japanese idealists]. Tokyo: Eihōsha.

1959 『明治哲学史研究』 [Studies in the history of Meiji philosophy]. Kyoto: Minerva Shobō.

HEISIG, James W.
  2001   *Philosophers of Nothingness*. Honolulu: University of Hawai'i Press.

HEISIG, James W., and John C. MARALDO
  1995   *Rude Awakenings: Zen, the Kyoto School, and the Question of Nationalism*. Honolulu: University of Hawai'i Press.

HISAMATSU Shin'ichi 久松真一
  1960   "Characteristics of Oriental Nothingness." *Philosophical Studies of Japan*, vol. 2. Tokyo: Japan Association for Promotion of Science, Commission for UNESCO, 65–97.

HSIUNG, Shih-li
  1944   *New Doctrine of Consciousness Only*. Chunking.

INOUE Enryō 井上円了
  1886–87 『哲学一夕話』 [An Evening of Philosophical Conversation]. Tokyo: Tetsugaku Shoin.

INOUE Tetsujirō 井上哲次郎
  1894   「我世界観の一塵」 [A particle of my world view]. 『哲学雑誌』 IX/89: 489–512.
  1897   「現象即実在論の要領」 [An outline of the phenomena-as-reality theory]. 『哲学雑誌』 XII/123: 377–96.

KIM, Ha Tai
  1952   "Nishida and Royce." *Philosophy East and West* I/4: 18–29.

KIMURA Soe 木村そえ
  1932   『西田先生の話』 [Conversations of Nishida Kitarō]. Tokyo.

KOMATSU Setsurō 小松節郎
  1948   『西田哲学の根本問題』 [Fundamental problems of Nishida's philosophy]. Tokyo: Sekai Hyōronsha.

KŌSAKA Masaaki 高坂正顕
  1947A   『西田幾多郎先生の追憶』 [Recollections of Professor Nishida]. Tokyo: Kokuritsu Sensho.
  1947B   『西田先生の生涯と思想』 [The life and thought of Nishida Kitarō]. Tokyo: Kobundo Shobō.

KŌYAMA Iwao 高山岩男
  1935   『西田哲学』 [Nishida philosophy]. Tokyo: Iwanami Shoten.
  1940   『続西田哲学』 [Nishida philosophy: A continuation]. Tokyo: Iwanami Shoten.

MIYAJIMA Hajime 宮島 啓
  1960   『明治的思想家の形成: 西田哲学設立史と思想史方法論の問題』 [The formation of a Meiji thinker's image: The history of the formation of

Nishida philosophy and problems in the methodology of the history of thought]. Tokyo: Miraisha.

MIYAKAWA Tōru 宮川 透
1956　『近代日本思想の構造』[The structure of modern Japanese thought]. Tokyo: Tokyo University Press.

1961　『近代日本の哲学』[Modern Japanese philosophy]. Tokyo: Keisei Shobō.

1963　「西田哲学に対する批判と反批判」[Criticism and counter criticism with respect to Nishida philosophy].『近代日本思想論争』[Recent Japanese ideological debates]. Tokyo: Aoki Shoten, 291–317.

MUTAI Risaku 務台理作
1944　『場所の論理学』[The logic of topos]. Tokyo: Kobundo Shobō.

1948A　『場所的逆対応について』[Concerning topological counterdependency].

1948B　『西田幾多郎: その人と学』[Nishida Kitarō: The man and the scholar]. Tokyo: Daitō Shuppansha, 139–46.

1949　『西田哲学』[Nishida philosophy]. Tokyo: Athena Bunko.

NISHIMURA Shigeki 西村茂樹
1887　『日本道徳論』[Essay on Japanese ethics]. Tokyo.

NISHITANI Keiji 西谷啓冶, ed.
1967　『禅の講座』[Lectures on Zen]. 8 vol. Tokyo: Chikuma Shobō.

NODA Matao 埜田又夫
1955　"East West Synthesis in Kitarō Nishida." *Philosophy East and West*. IV/3: 345–59.

OWEN, J.
1960　"Aristotle on Categories." *Review of Metaphysics* XIV: 65–90.

PIOVESANA, Gino K.
1968　*Recent Japanese Philosophical Thought 1862–1962: A Survey*. Monumenta Nipponica Monographs No. 29. Tokyo: Sophia University. Revised and reprinted *Recent Japanese Philosophical Thought 1862–1996: A Survey*. Curzon, Richmond, Surrey 1997.

QUINE, Willard Van Orman
1963A　*From a Logical Point of View*. New York: Harper Torchbooks.

1963B　*Set Theory and Its Logic*. Cambridge: Belknap Press.

RAMSEY, Frank Plumpton
1931　*Foundations of Mathematics*. London: Routledge and Kegan Paul.

ROYCE, Josiah
1899　*The World and the Individual*. New York: MacMillan and Co., Ltd.

SACK, David
  1948 "Does Aristotle Have a Doctrine of Secondary Substances?" *Mind*
        LVII: 221–5.

SHIMOMURA Toratarō 下村寅太郎
  1965 『西田幾多郎：人と思想』[Nishida Kitarō: The man and his thought].
        Tokyo: Tokai University.

SODA Sōkichi 曾田左右吉
  1926 「西田哲学の方法について：西田博士の教えを乞う」[Concerning the
        method of Nishida philosophy: Requesting Dr. Nihida's guidance].
        『哲学研究』133.

SONKENKAI, ed.
  1931 『井上先生喜寿記念論文集』[Essays in honor of Professor Inoue's sev-
        enty-seventh birthday]. Tokyo: Fujisanbo.

STENIUS, Erik
  1967 *Wittgenstein's Tractatus: A Critical Exposition of Its Main Lines of
        Thought.* Ithaca: Cornell Press.

SUZUKI Daisetsu Teitarō 鈴木大拙貞太郎
  1949 *The Zen Doctrine of No-Mind.* London: Rider and Co.
  1950 *Manual of Zen Buddhism.* London: Rider and Co.

TAKAHASHI Satomi 高橋里美
  1912 「意識現象の事実とその意味：西田産着善の研究お読む」[The meaning and
        fact of conscious phenomena: On reading Nishida's *An Inquiry into
        the of Good*].『哲学雑誌』1912: 303–4.

TAKEUCHI Yoshitomo 竹内良知
  1966 『西田幾多郎：近代日本の思想家』[Nishida Kitarō: Modern Japanese
        thinkers] No. 7. Tokyo: Tokyo University Press.

TANABE Hajime 田辺 元
  1930 「西田先生の教えを仰ぐ」[Requesting Professor Nishida's guidance].
        『哲学研究』170.

TOSAKA Jun 戸坂 潤
  1966 「無の論理は論理であるかぐ」[Is the logic of nothingness a logic?]
        『戸坂潤全集』[The collected works of Tosaka Jun]. Vol. 1. Tokyo:
        Keisei Shobō.

WALSH, W. H.
  1963 *Metaphysics.* New York: Harcourt Brace and World.

WITTGENSTEIN, Ludwig
  1961 *Tractatus Logico-Philosophicus.* Trans. Pears and McGuinness. Lon-
        don: Routledge and Kegan Paul.

YANAGIDA Kenjūrō 柳田謙十郎

1939   『実践哲学として西田哲学』 [Nishida's philosophy as the philosophy of practice]. Tokyo: Kobundō.

1946–47   『西田哲学体系』 [The system of Nishida's philosophy]. Part I, 『場の論理』 [The logic of place]. Part II, 『歴史的実在』 [Historical reality]. Part III 『特使哲学』 [Particular topics in philosophy]. Tokyo: Tokyo Shuppansha.

YUSA Michiko 遊佐道子

2002   *Zen and Philosophy: An Intellectual Biography of Nishida Kitarō.* Honolulu: University of Hawai'i Press.

Index

Printed in the United Kingdom
by Lightning Source UK Ltd.
124369UK00001B/212/A